The CareWise Guide

THE CAREWISE GUIDE

Self-Care From Head To Toe

Sixth Edition

Acamedica Press
A division of SHPS, Inc.
Seattle, Washington

Reviewed for medical accuracy by a
panel of board-certified physicians

Acamedica Press
A division of SHPS, Inc.
PO Box 34570, Seattle, WA 98124-1570

Printed in the United States of America
09 08 07 06 05 04 03 02 01   10 9 8 7 6 5 4 3 2 1

Library of Congress Control Number 2006901417
ISBN-13: 978-1-886444-08-9   ISBN-10: 1-886444-08-0

Decision helper charts © 1996, 1997, 1999, 2000, 2002, 2006
Acamedica Press and Reliance Medical Information, Inc. (RMI)

The medical information in this book was reviewed for accuracy by a panel
of board-certified physicians and was found to be consistent with generally
accepted medical practices at the time of review.

The CareWise Guide, intended to provide general information on common
medical topics, is not a comprehensive medical text and does not include
all the potential medical conditions that could be represented by certain
symptoms. In addition, medical practices may change periodically; therefore,
this guide cannot and should not be relied upon as a substitute for seeing
an appropriate healthcare professional.

Acamedica Press has made every effort to print trademarked product names
within this book in initial capital letters to indicate trademark and/or
registered trademark designation.

Design by Todd J.Y. Kubo
Cover illustration by Deborah Hanley
Interior illustrations by Confluence Communications

Contents

Turn to the first page of each section for specific topics and their page numbers. See the index, pages 347 to 368, for terminology and references as well as specific topics.

Section 4 Health Concerns (continued)

Section 5 Medications 323

How and when to use medications to get the best results

Section 6 Prevention 329

A variety of lifestyle tips and preventive decisions for getting and staying healthy

Section 7 Working With Your Doctor 339

Our best tips for becoming an effective partner with your healthcare professionals

Preface

Managing your own health and that of your family is undoubtedly one of your primary concerns. So it should be especially comforting to know that you have convenient access to healthcare information and the support you need to make the best possible decisions.

The CareWise Guide is your key resource. It provides you with the best available healthcare information to help you decide when to apply self-care, when to seek medical care, and how to work effectively with your doctor to get the most appropriate, cost-effective and highest quality healthcare.

This book is also a tool to help you take charge of your own health and the health of your family. Its focus is on self-care—making healthy lifestyle and preventive decisions, understanding your symptoms and medical concerns, participating with your doctor in shared decision making, and effectively managing your medical conditions.

We have taken our extensive health education experience, combined it with leading sources of health and medical information, and presented the material in an easy-to-understand format. The medical information has been developed by physicians, nurses and health educators in response to consumers' needs, and reviewed for accuracy by a panel of board-certified physicians.

Our goal is to help you become wiser about your healthcare, which means getting in the habit of weighing the benefits, risks and costs when it comes to your specific medical concerns. As you do, you will experience better health, greater satisfaction when you seek medical care, and—in the end—the highest quality care.

Healthcare decisions are personal and important, and they can have a tremendous impact on your overall well-being. *The CareWise Guide* is written to give you the information you need to take charge of your health—from head to toe.

Acknowledgments

We wish to acknowledge the many medical and communications professionals who contributed to the publication of *The CareWise Guide* including:

Editorial Staff
Randi Holland, R.N.
Jan Anderson, R.N.
Charmaine Adsero
Carrie C. Dennett

SHPS Clinical Content Certification Council
Lyle Graham, M.D.
Maureen Gregg, M.D.
William Mantle, M.D.
Jerry Osband, M.D.
Kenneth Peterson, M.D.
Todd Pruitt, M.D.
Jesse Samuels, M.D., F.A.C.E.P.
Christopher Scott Stanley, M.D.
Donald E. Stillwagon, M.D.

Research and Review Staff
Juliette A. Dahl, R.N., B.A.
Sandy Staats Evans, R.N., B.A.
Margaret M. Regan, R.N., B.S.N.
Johanna H. Wesneski, R.N.

Contributing Writers
Jan Anderson, R.N.
Charmaine Adsero
Peg Carver
Jennie Krull Gulian
Robert Miskimon
Kip Richards, R.N., M.N.

Special thanks to our many readers who are helping us continually improve our quality and who are taking the initiative for their own health.

Introduction

In today's rapidly changing world of healthcare there is one certainty—what you do to maintain or improve your health has a much greater impact on your quality of life than advances in medical science and the treatment of disease.

Taking Charge

The most effective way to reduce disease and disability is to address your lifestyle and personal health practices. You might be surprised to know that your lifestyle accounts for 53 percent of what affects your health, while medical care affects only 10 percent.* In fact, many of the leading causes of death may be preventable, and personal responsibility truly is the key to good health.

Why is it, then, that we too often leave the state of our health in the hands of fate, doctors or genetics and remain passive participants? Why are we content to treat illness rather than concentrating on becoming healthier? Simply put, we have the *desire* to be healthy, but lack the skills and information we need to *take charge*.

The goal of *The CareWise Guide: Self-Care From Head To Toe* is to help you develop the confidence to manage your medical concerns.

A Self-Care Approach

There is a common misconception that healthy living is hard work. In truth, an effective

self-care approach is much easier and more rewarding than falling into poor health and having to work back to good health.

A successful self-care strategy has three key ingredients: prevention, participation and education.

Prevention
Making healthy lifestyle and preventive decisions can have an enormous impact on reducing your risk of disease. The best place to start is with the behaviors that can make the biggest difference.

Common sense lifestyle measures are the cornerstone of prevention. Exercise regularly, eat a healthy diet, quit smoking, reduce or eliminate your consumption of alcohol and use of drugs, and control your weight to look and feel your best. In addition, keep your immunizations and screening tests up-to-date to help prevent health risks and identify and manage the onset of disease. (See *Prevention*, p. 329, to learn more about prevention and recommended immunizations and screenings.)

Of course, no amount of prevention can eliminate all disease, which is why your participation in the decision-making process is so important.

*The Wellness for Life Workbook

Participation

Unfortunately, our use of medical services is based on the hope that modern medicine can cure all our bad habits. The result is that we often overuse medical services for situations we can better handle at home (according to current findings, approximately 80 percent of all medical concerns can be effectively treated at home). Also, our expectations for medical care often go unmet because we don't fully understand the importance of our own active participation.

Making participation a part of your self-care strategy means taking charge of *how* you use medical services. This includes understanding your symptoms, making informed decisions about when to seek care, finding the right type of care, and working with your doctor to manage your health.

When you enter your doctor's office with a medical concern, you present a mystery. The more clues you can provide, the quicker your doctor can identify the culprit. Don't hesitate to offer information and ask questions. (See *Becoming Partners With Your Doctor*, p. 343, for more tips on how to work with your doctor.)

Education

When it comes to the health of you and your family, ignorance is not bliss. Learning what your self-care options are—when it is safe to treat health problems at home and when to see a doctor—saves everyone time and money. Being educated means sidestepping unnecessary treatment and testing, avoiding extra medical charges, and requesting generic drugs when possible. (They are less expensive but just as effective as name brands.)

Most important, working to improve your health and decrease your need for medical services is critical to solving our national concern over the cost of healthcare. You and your family can improve the quality of care you receive by combining it with a self-care approach—becoming part of the solution rather than part of the problem.

Using The CareWise Guide

Let's say it's 2 a.m. and your 4-year-old has a fever. Or it's Sunday afternoon and you've pulled a muscle playing volleyball. You're wondering whether to call your doctor or just wait. The problem is, you need help—now!

Open up *The CareWise Guide: Self-Care From Head To Toe*, a book that's designed to serve as your around-the-clock healthcare guide.

The CareWise Guide covers close to 200 topics, ranging from measles to menopause, from appendicitis to varicose veins. We suggest that you take a few moments, now, to browse through the book and familiarize yourself with its format and contents. We think you'll discover that it's filled with helpful information about all kinds of common, day-to-day health concerns—like what to do if your child has an ear infection or a fever, or if you have a funny-looking mole, or suddenly hurt your back or sprain your ankle.

Most topics include general information about the medical problem, as well as tips for:
- Prevention
- Treating the problem at home
- When to seek professional medical care

Where to find what you need

- **Emergencies and Injuries** are covered at the beginning of the book—where they are readily accessible. **In case of an emergency, call 911 or your local emergency services number. This book is not designed as a substitute for emergency or urgent care services.**
- **Health Concerns** come next, and are organized in a head-to-toe fashion—beginning with neurological problems and working all the way through the body, right down to foot and toe pain. The detailed index in the back of the book is designed to help you look up specific words and references and direct you to related topics.

    Other important sections include Infant/Child Health, Medications, Prevention and Working With Your Doctor.
- *Decision helper* sections, which accompany most topics, are designed to help you decide when self-care is appropriate, when to call a doctor, and when to apply emergency first aid and seek emergency help. Read on for details on how to use the *Decision helper* sections.

Using the *Decision helper* sections

- First, read all the general information about the topic. It will help you better understand *Decision helper*.
- Next, work your way through *Decision helper*. Don't skip from point to point; each point is based on the assumption that you have answered "yes" or "no" to the previous one. Follow the arrows that apply to each of your answers.

Decision helper: What does each action step mean?

Apply Emergency First Aid

Begin emergency first aid **immediately**.

Seek Emergency Care

Get professional medical help **immediately**.

Call Doctor Now

Call your doctor's office **now** and alert the doctor—or a nurse—to the problem. Ask them what you should do next. This is a situation that needs prompt, professional attention, but is not necessarily an emergency.

Call Doctor

Phone your doctor's office today and talk to the doctor or a nurse about the problem. Make an appointment if it's necessary.

Apply Self-Care

Follow the directions for self-care (listed in the *What You Can Do* section) carefully. If you become worried about your condition, call your doctor or healthcare provider.

Call Dentist

Phone your dentist's office today and talk to the dentist about the problem.

- Take action based on the "yes" arrow that most appropriately applies to your health concern. (See the *Decision helper* chart on the previous page.) Or, if *Decision helper* refers you to another topic in the book, you can turn to that page for additional information. For example, *Decision helper* for nausea and vomiting tells you to "see *Dehydration*, p. 236" for details on that particular side effect of nausea and vomiting.

Need more details?

After reading the section(s) covering your medical concern, you may have questions and want additional information. Ask your healthcare provider for additional medical information to help you evaluate treatment options.

The CareWise Guide is not intended to take the place of your doctor or other healthcare professionals. Instead, it is a resource to help you make the best decisions and get the most from the medical services available to you.

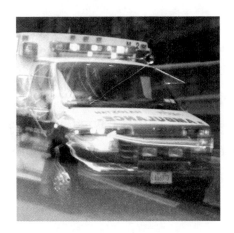

SECTION 1
Emergencies

Introduction

The time to prepare for a medical emergency is now—not at the scene of a car accident or on the doorstep of someone who is having a heart attack. An emergency by definition is an unexpected occurrence that demands immediate action. Knowing what to do ahead of time is your best defense against panic.

> **Reader's Note:** For every medical concern covered in *The CareWise Guide*, you'll find information that will help you determine whether you have an emergency. Look for this symbol.

Seek Emergency Care

Be Prepared

- Keep important phone numbers handy, including the Poison Control Center, your doctor's office and the nearest emergency room or urgent care facility.
- Know the best way to reach the emergency room by car, in case you need to drive yourself or someone else there.
- Take first-aid and CPR courses. Make both of them family affairs.
- Wear a medical-alert bracelet or necklace or carry emergency medical information in your wallet, especially if you have a condition such as diabetes, epilepsy or serious allergic reactions. This information could save your life if you are unable to speak.

Identifying an Emergency

In general, an emergency is any situation that places a person's health in serious jeopardy. If you think someone's symptoms appear critical or life-threatening, you are probably dealing with an emergency.

Emergency situations include:
- Unconsciousness
- Symptoms of a heart attack, such as chest pain, pressure or discomfort; shortness of breath; nausea; or sweating (see *Chest Pain*, p. 193)

- Severe breathing problems
- Severe, uncontrolled bleeding
- Symptoms of shock, such as pale, clammy skin, weakness, rapid heart rate (see *Shock*, p. 39)
- Possible spinal, neck or head injury (see *Head/Spinal Injury*, p. 56)

When to Call an Ambulance

Even if you know a situation is an emergency it may be difficult to determine whether to take the person to an emergency room or call an ambulance.

The American College of Emergency Physicians advises that you ask yourself a few questions before deciding which is appropriate:

- Is the person's situation life-threatening (as in a sudden loss of consciousness)?
- Could the person's condition become life-threatening on the way to the hospital?
- Could moving the person cause further injury?
- Does the person need immediate help from a paramedic or emergency medical technician?
- Would traffic, distance, or unreliable transportation cause a delay in getting the person to the hospital?

If the answer to any of these questions is "yes," or even if you're unsure, it's best to call an ambulance.

Emergencies that you may be driven to the emergency room for include:
- Deep wounds (see *Wounds*, p. 42)
- Some severe burns (see *Burns*, p. 28)
- Broken bones (see *Broken Bones*, p. 70)
- Some head injuries
- Sudden, severe pain
- New seizures in an adult (DO NOT drive yourself)

Cardiopulmonary Resuscitation (CPR)

Cardiopulmonary resuscitation (CPR) is an emergency first-aid technique for treating a person who suffers a cardiac or respiratory emergency. The American Heart Association (AHA) offers specific advice on how to handle such emergencies. In certain situations, the delivery of a shock with a portable defibrillator can greatly improve a person's chance for survival. Many basic life support classes now train people to use these devices, called "automatic external defibrillators" (AEDs). AEDs analyze the victim's heart rhythm and tell the rescuer whether to deliver a shock to restore the heartbeat. The rescuer is walked through the process with audio and visual prompts. The AHA encourages all household members to learn these techniques in a basic life support class.

The Chain of Survival

A four-step "chain of survival" approach (developed by the AHA) improves a person's prospects for surviving a cardiac or respiratory emergency. This approach also minimizes complications. The first three steps can be accomplished by a bystander:

- Early recognition of an emergency and activation of emergency medical services (EMS) by calling 911
- Early CPR
- Early delivery of a shock with an AED (if necessary)

The fourth step is provided by healthcare workers and involves life-saving care after CPR.

Note: CPR is a complex first-aid procedure. Although we describe CPR procedures, this section is not intended to replace a course that provides actual hands-on experience. Contact the American Red Cross, American Heart Association or your local community center for classes.

The Life Support Sequence

If you find an unresponsive person, or if you witness a person suddenly collapse, first make sure that the scene is safe for you and the victim. **Move a trauma victim only if absolutely necessary!**

Check for response
- Touch the victim on the shoulder and ask "Are you OK?"
- Check for movement.

Activate the EMS system
For adults, whether or not the victim is able to respond:
- Quickly activate the EMS system (phone 911).
- Get an AED (if one is available).
- Return to the victim.

Note: If two people are available, one should activate EMS and get the AED while the other begins CPR (if necessary).

For infants and children:
- Do five cycles (about two minutes) of CPR **BEFORE** activating EMS.

Open the airway (all ages)
- Place the victim face-up on a hard surface. (If you must move a person, avoid twisting the head; instead, log-roll the body and head at the same time, if possible.)
- Open the airway by gently tilting the head back with one hand and lifting the chin with the other. (Thrusting the jaw forward is no longer recommended.)
- Look, listen and feel for breathing; take no more than 10 seconds.
- If no breathing can be detected (or extreme breathing difficulty occurs), begin rescue breathing.

Begin rescue breathing

Take a normal breath before each rescue breath. Each rescue breath should take a full minute. Make sure the chest deflates between rescue breaths.

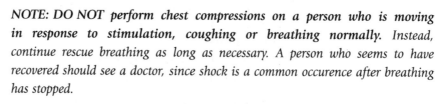

Figure 1

- Give two breaths that make the chest rise.
- If the chest doesn't rise, readjust the head-tilt and chin-lift positions and try again until you see the chest rise. (See Figure 1.)
- If the person does not respond to rescue breathing—indicated by no rising and falling of the chest—begin chest compressions.

NOTE: DO NOT perform chest compressions on a person who is moving in response to stimulation, coughing or breathing normally. Instead, continue rescue breathing as long as necessary. A person who seems to have recovered should see a doctor, since shock is a common occurence after breathing has stopped.

Figure 2

Begin chest compression (adults)

- Kneel beside the victim's chest.
- Place the heel of one hand over the heel of the other hand, on the middle of the chest between the nipples. (See Figure 2.)
- Keep your elbows straight and position your shoulders directly above your hands to make the best use of your weight. (See Figure 3.) (*Do not compress the chest with your fingers. This can damage the ribs.*)
- Push down with steady, firm thrusts, compressing the chest one to two inches at a rate of about 100 times a minute. The pushing down and letting up phase of each cycle should be equal in duration. Don't jab.
- Give two rescue breaths for every 30 chest compressions.

Figure 3

Begin chest compression (children ages 1 to 8)

Follow the instructions listed above for performing chest compressions on adults. However:

- Use one hand rather than both hands.
- Compress the chest to about one-third of its depth.

Note: Chest-compression-only CPR is recommended ONLY when the rescuer is unwilling or unable to perform mouth-to-mouth rescue breathing.

Figure 4

Final Notes

Take extra care when performing CPR on an infant

- Cover the baby's mouth and nose with your mouth and deliver a rescue breath. (Check that the chest is rising.)
- Compress the chest 1/2 to 1 inch, using only two fingers. (See Figure 4.)
- Give two breaths for every 30 chest compressions, compressing the chest AT LEAST 100 times a minute.
- Continue for as long as necessary until help arrives.

The American Heart Association no longer recommends checking for a person's pulse when performing CPR. Life support classes now emphasize rescue breathing and chest compressions if no signs of circulation are present (breathing, coughing or movement in response to two rescue breaths). This simplified teaching technique is recommended to improve a victim's chance of recovery and to simplify teaching CPR skills.

There are many details to take into account when performing CPR. To learn how it's done, take a first-aid training course. Many organizations, such as the American Red Cross and the American Heart Association, sponsor such courses.

Choking

Thousands of Americans choke to death needlessly every year. Anyone of any age can choke on pieces of food, vomit or small objects that become lodged in the windpipe.

For Yourself

Choking can usually be avoided by following a few common sense guidelines:

- Take small bites and chew food thoroughly. Cut meat into small pieces.
- Don't eat too fast, or talk and/or laugh while you're chewing or swallowing.
- Don't lie down with food in your mouth.
- Don't drink too much alcohol before or while eating.
- If you smoke, wait until after you've finished eating to light up.

If You're a Parent or Guardian

- Always supervise children while they eat.
- Keep objects that could make a child choke (such as toys with small, removable parts) out of the reach of small children; instruct older children about the dangers of choking for their younger siblings.
- Never give balloons to children younger than 3 years of age.
- Make sure small children sit in a high chair while they eat and drink.
- Do not let children lie down, run or jump with food or any other object in their mouths.
- Do not feed an infant any food that won't soften or dissolve easily in the baby's mouth or can't be swallowed whole (like yogurt, applesauce or pieces of soft banana). Ask the child's doctor what foods are appropriate for infants. Not all table foods are soft enough for infants to eat safely.

If Someone is Choking

You may have only four to eight minutes in which to save a choking person's life, so you should know how to administer the Heimlich maneuver. This procedure forces the diaphram up toward the lungs, creating an "artificial" cough.

Both children and adults who are choking but still concious will try to breathe in an exaggerated way. They may gasp for breath, turn purple or blue, and grasp the throat. They are unable to speak or cough and will probably nod "yes" if asked "Are you choking?" Choking people who can cough or speak are still getting some air into their lungs and should be encouraged to cough vigorously, as this may dislodge the object. DO NOT perform the Heimlich maneuver if this occurs. Also, do not hit or pat some-one on the back—it may cause the object to slide further down the airway.

Choking Rescue for a Conscious Adult or Child

Establish whether the person can speak or cough by asking, "Are you choking?" If the person nods:

- Stand behind the person and wrap your arms around his or her waist.
- Form a fist with one hand and place it (with the thumb on the inside), just below the person's rib cage; grab your fist with the other hand.
- Give four forceful and quick inward and upward thrusts (making sure to keep your arms off the person's rib cage). (See Figure 5.)
- Repeat the thrusts until the object is dislodged.
- If the person becomes unconscious, gently ease him or her to the floor.

Figure 5

Choking Rescue for an Unconscious Adult or Child

- Call 911 or your local emergency services number.
- Lay the victim on his or her back.
- Straddle the individual with your knees situated on either side of the person's hips.
- Place the heel of one hand just above the person's waistline, with the other hand directly on top of it. (See Figure 6)
- Give four forceful, quick upward thrusts, keeping your arms straight.
- Repeat the procedure until the object is dislodged.

Figure 6

Obstructed Airway in Infant or Child Less than 1 Year of Age

The following steps are appropriate if there is complete airway obstruction due to a witnessed or strongly suspected obstruction by an object. **DO NOT PERFORM these maneuvers to clear an airway that is obstructed due to swelling caused by infection. SEEK EMERGENCY CARE.**

Figure 7

- Hold the infant or child face down along your forearm, supporting the head and neck with one hand. Rest your forearm on your thigh for support.
- Give five back blows forcefully between the shoulder blades with the heel of your hand. (See Figure 7.)
- Repeat several times, if necessary, until the object is dislodged.

IMPORTANT: If this technique fails to dislodge the object, turn the baby over. (See Figure 8.)

Figure 8

If back blows fail:
- Turn the baby over.
- Place two fingers on the chest, just below an imaginary line connecting the infant's nipples.
- Give four forceful thrusts to the chest (to a depth of one inch).
- Repeat several times, if necessary, until the object is dislodged or emergency help arrives.

If the baby is still unable to breathe, CALL 911 AND BEGIN CPR:
- Place the infant or child on a firm surface.
- Open the airway. (Push down and back on the forehead while gently lifting the chin by placing your fingers on either side of the jaw bone.) *Note: Be careful not to extend the head back too far, as this can shut off the airway.*
- Begin rescue breathing:
  - Cover the baby's mouth and nose with your mouth.
  - Give five chest compressions, using only two fingers, followed by one rescue breath (compress the chest to a depth of 1/2 to 1 inch).
  - Continue this technique until help arrives, compressing the chest approximately 100 times a minute.

Figure 9

If You are Alone and Begin to Choke

- Do not panic.
- Try coughing vigorously.
- Position your fist slightly above your navel.
- Grasp your fist with your other hand and thrust upward into your abdomen until the object is expelled, or lean forward over the back of a chair to produce this effect. (See Figure 9.)
- Repeat until the item is dislodged.

For a Pregnant or Obese Person

- Stand behind the person and place your arms under his or her armpits.
- Place your fist on the middle of the breastbone, but not over the ribs.
- Place your other hand on top of it.
- Give five quick, forceful movements with your fist; do not squeeze with your arms.

Final Notes

Seek emergency care if a choking person becomes unconcious (unresponsive to voice or touch) or has been unable to breathe due to choking, but starts breathing again. **Also seek emergency care** if a person has a sudden onset of coughing or gagging with breathing difficulty, is grasping the throat and has a bluish discoloration of the skin or lips, appears extremely anxious, makes raspy or wheezing sounds when inhaling, or is unable to cough, speak or breathe.

Call your doctor right away if the Heimlich maneuver has just been performed on a choking person whose voice now sounds strained or "mechanical" or who has persistant throat, chest or abdominal pain. (The maneuver can cause trauma to the chest or abdomen, and the object may have damaged the throat.)

Call your doctor if a person has choked and had a successful choking rescue procedure performed (Heimlich maneuver) or was unable to remove or expel the object blocking the windpipe. This is important because the maneuver itself can cause trauma to the chest or abdomen. It is also possible that the object has damaged the individual's throat.

Call your local hospital or Red Cross chapter for more information and instruction on these procedures.

Poisoning

Call the National Poison Control Center, 1-800-222-1222, hospital or emergency services number **the minute you suspect a poisoning**. Specially trained Poison Control staff are always available to ask pertinent questions, give first aid instructions and direct you to the appropriate level of care. Poison Control also can call 911 for the person, call the person's doctor or call ahead to the emergency room with information, if needed. Poison centers answer non-emergency calls, too, including calls for poison prevention information. Among other things, you can call to find out about drug interactions, whether a plant or spoiled food is poisonous, how to use a pesticide safely, and how to poison-proof the home.

What You Can Do

Be ready to give the person who answers as much information as possible:
- What substance was taken
- How much
- When
- Person's age and health status
- Whether the person has vomited
- How far away you are from emergency help

If the Person Becomes Unconscious or Stops Breathing

- See *Unconsciousness*, p. 37, or *CPR*, p. 18.

If the Person is Having Convulsions

- Remove any objects that could cause injury.
- Do not put anything in the person's mouth.

If you go to the hospital, take the remains of the suspected poison with you, along with any substance that has been vomited.

Children ages 1 to 4 account for 80 percent of all poisonings. To protect them:

- Never leave children unattended with potentially harmful substances. These include medications, antifreeze, household cleaners, insecticides, organic solvents and fuels.
- Childproof all cupboards with plastic latch locks.
- Keep items in their original containers. This will help your child associate containers and their contents with substances that are off-limits.
- Apply "Mr. Yuk" stickers to containers of poisonous substances, and make sure your child understands their meaning.
- Check walls for peeling paint that a child could rip off and suck. Lead paint is especially dangerous.
- Teach children where to find and how to use emergency numbers, as well as how to get help in general.
- Post the Poison Control Center telephone number before you need to use it.

See **Food Poisoning**, p. 219.

Burns

The skin is the body's largest organ, protecting it from infection and helping to regulate the balance of water and temperature. Burns—whether caused by fire, hot objects or fluids, electricity, chemicals, radiation or other sources—threaten these vital functions. For the very young or old, or those with other medical conditions, burns can be even more serious.

Burns are classified based on their depth of penetration of the skin.

- *First-degree burns* involve only the tough, outer layer of skin. The skin turns bright red and becomes sensitive and painful. It may be dry, but it does not blister.
- *Second-degree burns* are deeper than first-degree burns and are very painful, red and mottled. The burned area may blister and/or be swollen and puffy.
- *Third-degree burns* are still deeper and can involve muscle, internal organs and bone. The skin looks charred and dry and may break open. Underlying muscle or tendons may be visible. Pain may be severe. If nerves have been damaged, however, there may be no pain except around the edges of the burn.

First- and second-degree burns are also called "partial thickness" burns, and third-degree burns are called "full thickness" burns.

If Someone is on Fire

- Stay calm.
- Help the person drop down and roll in a blanket, rug, coat, or some type of covering to smother the flames. Do not let the person run—this will fuel the fire.
- Completely extinguish the fire and stop skin and clothes from smoldering by soaking them with water. Do not remove burned clothing.
- Cover the burn with a cool, damp, sterile bandage or a clean, non-fibrous cloth such as a sheet.
- **Seek emergency care.**

For Severe Burns of Any Kind

Seek emergency care if:

- The person is not breathing. **(Start CPR, see p. 18.)**
- Bleeding is not controlled (see *Control Severe Bleeding*, p. 43)
- Signs of shock are present: altered consciousness; faintness; paleness; rapid and shallow breathing; rapid and weak pulse; cool and clammy skin (see *Shock*, p. 39)
- Signs of charring are present in the mouth or nasal hairs. Check for sooty residue on the face, shortness of breath, a cough or hoarseness. These signs may indicate damage of the respiratory tract.

For Other Burns

Electrical burns

- Turn off the power before touching someone who is in contact with an electrical wire or appliance. Assume a downed power line is live.
- Try not to move the person.
- If a power line has fallen across a car, passengers remain safest if they stay inside. If they have to leave because of fire or some other reason, they should jump clear of the car.

An electrical burn can appear minor even when it has caused major internal injuries. Generally, there will be wounds at the places of entry and exit of the electrical current, unless the person was in contact with water. All electrical shocks that cause burns or that occur with water require emergency care.

(See the following information on first-, second- and third-degree burns.)

Chemical burns

- Flush the skin with cool, running water for 10 to 15 minutes or until the burning pain has stopped for at least 10 minutes. If the chemical is a dry solid, brush it off first.
- Remove any contaminated clothing, jewelry or other items.
- Cover the area with a cool, damp, sterile dressing or clean cloth and **seek emergency care.**
- If an eye has been burned, flush it immediately with lukewarm water for 20 minutes. Angle the head so the contaminant does not flow into the

other eye. After flushing, close the eye and cover it with a loose, moist dressing and **seek emergency care.**

First-degree or partial thickness burns

- Run cool water over the area or soak it in a cool-water bath as often as necessary to control the pain. If this is not possible, apply cold compresses.
- Cover the area with a cool, moist, clean bandage or clean cloth.
- Take pain relievers—such as aspirin, ibuprofen (Advil, Motrin) and acetaminophen (Tylenol)—to help reduce pain and swelling. **NEVER give aspirin to children/teenagers unless your healthcare provider orders it. It can cause Reye's syndrome, a rare but often fatal condition.**
- Apply a broken aloe vera leaf or aloe vera gel to the burned area to soothe the pain.
- While caring for your burn at home, be aware of signs of infection, which can develop in 24 to 48 hours. (See *Infected Wounds*, p. 73.)

Second-degree or partial thickness burns

- Treat like first-degree burns if they are no bigger than 2 to 3 inches (5 to 8 centimeters) in diameter and not located on the face, hands, feet, groin, buttocks, a major joint or completely encircling a digit or extremity—in which case you should **seek emergency care.**

Third-degree or full thickness burns

- **Cover the burned area with a cool, damp, sterile dressing or clean cloth and seek emergency care.**

For Adults and Children

- Conduct fire drills at home and work. Know the location of fire escapes when you sleep away from home.
- Install smoke detectors in every bedroom and on every floor and test them periodically.
- Keep emergency numbers near the telephone.
- Place a fire extinguisher in the kitchen and check its expiration date on a routine basis. Make sure the extinguisher is rated for kitchen fires.
- Keep a large box of baking soda within easy reach of the stove.
- Keep a potted aloe vera plant or aloe vera gel in the kitchen (where most burns occur) to use the jelly for treating minor burns.

- Never put lighter fluid on lit charcoal briquettes.
- Use only kerosene or other space heaters that have the UL (Underwriter's Laboratory) seal of approval.
- Always follow safety instructions when using chemicals and note any warnings or precautions on the container.
- Learn how to deal with an overheated engine, car fire, or live wire on a car.
- Never touch a downed electrical wire.
- Know where all electrical wiring is located before starting construction or renovation. This also applies to any kind of outdoor digging.
- Check with your utility company if you are unsure about the location of power lines in your area.

For Children

- Never leave a young child at home alone.
- Keep matches and chemicals out of reach.
- Turn pot handles toward the back of the stove while cooking.
- Never drink hot beverages with a child on your lap.
- Never place hot beverages or liquids near a table edge.
- Don't use mats or tablecloths that can be pulled easily off a table.
- Make sure pajamas are flame-retardant.
- Cover electrical outlets when they are not in use.
- Set water heater thermostats no higher than 120° to 125° F (48.8° to 51.6° C).

For All Types of Burns

- NEVER apply ointments, such as Vaseline, sprays, butter, oils or creams. They may slow healing and increase the risk of infection. Flush with cool water instead.
- NEVER cover a burn with materials such as blankets, towels or tissue, since fibers can stick to the wound. Use a clean sheet or sterile dressing.
- NEVER break blisters. They protect the burn from infection and should only be ruptured if swelling constricts circulation.

Heat Exhaustion

Heat exhaustion occurs when your body is not able to cool off and maintain a comfortable temperature. Hot weather, excessive exercise and dehydration can cause the body to overheat. Small children, older adults or people who are frail, obese or have a chronic illness are at risk, as are people in poor condition who overexert themselves.

- Headache
- Weakness
- Fatigue
- Dizziness
- Nausea
- Shallow breathing
- Muscle cramps
- Profuse sweating, cool, clammy skin, or a body temperature slightly elevated or lower than normal

If you are overheating:
- Move to a cooler place and remain quiet.
- Loosen clothing.
- If you are dizzy, lie down with your head lower than your feet.
- Drink small amounts of liquid frequently.
- Place a cool, wet cloth on your forehead.
- Watch for signs of shock and heatstroke. (See *Shock*, p. 39.)
- Do not consume alcohol or apply it to the skin.

- Drink at least 10 eight-ounce glasses of water a day if you exercise or work in hot weather.
- Stay in the shade or air-conditioned areas. Avoid sudden changes of temperature.

- Wear loose-fitting, light-colored clothing of natural fibers such as cotton or linen.
- Limit your activity and exercise during the hottest time of the day.
- Never leave an infant or child alone in a closed auto in hot weather.

Decision *helper*

Heat Exhaustion
Do these apply:

Heatstroke is the critical stage of heat exhaustion and is a medical emergency. All of the body's cooling systems are overloaded when the body temperature reaches 104° F (40° C) and continues to rise. Symptoms of heatstroke are:
- Hot, dry skin
- Bright red or flushed skin
- Body temperature of 104° F (40° C) or greater
- Delirium, disorientation or unconsciousness
- Heat exhaustion symptoms are severe, become worse in spite of self-care or last longer than one hour.

Until help arrives:
Sponge the person's body with cool water or wrap the individual in cool, wet sheets; monitor the person's temperature every 10 minutes. Stop cooling if the temperature drops suddenly or signs of shock develop, such as cool, clammy skin and a weak, rapid pulse. (See **Shock,** p. 39.)

yes

Seek Emergency Care

Apply Emergency First Aid

Hypothermia and Frostbite

In hypothermia, body temperature drops below normal because body heat is lost faster than it can be produced. Frostbite is the freezing of the skin or tissue near the skin surface. These conditions usually occur in freezing weather, but hypothermia can also occur when the weather is windy or wet, yet still above freezing. Frail, inactive people, older adults and small children are particularly susceptible.

Hypothermia

This condition can develop quickly and become a serious problem with little warning. Early symptoms include severe shivering, slurred speech, apathy, impaired judgment and cold, pale skin. As the body temperature continues to drop, shivering may stop; abdomen and chest muscles become hard, and there is slowing of the pulse and breathing. Weakness, drowsiness and confusion may quickly lead to unconsciousness.

Frostbite

Initially the skin feels soft to the touch but is numb and tingly and may turn white. As the skin freezes and becomes hard, blisters may develop. In third-degree frostbite the skin may look blue or blotchy and the underlying tissue is hard and very cold.

Treat for hypothermia before treating frostbite.

Hypothermia

- Get the person to warm, dry shelter.
- Rewarm the individual slowly. Keep him or her awake.
- Replace wet clothing with dry clothes, sleeping bags or blankets, and apply body heat from another person, if possible.
- If the person is alert, give him or her warm liquids and high-calorie food. **Do not give alcohol.**

Frostbite

- Rewarm the person as soon as possible if refreezing **will not** occur.
- Warm small areas with your breath or by placing your hands next to bare skin.
- Immerse body parts in warm (not hot) water (104° to 108° F [40° to 42.2° C]) for 20 to 40 minutes.
- Elevate and protect the warmed part.
- Do not rub or massage a frozen area—further damage can occur.
- Protect blisters. Do not break them.
- Aspirin or acetaminophen (Tylenol) may ease painful burning. **NEVER give aspirin to children/teenagers unless your healthcare provider orders it. It can cause Reye's syndrome, a rare but often fatal condition.**
- Watch for signs of infection. (See *Infected Wounds*, p. 73.)

- Dress warmly in layers with wool and/or polypropylene for insulation and an outer layer that is windproof and waterproof. Polyester fleece garments provide the same or better protection as wool, but they dry much more rapidly than wool.
- Wear a warm hat with ear protection. Wear mittens rather than gloves.
- Pace your activities. Do not become exhausted or sweaty.
- Avoid alcohol and smoking before spending time in the cold.
- Eat well and carry extra high-calorie food.
- Plan ahead and carry provisions in case of an emergency or sudden weather changes.

See **Decision helper,** p. 36.

Hypothermia and Frostbite

Do these apply:

- Unconsciousness
- Slowing in pulse and breathing
- Rigid or stiff body
- Dilated pupils
- Weakness, drowsiness or confusion
- Severe shivering or shivering that has stopped without warming having occurred
- Slurred speech
- Cold, blue extremities
- White and very hard skin (like a block of wood)
- No feeling or function in the affected body part

Until help arrives:
See ***What You Can Do, Hypothermia,*** p. 35.

Seek Emergency Care

Apply Emergency First Aid

- Possible hypothermia occurs in a small child, older adult or frail person
- After the skin thaws:
  - There is considerable pain, numbness or tingling or the skin is mottled red, purplish, blotchy blue or black
  - Blisters develop
- Signs of infection occur 24 to 48 hours after frostbite:
  - Redness around the area or red streaks leading away from it
  - Swelling
  - Warmth or tenderness
  - Pus
  - Fever of 101° F (38.3° C) or higher
  - Tender or swollen lymph nodes

Until you are seen by a doctor:
See ***What You Can Do, Frostbite,*** p. 35.

Call Doctor Now

Unconsciousness

When people are unconscious, they are completely unaware of themselves and their surroundings. They have no control over body functions or movement. Usually they are not able to recall or remember any of the time spent in an unconscious state. Causes of unconsciousness include stroke, epilepsy, diabetic coma, head injury, alcohol intoxication, poisoning, heart attack, bleeding, electrocution and shock.

What You Can Do

If Someone has Lost Consciousness

- Call for emergency medical assistance.
- Check for breathing. If necessary, open the airway and begin rescue breathing. (See *CPR*, p. 18 and *Choking*, p. 22.)
- Check for movement in response to stimulation. If there is none, begin CPR. (See *CPR*, p. 18.)
- Keep the person warm unless you suspect heatstroke. (See *Heat Exhaustion*, p. 32.)
- Roll the person to their side with the lower arm out front. Move the individual as little as possible and only to provide life support or safety. Do not move the person if you suspect a head or neck injury. (See *Head/ Spinal Injury*, p. 56.)
- If the person vomits, turn him or her to one side to allow fluids to drain out.
- Look for medical identification or a possible cause of unconsciousness.
- Do not give the individual anything to eat or drink.

See **Decision helper,** p. 38.

Decision
helper

Unconsciousness
Do these apply:

- There is no response to shout or touch
  (Check breathing. Start CPR if necessary, p. 18.)
- There is only a vague response to shouting and touch
- The person loses bladder and bowel control
- The person cannot recall the time and may have
  a head injury

Seek Emergency Care

(no) (yes)

**Apply Emergency
First Aid**

- The person is awake and responsive after a period of
  complete unconsciousness

(yes)

Call Doctor Now

Shock

If your vital organs are unable to get the blood and oxygen they need, your body can go into shock. Many conditions can cause this urgent situation, including an injury, bleeding, pain, poisoning, extremely high or low body temperature, allergic reaction or severe illness. *Shock is always an emergency and requires professional medical help immediately.*

Preparing for an Emergency

- Learn your local emergency phone numbers. Post them somewhere handy.
- Wear identification to alert medical help if you have any allergies or chronic medical conditions.

When You See Signs of Shock

- Act immediately when you see any signs of shock. Do not wait to see if the person improves on his or her own.
- Call your local emergency services number. While you wait for help to arrive:
  - Have the person lie down and elevate the legs higher than the heart, with support. **If a head or neck injury is suspected, keep the person flat and do not move him or her.** (See *Head/Spinal Injury*, p. 56.)
  - If vomiting begins, roll the person onto his or her side to allow fluid to drain out.
  - Control bleeding by applying direct pressure to the wound. (See *Control Severe Bleeding*, p. 43.)
  - Keep the person warm unless the cause of shock is heatstroke. (See *Heat Exhaustion*, p. 32.)
  - Note the time. Take and record the person's pulse rate every five minutes. (Feel for the heartbeat in the person's wrist or side of the neck with the tips of your index and middle fingers. Count the number of beats in 15 seconds and multiply by four: 30 beats in 15 seconds x 4 = a pulse rate of 120 beats/minute.)

- Do not give the individual anything to eat or drink.
- Comfort and reassure the person while waiting for medical assistance.
- Look for evidence of a cause, such as poison nearby. (See *Poisoning,* p. 26.)
- Check for medical-alert identification.

Shock

Do these apply:

- Cool, pale, clammy skin
- Weak, rapid pulse
- Shallow, rapid breathing
- Confusion, anxiety or restlessness
- Faintness, weakness, dizziness or loss of consciousness
- Dilated pupils
- Nausea, vomiting or thirst

See **What You Can Do,** pp. 39 - 40.

yes

Apply Emergency
First Aid

Seek Emergency Care

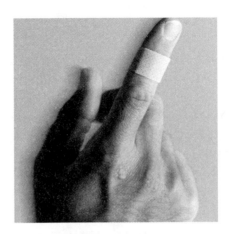

SECTION 2
Injuries

Wounds

There are three kinds of wounds: cuts, abrasions and punctures. All of them—no matter how small—should be cared for quickly to promote healing, prevent infection and reduce scarring.

With every wound there is the potential for infection. (For prevention and care of infected wounds, see Infected Wounds, p. 73.) Get a routine tetanus booster every 10 years and keep up-to-date immunization records. If you have a dirty wound or a puncture and have not had a tetanus booster within the last five years, or if you have not completed your primary series, your doctor will probably recommend a booster injection.

Cuts

There is rarely permanent damage from shallow, minor cuts (*lacerations*) in which the wound is limited to the skin and the fatty tissue beneath it, and they usually can be treated easily at home.

In most minor cuts, bleeding is slow and stops on its own after a few minutes. Slightly deeper cuts can reach the veins, and cause steady blood flow that is slow and dark red. Pressure on the wound usually stops bleeding after a short period. The most serious type of external bleeding, however, is from a cut that strikes an artery. Bleeding is profuse and can be difficult to control even with pressure on the wound. Blood will be bright red and come in spurts as the heart beats. A person with severe bleeding can slip into shock. (See *Shock*, p. 39, and *Control Severe Bleeding*, p. 43.)

Stitches are usually not necessary if the edges of the cut can be pulled together with a bandage or sterile adhesive tape—except on the face, where scarring may be a problem. However, your doctor may *suture* (stitch) cuts in areas subject to frequent movement, such as a finger; in young children, who would pull off bandages; or when a cut is deep, more than one inch (2.54 cm) long, or has jagged edges. Generally, suturing should take place within eight hours of injury for best results. Call your doctor if you're not sure whether you need stitches.

What You Can Do

Control Severe Bleeding

- Dial 911 or your local emergency services number. While waiting for help to arrive:
  - Have the injured person lie down flat and face up with the head slightly lower than the body. Elevate the legs and the site of the bleeding.
  - Keep the person warm to lessen the possibility of shock. (See *Shock*, p. 39.)
  - Remove large pieces of dirt and debris from the wound, but only if this can be done easily. DO NOT remove any embedded objects or try to clean the wound. (See *Punctures*, p. 46.)
  - Place a clean cloth over the wound and apply direct, steady pressure for 15 minutes. To avoid infection, use your bare hands only if necessary. Wash your hands after contact with blood.
  - DO NOT apply direct pressure if there is an object in the wound or a bone is protruding or visible. Apply pressure around the wound instead.
  - If the first cloth becomes soaked with blood, apply a fresh one over it while continuing steady pressure. Do not remove used bandages.
  - If bleeding does not slow or stop after 15 minutes, continue to apply firm, continuous, direct pressure.
  - DO NOT apply a tourniquet, which can result in loss of a limb due to lack of circulation.

Give Prompt Attention to Minor Wounds

- Apply pressure on the wound for 10 or 15 minutes to stop bleeding, if necessary.
- Gently clean the cut with clean running tap water for at least five minutes or until the wound appears clean (to remove dirt, glass and other particles).
- If the wound is slightly gaping, pull its edges together with a regular or butterfly bandage. Cover the wound with dry gauze and tape. Change gauze daily, but don't take the butterfly bandage off until the wound is knit together.
- Cover a cut with a Band-Aid or gauze pad and tape until a scab has formed. Use triple antibiotic ointment for wounds, applied to the dressing, not directly to the wound. Change the dressing and gently wash the wound once a day or whenever the dressing becomes wet or dirty.

Watch for Signs of Infection

Thorough cleansing of the wound is the best way to prevent infection and speed healing. Infection is more likely when a cut occurs in an area that is difficult to keep clean and dry, such as a hand, foot or near a child's mouth. Signs of infection may begin about 24 to 48 hours after the injury. They include redness around the area or red streaks leading away from it, swelling, warmth or tenderness, pus, fever of 101° F (38.3° C) or higher and tender or swollen lymph nodes. (See *Infected Wounds*, p. 73.)

Deep cuts can sever or damage major blood vessels, nerves or tendons, so it is important to know the signs of a serious laceration. In general, be concerned more with cuts to the face, hands, chest, abdomen or back, which have the potential to be more critical than lacerations to other areas.

See *Decision helper,* p. 47.

Abrasions

Scrapes, or *abrasions*, are common injuries, especially among young children. These injuries often result from falls and other minor accidents that typically scratch and tear the outermost layers of skin. The injury is shallow but can be painful because millions of nerve endings are exposed. The pain usually subsides within a few days as scabs form. These injuries are usually dirty and must be cleaned thoroughly to prevent infection.

- Place an ice pack over the wound for a few minutes to alleviate most of the pain. For protection, place a washcloth between bare skin and ice.
- Use a pain reliever such as aspirin, acetaminophen (Tylenol) or ibuprofen (Advil, Motrin) if pain persists. **NEVER give aspirin to children/ teenagers unless your healthcare provider orders it. It can cause Reye's syndrome, a rare but often fatal condition.**
- Clean the area with running tap water for at least five minutes, making sure to remove all dirt and foreign particles.
- Leave skin flaps in place to act as a natural bandage. Dirty skin flaps can be cut away carefully with nail scissors. Stop cutting if it hurts.
- Apply a hydrogel dressing (such as Bioclusive, Tegaderm or Duoderm) to keep the wound moist. Follow package directions. If one of these is not available, apply triple antibiotic ointment to a sterile, nonstick dressing and apply it to the wound.
- If a dressing has become stuck to a scrape, soak the area with warm water before trying to remove it.
- Watch for signs of infection. (See *Infected Wounds*, p. 73.)

See **Decision helper,** p. 47.

Punctures

A puncture wound is a penetrating injury with a sharp-pointed object such as a nail. Seemingly minor puncture wounds sometimes can cause considerable internal damage and—because they can be hard to clean—can become easily infected. If you have not had a tetanus booster within the last five years or if you have not completed your primary series, your doctor will probably recommend a tetanus shot to prevent tetanus ("lockjaw").

What You Can Do

- **Seek emergency medical care if an object, such as a knife, projects from or is embedded in the skin.** Never try to pull the object out, since this could cause further injury. Very gently place a clean, damp cloth around the wound. (For smaller objects, see *Splinters,* p. 62.)
- Allow the wound to bleed freely to cleanse itself. Don't apply pressure unless blood is spurting out or is excessive. (See *Control Severe Bleeding,* p. 43.)
- If the puncture wound isn't serious enough to need emergency medical attention, wash it thoroughly with running tap water. Remove dirt carefully, using tweezers wiped with alcohol to extract debris. Pat the wound dry with clean cloth to stop bleeding. Small wounds will stop bleeding on their own. For others, you may need to apply pressure with a gauze pad or clean cloth and elevate the area above the level of the heart. Avoid contact with blood if possible. Wash your hands thoroughly after touching blood.
- Strong antiseptics, such as Mercurochrome and Merthiolate, aren't necessary and may cause pain. Nonprescription triple antibiotic ointments may help prevent infection. Apply them to the side of the bandage that touches the wound, rather than to the wound itself.
- Cover the wound with a sterile bandage. Change the dressing at least once a day and keep the area clean and dry.
- Watch closely for signs of infection. (See *Infected Wounds,* p. 73.)
- Keep a well-stocked first-aid kit on hand. (See *Home Pharmacy,* p. 325.)

Final Notes   Any wound that doesn't heal well in two weeks should be seen by a doctor. Infection is a common and potentially serious complication that can occur even with minor wounds. (See *Infected Wounds*, p. 73.) An infected wound takes longer to heal and is more likely to scar.

Cuts/Abrasions/Punctures
Do these apply:

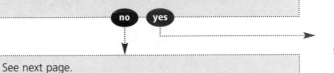

- Bleeding is steady, profuse, or occurs in rhythmic spurts
- Signs of shock are present: weakness; confusion; cold, pale, moist skin (see **Shock,** p. 39)
- Breathing is shallow and the pulse is weak and rapid
- The wound is deep and penetrates to muscle or bone
- An object, such as a knife, projects from or is embedded in the wound (see **What You Can Do, Punctures,** p. 46)

no · · · yes

Seek Emergency Care

See next page.

Do these apply: See previous page.

- Bleeding persists despite applying pressure and elevating the wound for 10 to 15 minutes
- The wound is severe and you have difficulty moving the limb or digit, or you have numbness or tingling near the injury
- The wound edges cannot be pulled together easily
- You suspect the wound needs stiches
- The wound involves the head, face, chest, hand or abdomen
- The wound is difficult to clean thoroughly
- The wound is extremely dirty and/or you are uncertain whether there is foreign material in it
- Signs of infection are present: redness around the area or red streaks leading away from it, swelling, warmth or tenderness, pus, fever of 101° F (38.3° C) or higher, tender or swollen lymph nodes (see *Infected Wounds,* p. 73)

Call Doctor Now

- The wound has not healed in two weeks
- You have a serious chronic health condition and have sustained a wound
- You think you need a tetanus booster or you have not completed your primary series (see *Wounds,* p. 42)

Call Doctor

See *What You Can Do,* pp. 43 - 44, 45, 46.

Apply Self-Care

Bites/Stings

If you have ever experienced an allergic reaction to a bite or sting, ask your doctor about wearing a medical-alert bracelet and getting a prescription for a kit to prevent anaphylaxis, a severe and sometimes fatal allergic reaction. If you're planning outdoor activities such as camping, contact your local health department before you depart to get specific rabies information for the area you will visit.

Animal/Human Bites

The most common type of animal bites involve young children bitten by pets—usually dogs. Overall, about 5 percent of bites become infected. Cat bites become infected 20 to 50 percent of the time. Adult human bites, which become infected in 15 to 30 percent of cases, most frequently result from injuries sustained in fist fights. Bites like these, which break the skin, can cause several types of serious infections:

- Infection caused by various bacteria or microorganisms that can enter the wound
- Pasteurella infection, commonly caused by cat bites
- Tetanus, which can develop after any kind of bite if you have not been inoculated within the last five years or if you have not completed your primary series of tetanus shots
- Rabies, most commonly from bites by skunks, bats, raccoons, coyotes, foxes and other wild mammals and by unvaccinated cats and dogs

Immediately After Being Bitten

- Get emergency care if the bite seems serious or affects the face or hands.
- Rinse and clean the wound immediately.
- Blood flow helps cleanse the wound. Control excessive bleeding by wrapping the wound with a bandage and applying direct pressure. (See *Control Severe Bleeding*, p. 43.)

- Watch for signs of infection, which usually occur within 24 to 48 hours. (See *Infected Wounds,* p. 73.)
- Report all animal bites to the local health department, especially if the bite is from a wild animal or a domestic animal whose rabies vaccination status is unknown. A domestic animal with uncertain rabies vaccination status should be observed for 15 days even if the animal appears healthy.

- Treat all unfamiliar pets with caution.
- Don't try to touch any wild animal, especially if it appears sick.
- Obey "Beware of Dog" signs.
- Teach children not to touch or feed any wild animal or any domestic animal they do not know.
- Never leave an infant, young child or defenseless person unattended with a pet, especially a large dog.

See **Decision helper,** p. 54.

Insects, Spiders and Scorpions

Most insect bites and stings are minor and cause reactions that are *localized* (affecting a limited area). However, a bite from a poisonous spider such as a black widow or brown recluse, or a sting from a scorpion, can cause serious problems.

Even a seemingly harmless bite or sting can be dangerous to people with allergies. Some people are so sensitive to bites and stings that *anaphylaxis* can occur quickly. This potentially life-threatening complication involves extreme breathing difficulty, constriction of the chest, swelling of the mouth, lips, tongue or throat, erratic pulse, severe hives and itching, or violent coughing.

What You Can Do

To know whether you need emergency care, see *Decision helper*, p. 54.

If Emergency Care is Required

Until emergency care can be obtained:
- Use an anaphylactic kit if one is available.
- Apply ice or cold water to the bite for five minutes. For protection, place a washcloth between the bare skin and the ice.
- If the bite is on a hand or foot, keep the limb snugly bandaged above the bite for five minutes (but make sure you can feel a pulse below the bandage). Do not apply a tourniquet.
- Keep the limb below the level of the heart.
- Remove any stinger left in the skin. (See below.)

When Emergency Care is Not Required

- Scrape or flick out any stinger that may be left in the skin with a credit card or your fingernail. Avoid squeezing the stinger.

- Apply ice for 15 to 20 minutes at a time, more frequently initially, then three to four times a day for up to 48 hours. Leave ice off for at least 20 minutes between applications. For protection, place a washcloth between bare skin and ice and change the cloth if it becomes wet.
- Wash the area with soap and water.
- Use calamine lotion or over-the-counter (OTC) hydrocortisone cream to reduce itching and inflammation.
- If itching becomes severe, try an OTC oral antihistamine such as Benadryl or Chlor-Trimeton. Many antihistamines, especially over-the-counter ones, may cause drowsiness or inattention and lead to accidents. Talk to your physician or pharmacist about the risk of sedation and do not give antihistamines to a child under 1 year of age without consulting your doctor.

General Precautions

- Avoid wearing perfume if you'll be spending time outdoors—it attracts bees.
- Get reliable instructions before trying to remove a beehive or nest. Follow directions on commercial products.
- If you are allergic to bees, always carry an anaphylactic kit. You can get one with a prescription from your doctor.

See **Decision helper,** p. 54.

Snake Bites

Thousands of people in the United States are bitten by snakes each year, but few of these bites are from poisonous snakes. Fewer than 15 fatalities result from snake bites annually, and many of those occur because the bites are not treated.

Most people cannot tell a poisonous from a nonpoisonous snake. Therefore ALL snake bites that break the skin should receive emergency medical care.

Identifying a Poisonous Snake

Most venomous snakes in the United States (such as rattlesnakes, copperheads and water moccasins) are characterized by:
- Triangular-shaped heads
- Elliptical-shaped (slit-like) eyes
- A depression (or pit) midway between the nostrils and eyes

Rattlesnakes produce a characteristic rattling sound with their tail. The water moccasin has a whitish, cottony lining in its mouth. The copperhead has a large, coppery head. Poisonous coral snakes have red, yellow and black rings along their bodies.

If you think you have been bitten by a poisonous snake, it is especially important to seek emergency medical care. Never use your mouth to suction the wound.

After Being Bitten

Seek emergency care for any snake bite that breaks the skin. The wound from a snake bite, even if it isn't poisonous, can become infected or cause a severe allergic reaction. To treat such bites:
- Rinse and clean the wound with soap and water.
- Don't try to stop the bleeding unless it is severe.
- Get a tetanus shot if you haven't had one in five or more years or if you didn't complete your primary series of tetanus shots.
- Watch for signs of infection. (See *Infected Wounds*, p. 73.)

What You Can Do

While You Wait for Medical Attention

- Lie down and try to remain calm. Stay as quiet as possible.
- Keep your body warm.
- Keep the bitten area lower than the level of the heart.
- Remove all jewelry. Any part of the body can swell after a snake bite.
- Snugly wrap a bandage around the entire arm or leg (but make sure you can feel a pulse below the bandage).
- Do not move the wounded area. Use a splint if possible.
- DO NOT take any drugs, including aspirin or alcohol. DO NOT apply heat or ice to the wound. DO NOT use a tourniquet. DO NOT cut into the wound to try to drain or suck out the venom.

Decision *helper*

Bites/Stings
Do these apply:

- You experience symptoms of an allergic reaction following a bite: extreme breathing difficulty, constriction in the chest, swelling of the mouth, lips, tongue or throat, erratic pulse, severe hives and itching or violent coughing
- Severe pain or itching, increased perspiration, weakness or listlessness, nausea or paralysis follow a snake bite
- You are bitten by a black widow or brown recluse spider, poisonous insect or marine animal or reptile
- You have a known sensitivity or allergy to an insect, spider, scorpion, reptile or mammal
- A snake bite breaks the skin
- You have a serious bite, especially if it affects the face or hand

See **What You Can Do**, pp. 49 - 50, 51 - 52, 54.

no · · · yes

See next page.

Seek Emergency Care

Apply Emergency First Aid

Do these apply: See previous page.

- An animal or human bite or scratch breaks the skin
- A bite that doesn't break the skin is from a wild animal, a domestic cat or dog whose rabies status is unknown or any animal that displays bizarre behavior
- Signs of infection are present: redness around the area or red streaks leading away from it, swelling, warmth or tenderness, pus, fever of 101° F (38.3° C) or higher, tender or swollen lymph nodes

Call Doctor Now

- You are exposed to a bat, but are not bitten or scratched
- You are bitten by a human or animal and you have not had a tetanus shot in five or more years or you have not completed your primary series
- Illness occurs one to two weeks after a cat bite or scratch or a rat bite

Call Doctor

See *What You Can Do,* pp. 49 - 50, 51 - 52, 54.
See *Punctures,* p. 46.

Apply Self-Care

Other Injuries

Head/Spinal Injury

Any significant trauma to the head or spine is cause for concern because of the potential for injury to the delicate structures within the brain and spinal cord. This can be serious and requires professional medical assistance. Fortunately, most injuries are minor, limited to the surrounding protective tissues, and can be treated with self-care.

Head Injury

Following an injury to the head, treat any surface injury, protect it from additional damage, and watch for signs of internal bleeding. Observation for at least 72 hours is important since bleeding inside the skull may be slow and symptoms may develop gradually.

- If there is external bleeding, apply pressure on the wound for 15 minutes or until the bleeding stops completely. Use a clean cloth; if the blood soaks through, apply additional cloths over the first one.
- Apply ice or cold packs to ease pain and reduce swelling. For protection, place a washcloth between bare skin and ice. A "goose egg" may develop.
- Check for other injuries, especially to the neck and back.
- Keep the person sitting or lying down with the head slightly elevated.
- Check for signs of bleeding inside the skull immediately after the injury, then every two hours for the first 24 hours, every four hours for the following 24 hours, and every eight hours through the third day. Signs include:
  - **Changes in mental state,** which may include unconsciousness, confusion, a decrease in alertness, abnormally deep sleep, or difficulty waking up
  - **Unequal size of pupils after the injury;** some people normally have different pupil sizes, but a change after an injury can be a serious sign
  - **Severe, forceful vomiting** that is repeated or continuous (one single episode of vomiting may be a reaction to the pain)
  - **A change or decrease in the ability** to move parts of the body or a change in the ability to see, smell, hear, taste or touch

- Watch for bleeding or clear drainage from the nose or ears, and for fever.
- Avoid heavy exercise or exertion for at least 72 hours.
- Be alert to chronic headache or changes in personality for weeks to months after a head injury. These may be signs of very slow internal bleeding, which can cause pressure on the brain much later.

Spinal Injury

Injury to the spine can occur in any accident involving the head, neck or back. Self-care is directed toward preventing additional damage and permanent paralysis, decreasing symptoms and eliminating future injury.

What You Can Do

If you suspect an injury to the spine:
- DO NOT MOVE THE PERSON unless there is an immediate threat to life, such as a fire.
- Call for professional medical help to move the person. Keep the person still and warm. Do not give the individual anything to eat or drink.
- If there is immediate danger and you must move the person, **immobilize the neck and back.** Slide a board or other firm surface under the person's head and back without moving the neck or back from the position it was in. Place soft, bulky material on each side of the head to prevent rotation.
- In a diving or surfing accident, do not pull the person from the water unless his or her life is endangered. Float the person face up. If you must move the person, use a board that supports the area from the head to the buttocks. Lift him or her out of the water on the board.
- If there is much bleeding from the nose or mouth, roll the person onto his or her side (the entire body needs to roll in one even movement) without twisting the neck or back. If the bleeding is minor, wipe out the mouth and nose without moving the person.

Prevention

- Wear your seat belt while in all motor vehicles and place children in proper car seats.
- Wear a helmet while biking, motorcycling, skating, skateboarding or horseback riding.
- Don't dive into shallow or unfamiliar water.

See **Decision helper,** p. 58.

Decision *helper*

Head/Spinal Injury

Do these apply:

- There is cessation of breathing or no pulse; start CPR (see **CPR,** p. 18)
- Bleeding is uncontrolled
- There is an obvious severe head or neck injury, including a stiff or painful neck
- Any loss of consciousness occurs, even if the person is now awake
- Seizure
- Bowel or bladder control is lost
- Visual changes occur or pupils are fixed or unequal
- The person has trouble walking or speaking
- There is a change in mental status (confusion, disorientation, extreme drowsiness or lack of responsiveness, irritation or agitation)
- An infant has a bulging soft spot or cries for more than 15 minutes

 no · **yes**

Seek Emergency Care

FIRST AID

Apply Emergency
First Aid

- A laceration may need stitches
- Fluid drains from the nose or an ear
- Vomiting occurs more than twice
- The person has a severe headache
- Someone's head has been forcfully struck with a very hard object
- A fall results in a forceful impact on the head or neck
- New bruising appears around the eyes or behind both ears
- A past head injury later results in increasing or recurrent headache, difficulty concentrating, memory loss, or personality change

 no · **yes**

Call Doctor Now

- A minor head injury has no immediate signs of brain or spinal injury

See **What You Can Do, Head Injury,** pp. 56 - 57;
What You Can Do, Spinal Injury, p. 57.

Apply Self-Care

Accidental Tooth Loss

When a permanent tooth is knocked out, your dentist may be able to re-implant it successfully if the tooth tissue is kept alive. Your chances of saving a tooth are good up to one hour after injury. Baby teeth are not usually re-implanted since they eventually come out anyway.

When You Injure or Lose a Permanent Tooth

- Avoid touching the root end of the tooth.
- Rinse the tooth in water (do not scrub it).
- Put the tooth in cold milk and bring it with you.

- Wear a protective dental guard or headgear when participating in sports.
- Know when and how to reach your dentist in an emergency.

Accidental Tooth Loss
Do these apply:

- A permanent tooth is knocked out with no other signs of head or facial injury

See **What You Can Do,** this page.

Request an emergency appointment for re-implantation by your dentist. Bring the tooth with you.

- A baby tooth is knocked out

Request an appointment to determine the need for a spacer.

 yes

Call Dentist

Fishhooks

Fishhooks are designed with a barb to keep fish hooked. Unfortunately, the barb works the same way on people once the skin is punctured. It is useful to know how to remove a fishhook for yourself or a companion, especially if you are any distance from medical help.

If the Hook is Near the Skin Surface

- **Step 1:** Clean the hook and skin with soap and water.
- **Step 2:** Apply ice or cold water to provide temporary numbing.
- **Step 3:** Loop a piece of fishing line through the hook (Figure 10). Make the line long enough to grasp securely with your hand.
- **Step 4:** Grasp the eye or shaft of the hook with one hand and press down about one-eighth inch (.32 cm) to disengage the barb.
- **Step 5:** While still pressing down on hook, pull the line parallel to the skin's surface so the hook shaft leads the barb out of the skin (Figure 11).
- **Step 6:** Wash the wound thoroughly with soap and water. Treat it as you would a puncture wound. (See *Punctures*, p. 46.)

If the Hook is Deeply Embedded

Figure 10

Note: only attempt a difficult hook removal if medical care is unavailable.
- **Step 1:** Clean the hook and skin with running water.
- **Step 2:** Apply ice or cold water to provide temporary numbing.
- **Step 3:** Push the hook through the skin.
- **Step 4:** Cut off the barb with wire cutters.
- **Step 5:** Pull the hook back out.
- **Step 6:** Wash the wound thoroughly with soap and water. Treat it as you would a puncture wound. (See *Punctures*, p. 46.)

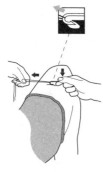

Figure 11

Fishhooks

Do these apply:

- The hook is in the eye
  Do not try to remove the hook. Keep the person still. Secure a cup over the injured eye and cover both eyes to prevent eye movement.

 no yes

Seek Emergency Care

- The hook is embedded in the skin and medical care is available
- Signs of infection develop (see ***Infected Wounds,*** p. 73)
- You are unable to remove the fishhook

no yes

Call Doctor Now

- Five or more years have passed since your last tetanus shot or you have not completed your primary series

no yes

Call Doctor

- The person is able to cooperate
- The hook is embedded near the skin surface and can be reached

See ***What You Can Do,*** p. 60.

Apply Self-Care

Splinters

A sharp, slender piece of wood, metal or glass can easily pierce the skin and become lodged. This type of injury usually can be treated at home by removing the splinter and cleaning the area. In some instances, infection may develop or a nerve may be damaged, both of which require medical evaluation.

If the Splinter Can be Reached

- Grasp the end of the splinter with tweezers and gently pull it out along the entry track.
- Cleanse the area with running tap water.
- Keep the area clean and dry; apply a dry bandage if necessary.
- Watch for signs of infection:
  - Redness around the area or red streaks leading away from it
  - Swelling
  - Warmth and tenderness
  - Pus
  - Fever of 101° F (38.3° C) or higher
  - Tender or swollen lymph nodes

If the Splinter is Deeply Embedded

- Clean a needle by dipping it in alcohol or holding it in a match flame.
- Cleanse the skin with soap and water, then pick the skin over the end of the splinter and make a small hole.
- Lift the splinter with the tip of a needle until it can be grasped by tweezers. Withdraw it along the entry track.
- Cleanse again and care for the wound, as outlined above.

Splinters

Do these apply:

- A splinter is in the eye
  Cover both eyes to prevent eye movement.

no **yes**

Seek Emergency Care

- A splinter is large, of toxic material or deeply embedded
- You have unusual trouble moving a finger, toe or limb where the splinter was embedded
- Signs of infection develop (see **Infected Wounds,** p. 73)

no **yes**

Call Doctor Now

- Five or more years have passed since your last tetanus shot or you have not completed your primary series

no **yes**

Call Doctor

See **What You Can Do,** p. 62.
See **Punctures,** p. 46.

Apply Self-Care

Smashed Fingers

Fingers often get smashed, pinched or jammed during daily activities. Most finger injuries are not serious. Although they may be quite painful and inconvenient, these injuries heal well with self-care at home. Serious injuries with possible bone fractures, severe bleeding or severed parts require professional medical help.

What You Can Do

- Immediately insert the fingers into ice-cold water to decrease the pain and reduce swelling. Then, apply ice for 15 to 20 minutes at a time, more frequently initially, then three to four times a day for up to 48 hours. Leave ice off for at least 20 minutes between applications. For protection, place a washcloth between bare skin and ice and change the cloth if it becomes wet.
- Remove any jewelry if you can do so without causing additional pain.
- If the skin is broken, wash with soap and water, then dry. Apply a soft, clean dressing.
- Splint and support an injured finger by taping it to a finger splint.
- Rest and elevate the hand above the level of the heart for 24 to 48 hours; use it as little as possible.
- Take aspirin or ibuprofen (Advil, Motrin) to reduce swelling and pain. **NEVER give aspirin to children/teenagers unless your healthcare provider orders it. It can cause Reye's syndrome, a rare but often fatal condition**.
- Once swelling stops, apply warm compresses at intervals for comfort.

"Torn" or "Torn-Off" Fingernails

- If a nail is only partially attached or is completely torn off, seek care. The nail bed needs to be cleaned and smoothed and any lacerations repaired to help the new nail grow back smoothly. The torn-off nail may be used to protect the nail bed, so place it in cool water and take it with you to the doctor.
- Keep the area clean; watch for signs of infection. (See *Infected Wounds*, p. 73.)
- Protect the tip of the finger with a soft cloth or covering to which antibiotic ointment has been applied.

For a Minor Torn Nail

- Trim any jagged edges that might catch on a bandage or clothing.
- Clean with peroxide; it will make up for scrubbing with soap and water, which might be too painful. **Note: Peroxide is not typically suggested for cleaning other injuries; soap and water generally works best.**
- Cover the nailbed with Neosporin ointment and then with a non-stick bandage.

Blood Under a Nail

- Apply ice as soon as possible. For protection, place a washcloth between bare skin and ice.
- Clean the nail with soap and water.
- Make a hole in the nail to relieve pressure and pain:
  - Straighten a paper clip and use a pair of pliers to hold it in a flame until it is red hot.
  - Place the tip of the paper clip on the nail firmly but gently and let it melt through. You need not push. A thick nail may take several tries. As soon as the hole is complete, blood will escape and the pain and pressure will ease.
- Soak the finger for several minutes four and eight hours after making the hole in a solution of equal parts warm water and hydrogen peroxide. This keeps the hole open.
- If the blood and pressure build up again, repeat the procedure using the same hole.

Decision *helper*

Smashed Fingers
Do these apply:

- The finger is severed
  Apply direct pressure with a sterile bandage to control bleeding. Wrap the finger in clean or sterile gauze and place it in a plastic bag. Place the bag in cold water; do not let the tissue freeze. Bring the severed finger with the injured person.
- Severe bleeding or hemorrhage occurs
  Apply direct pressure with a sterile bandage.
- A finger is deformed or bent into an abnormal shape or bone protrudes through the skin
  Immobilize the hand. Avoid unnecessary movement. Do not move or reposition the finger.
- You have a penetrating finger injury
  Do not attempt to remove an object that is stuck in a finger. Control bleeding and immobilize the hand.

 no **yes**

Seek Emergency Care

- The nail is completely or partially torn off
- Stiches are needed
- There was immediate pain with a tearing, cracking or popping sound
- Signs of infection are present (see **Infected Wounds,** p. 73)
- Movement is painful for 24 hours or more
- Swelling prevents removal of jewelry

no **yes**

Apply Emergency First Aid

- Numbness or a sensation of pins and needles occurs in a finger or hand
- Five or more years have passed since your last tetanus shot or you have not completed your primary series
- Pain and swelling do not ease with self-care

no **yes**

Call Doctor Now

See **What You Can Do,** pp. 64 - 65.

Call Doctor

Apply Self-Care

Strains and Sprains

A *strain* is an injury to a muscle caused by over-stretching. Also called a "pulled muscle," a strain occurs when a muscle's elastic fibers are overextended and contract, tear and bleed. A *sprain* is an injury to a ligament and other soft tissue surrounding a joint. *Ligaments* are bands of fiber that connect the bones at a joint. They can be stretched or torn when a joint is twisted, "jammed" or overextended. With either injury, bleeding may produce a bruise that resolves slowly.

The basic treatment for strains and sprains is a two-part process: **RICE** (rest, ice, compression, elevation) to treat the immediate injury and **MSA** (movement, strength, alternate activity) to help the injury heal and prevent further problems. Begin the **RICE** process **immediately** following the injury:

- **Rest.** Do not put weight on the injured joint or muscle, and limit movement in the area of the injury. Use crutches, splints or a sling as needed.
- **Ice.** Apply ice for 15 to 20 minutes at a time, more frequently initially, then three to four times a day for up to 48 hours. Leave ice off for at least 20 minutes between applications. For protection, place a washcloth between bare skin and ice and change the cloth if it becomes wet.
- **Compress.** Wrap the injured area in an elastic bandage for support and protection. Don't wrap it so tightly that circulation is cut off.
- **Elevate.** Place the injured part on pillows while you apply ice and anytime you are seated or lying down. Raise the injured area above the level of your heart whenever possible.

Aspirin and ibuprofen (Advil, Motrin) may ease pain and inflammation. Acetaminophen (Tylenol) eases discomfort but does not decrease inflammation. Do not use other drugs to mask pain in order to continue using the injured part. **NEVER give aspirin to children/teenagers unless your healthcare provider orders it. It can cause Reye's syndrome, a rare but often fatal condition.**

The MSA process should be started only if the initial swelling is gone:

- **Movement.** Begin gently moving the joint to resume full range of motion.
- **Strength.** After the swelling is gone and full range of motion is restored, gradually begin to strengthen the injured part. Slow, gentle stretching during the healing process will make scar tissue flexible and prevent limited movement later.
- **Alternate activities.** Resume regular exercise through activities and sports that do not place a strain on the injured area. Go slowly and stop any activity that causes discomfort.

Any increase in pain or return of swelling is a sign to stop **MSA** and resume **RICE**.

Heat can be applied once swelling stops increasing to relieve muscle spasm and increase circulation. Place a warm washcloth, water bottle or heating pad directly on the injured area for 20 minutes at a time. Use caution with heat to prevent burns. Never leave a child unattended with a heating pad.

Prevention

- Use correct form in all work and play activities.
- Adjust equipment and furniture to fit your needs.
- Go slowly when starting a new activity or sport.
- Use warm-up and cool-down exercises to help your body prepare and recover safely. Don't forget to stretch.
- Take frequent breaks when performing any continuous activity.
- Do not push beyond your strength or ability; advance your skill level gradually.

Decision *helper*

Strains and Sprains
Do these apply:

After an injury there is:
- Immediate pain with a popping, cracking or tearing sound
- A feeling of instability in a joint or extremity
- Severe pain
- Inability to use an extremity for more than two hours
- Pain that has prevented the use of a joint for 24 hours or more

no   **yes**

Call Doctor Now

- Numbness or tingling is felt in an extremity
- The following symptoms last longer than 72 hours:
  - Mild to moderate pain
  - Limited movement
  - No improvement with self-care

no   **yes**

Call Doctor

- Pain or swelling in a joint or muscle follows activity or movement
  Start RICE immediately (see p. 67).
- Pain is decreasing and swelling is going away with RICE
  Continue until swelling is gone and then start MSA. Full healing may take four or more weeks.

See **What You Can Do,** pp. 67 - 68.

Apply Self-Care

Broken Bones

It is often difficult to tell if a bone has been *fractured* (broken) in an injury. Unless the fracture is obvious, an x-ray may be needed to be sure. The break may be a small crack such as a *stress fracture* caused by overuse, a *greenstick fracture* (often found in children, where the bone is only partially broken), a *simple fracture* in which the bone ends separate but stay in alignment, or a *compound fracture*, where the soft tissue in the area is torn and the bone protrudes through the skin. The seriousness of a break varies depending on which bone is broken, the type of break involved and whether there are associated injuries.

Suspect a Fracture if:

- The injured part is bent or deformed
- A bone pokes through the skin
- There is a bump or irregularity along the bone
- A cracking or snapping sound was heard at the time of injury
- There is rapid swelling or bruising immediately after the injury

- Assume there may be a fracture.
- Immobilize and support the injured area with a splint. To splint, attach a stiff object (such as a rolled magazine or newspaper or a cane) to the injured limb with a rope or belt. Position the splint so the injured limb cannot bend.
- Do not attempt to move an abnormally bent or displaced bone back into place. Splint it as it is.
- Apply ice for 15 to 20 minutes at a time, more frequently initially, then three to four times a day for up to 48 hours. Leave ice off for at least 20 minutes between applications. For protection, place a washcloth between bare skin and ice and change the cloth if it becomes wet.
- To immobilize and support a possible fractured toe, gently tape it to an adjacent toe.

- Wrap the injury with an elastic bandage to immobilize and compress the area. Loosen the bandage if it becomes too tight.
- Elevate the injured area.
- Avoid any unnecessary movement. Rest the injury for at least 24 to 48 hours.

Use aspirin or ibuprofen (Advil, Motrin) to ease pain and inflammation. **NEVER give aspirin to children/teenagers unless your healthcare provider orders it. It can cause Reye's syndrome, a rare but often fatal condition.**

Broken Bones
Do these apply:

- The limb is cold, blue or numb
- The pelvis or thigh is injured
- Signs of shock occur (cool, clammy, pale skin; dizziness or light-headedness; thirst)
  Keep the person lying down and covered to stay warm.
  Do not give the person anything to eat or drink.
- Shortness of breath or difficulty breathing occur after a chest injury
  Keep the person quiet and place in a seated position to assist breathing.
- Bone protrudes through the skin
- You suspect fracture near a joint
- The injured part is crooked or deformed
- Heavy bleeding occurs or blood spurts out
  Cover an open wound with a clean, dry cloth. Apply direct pressure on the bleeding with a sterile or clean cloth. Apply only enough pressure to stop the bleeding. If blood soaks through, apply another bandage. Do not remove the first one nor apply a tourniquet.

no   yes

Seek Emergency Care

See next page.

Apply Emergency
First Aid

Do these apply: See previous page.

• The injured part is unstable or unable to bear weight
• Large amount of swelling or bruising occurs immediately after the injury

See *What You Can Do,* pp. 70 - 71.

no   yes

Call Doctor Now

• An injury does not improve after 48 hours of self-care

yes

Call Doctor

Infected Wounds

Any wound can become infected, particularly if it has not been thoroughly cleaned. An infected wound takes longer to heal, is more likely to scar and can result in serious complications, including death. Take the treatment of any wound seriously and be alert for signs of infection.

Signs of an infected wound include:
- Redness around the area or red streaks leading away from it
- Swelling
- Warmth and tenderness
- Pus
- Fever of 101° F (38.3° C) or higher
- Tender or swollen lymph nodes

With your doctor's approval:
- Use a sterile bandage and change it daily or once it becomes wet.
- Remove the bandage and soak the wound in warm water several times a day.

Ward off infection by taking some simple steps as soon as the injury occurs. If the wound does not require emergency care:
- Clean it thoroughly with mild soap and warm water.
- Remove foreign objects and large particles of dirt with tweezers if necessary. Wipe the tweezers with alcohol first to disinfect them.
- Avoid using strong antiseptics, such as Mercurochrome, iodine and full-strength hydrogen peroxide, which can damage skin tissue.
- Keep your tetanus immunization up to date. You should get a routine tetanus booster every 10 years. However, if you have a dirty wound and have not had a booster within the last five years, or if you have not completed your primary series, your doctor may recommend a booster injection.

Final Notes

Symptoms of infection generally begin to appear about 24 to 48 hours after an injury, although potentially, the infection can occur at any time until healing is complete. People with diabetes and patients with organ transplants, immune system disorders or cancer are at higher risk of infection.

Decision *helper*

Infected Wounds
Do these apply:

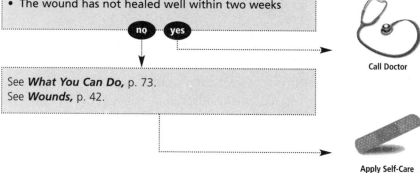

- Signs of infection develop:
  - Redness around the area or red streaks leading away from it
  - Swelling
  - Warmth or tenderness
  - Pus
  - Fever of 101° F (38.3° C) or higher
  - Tender or swollen lymph nodes
- The wound has not healed well within two weeks

no · · yes

See *What You Can Do,* p. 73.
See *Wounds,* p. 42.

Call Doctor

Apply Self-Care

SECTION 3
Infant/Child

Infant Rashes

Infant Rashes

The bumps and splotches on a new baby may be worrisome to a parent, but they aren't usually harmful. The following chart lists the most common infant rashes.

Symptoms	Self-Care
Acne	
Acne on forehead, cheeks and chin, beginning at 2 to 4 weeks of age	Wash the face daily with cloth, water and mild soap; acne usually clears up within six months to one year
Cradle Cap	
Thick yellow crust on scalp; in severe cases, cradle cap may be present on the face and behind the ears; scalp can also look red and inflamed; no fever; may also appear as reddened areas in skin folds	Use mild baby shampoo daily; apply warm mineral or olive oil to the scalp 10 minutes before shampooing. To loosen scales, gently comb with a fine-toothed baby comb. Cradle cap tends to recur
Diaper Rash	
Redness in the diaper area - Redness extending beyond the diaper area with small red spots or blisters may indicate a yeast or bacterial infection; call doctor	Change cloth and disposable diapers frequently; wash the skin with soap and water after stools, dry well; avoid plastic pants until healed; Desitin or A&D ointment can help protect the skin and promote healing
Erythema Toxicum	
Flat, red splotches on the arms, legs, chest, back and face, appearing before 5 days of age	No treatment needed
Milia	
Small white bumps on the forehead, nose and cheeks	No treatment needed
Prickly Heat (Sweat) Rash	
Small, red bumps in skin folds, especially on the head, neck and shoulders	Dress baby lightly; provide less-humid environment; avoid ointments or creams that block pores

If a rash is accompanied by fever or signs of illness, consult your doctor. (See *Fever*, p. 100.)

Childhood Diseases

Chickenpox

Chickenpox (or *varicella*) is a common, highly contagious viral disease most likely to occur in children ages 2 to 10. For adults it's relatively uncommon but can create serious complications when contracted, especially for people with immune disorders, pregnant women and their unborn children. The chickenpox vaccine has made this disease far less common than it was in the past.

Chickenpox is contagious for about a week, from 24 to 36 hours before the rash appears until all the pox sores have scabbed over. Upon exposure, it takes an average of 14 to 16 days for symptoms to develop.

After you've had chickenpox, the virus takes up residence in a bundle of sensory nerve cells connected to the spinal cord. For most people the virus remains dormant. However, in some cases it is reactivated and travels down the nerve, causing a skin rash in that area that turns into blisters. This is called *shingles*. No one knows what reactivates the virus, but stress, aging, trauma and certain illnesses can be triggers. Shingles usually occurs on one side of the body (most often on the torso) and is accompanied by sharp nerve pain. Acyclovir (Zovirax) is often prescribed to relieve symptoms.

If you have shingles, it is possible to pass chickenpox on to someone who has never had the disease, although the virus is not often spread this way.

Note the Symptoms

Early signs of chickenpox include a vague feeling of discomfort, mild headache, a cough and a low-grade fever. The rash appears as red bumps with tiny fluid-filled blisters. The blisters crust over within six to eight hours. For five or six days, the rash appears on various sites of the body, which can include the mucous membranes of the eyes, mouth and vagina. The rash is extremely itchy and can cause permanent scars (slight, round depressions in the skin), especially if the scabs are scratched off. The scabs are present even after chickenpox is no longer contagious. Usually people start to feel better before they look better.

Chickenpox is usually mild in healthy children, but can be more serious in adults or those with immune-system disorders.

Complications from chickenpox include infected pox, pneumonia and, on rare occasions, *encephalitis* (an inflammation of the brain) or *necrotizing fasciitis* (a serious bacterial infection of connective tissue).

Chickenpox is very serious in newborns. If a mother has chickenpox within a week before delivery, or within two days after delivery, there is a 50 percent chance that the infant will be infected with the disease. This can be fatal for the infant.

Prevention

The American Academy of Pediatrics recommends including the chickenpox vaccine, Varivax, as part of a child's immunization program. The recommended schedule is:

- One dose given to infants between the ages of 12 and 18 months and to any child up to age 13 who has not been immunized and who has not had chickenpox.
- Two doses given four to eight weeks apart to children over age 13 and adults who have not been immunized and who have not had chickenpox.

What You Can Do

Treatment for chickenpox is directed toward relieving symptoms and watching for complications. Apply cool, wet compresses. Take an oatmeal bath (one-half to one cup [115 to 230 mL] of oatmeal in a tub of lukewarm water). Apply calamine lotion with a cotton swab to the itchy areas, except the mucous membranes (such as the mouth, eyes or vagina). Adults can take an antihistamine, but a pediatrician should be consulted about its use in young children. Use mitts on infants and very young children to avoid skin damage from scratching.

Acetaminophen (Tylenol) will reduce fever and discomfort. **NEVER give aspirin to children/ teenagers unless your healthcare provider orders it. It can cause Reye's syndrome, a rare but often fatal condition. Children with chickenpox are at increased risk for Reye's syndrome.** If necessary, talk with your doctor about chickenpox over the phone instead of taking your child into the office. This eliminates the risk of exposing others to the disease.

Chickenpox

Do these apply:

- Severe respiratory distress accompanies chickenpox, such as a feeling of suffocation, gasping or straining to get a breath or a bluish discoloration of the lips or skin
- The level of consciousness changes, such as confusion, disorientation or a lack of responsiveness
- General symptoms occur, such as a severe headache, stiff neck, repeated vomiting, fever and very tender skin, red rash that is separate from chickenpox or large blisters along with peeling skin
- A child under age 2 has any of the following: very unusual crying (inconsolable, high-pitched, weak, continual), a bulging soft spot, seizure or a limp or floppy body
- An infant under 3 months of age has had a fever of 100.4° F (38° C) or higher in the past 24 hours (even if the temperature has returned to normal)

no **yes**

Seek Emergency Care

- Difficulty breathing or shortness of breath occur
- Signs of infection are present: redness around the area or red streaks leading away from it, swelling, warmth or tenderness, pus, fever of 101° F (38.3° C) or higher, tender or swollen lymph nodes
- Eye pain or a sore in the eye develops
- A high-risk child or adult has, or is exposed to, chickenpox. High-risk people include those who: have/had cancer, have received a transplant, are newborn, pregnant or elderly, have a chronic illness/condition, have weakened immune systems

no **yes**

Call Doctor Now

- A fever lasts more than four days
- Persistent or recurring cough develops

no **yes**

Call Doctor

See *What You Can Do,* p. 78.

Apply Self-Care

Rubella

Rubella, also known as *German measles* and three-day measles, is a mild virus often characterized by a flat or slightly raised pink or red rash.

The greatest danger is to an unborn child, who may develop *congenital rubella syndrome* if the mother contracts rubella during pregnancy. This can result in birth defects—or even death—for the baby. If a pregnant woman contracts rubella during the first trimester of pregnancy, there is a chance that the fetus will develop abnormally in some way.

The virus is usually spread through coughing and sneezing or through close contact with an infected person. Rubella can be transmitted to others one week before and up to four days after the onset of the rash.

Symptoms develop about 16 days after exposure. About five to 10 days before the rash appears, you may have swollen and tender lymph glands in the neck and behind the ears, mild fever, *malaise* (feeling lousy), sneezing and irritated eyes.

Other symptoms include:

- A rash that starts on the face and forehead, spreading quickly to the torso, arms and legs, and lasting about one day in each area
- A flushed face
- Redness of the *soft palate* (the back of the roof of the mouth) and throat

Some adults also experience headache, joint pain, weariness and a stuffy and runny nose.

Prevention

Immunization is the safest and most effective way to prevent rubella. The vaccine is usually given in combination with those for measles and mumps in the MMR vaccine. All babies should be immunized between 12 and 15 months. A second dose should be given between 4 and 6 years of age. If the second dose has not been given as scheduled, have your doctor give it during any office visit by the child's 11th or 12th birthday.

Women should make sure they are not pregnant before receiving the rubella vaccine and diligently practice a reliable form of birth control for at least three months after the immunization. Some adults may experience mild joint pain following the vaccination.

To treat symptoms and avoid spreading the infection:
- Stay at home until the rash subsides or as recommended by your doctor.
- If a fever rises above 101° F (38.3° C), drink plenty of fluids. Take a lukewarm bath or shower.
- Try acetaminophen (Tylenol) or anti-inflammatories, such as ibuprofen (Advil, Motrin) to provide comfort. **NEVER give aspirin to children/ teenagers unless your healthcare provider orders it. It can cause Reye's syndrome, a rare but often fatal condition.**

Rubella
Do these apply:

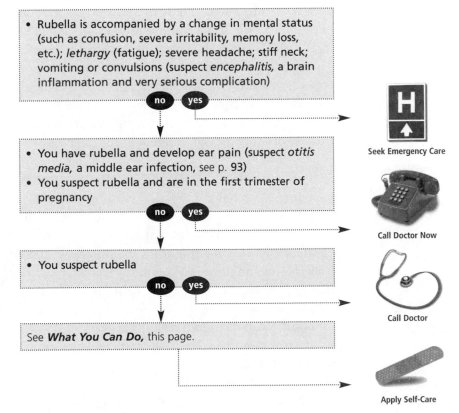

- Rubella is accompanied by a change in mental status (such as confusion, severe irritability, memory loss, etc.); *lethargy* (fatigue); severe headache; stiff neck; vomiting or convulsions (suspect *encephalitis,* a brain inflammation and very serious complication)

no   yes

Seek Emergency Care

- You have rubella and develop ear pain (suspect *otitis media,* a middle ear infection, see p. 93)
- You suspect rubella and are in the first trimester of pregnancy

no   yes

Call Doctor Now

- You suspect rubella

no   yes

Call Doctor

See **What You Can Do,** this page.

Apply Self-Care

Measles

Measles, also known as *rubeola* or red measles, is one of the most common and contagious diseases in the world. Although a person of any age can be affected, measles occurs most often in children, killing 1 million young people worldwide every year.

Widespread immunization programs in the mid-1960s caused a sharp decline in the number of children affected. However, in the United States outbreaks still occur in preschool-aged children who have not been immunized, as well as in previously immunized teenagers and young adults. Because of this, a second dose of MMR is now recommended. There have been no reported deaths from measles in the United States since 1992.

The virus is extremely contagious and is spread by coughing and sneezing. An infected person can infect others for two to four days before the rash appears—the most contagious period—and up to five days afterward. Once individuals have been infected, they are usually immune to the disease for the rest of their lives. An infant usually is protected for the first year of life because of antibodies it has received from its mother.

Note the Symptoms

Symptoms develop seven to 18 days after exposure to the virus and can include fever, sneezing, sore throat, persistent coughing and *malaise* (feeling lousy). There may be eye irritation with redness, swelling and discharge.

Two to four days later, tiny red spots—with centers that look like grains of white sand or salt—appear on the insides of the cheeks by the upper back molars, and sometimes on the eyes and vaginal area. They last one to four days. A sore, red throat, yellowish coating on the tonsils and swollen glands also may occcur.

A brick-red, blotchy rash typically appears one to two days after the spots in the mouth appear. The rash starts on the face and behind the ears, spreading to the torso and extremities. It fades in the same order it appears. Often there is mild itching.

At the peak of illness, you may develop a fever of 104° F (40° C) or higher, swelling around the mouth, a hacking cough and sensitivity to bright light. The fever should fall and the rash start to fade about three to five days after it appears. It may leave a coppery-brown discoloration and some scaliness, which gradually fades. Measles usually lasts 10 to 14 days.

Prevention

Vaccination for measles is the key to prevention. The live virus vaccine is usually given in combination with mumps and rubella (MMR) vaccines. It is very safe, although a small number of people develop a fever over 101°F (38.3°C) five to 12 days after the injection. This is sometimes followed by a rash.

All babies should be immunized between 12 and 15 months; a second dose should be given between ages 4 and 6. If this does not occur, have your doctor give it during any office visit by the child's 11th or 12th birthday.

People who have not been vaccinated and are exposed to measles may be protected if they are given the live vaccine within three days of exposure. The illness also may be averted by a measles immune globulin or immune serum globulin shot given immediately after exposure. (These injections are of no use once symptoms appear.)

What You Can Do

- Stay home for a few days after the rash appears to prevent infecting others.
- Rest in bed (a darkened room may be most comfortable) until the fever disappears. However, it is not necessary to force bed rest on a child who is happy playing quietly.
- If the fever rises above 105°F (40.5°C), sponge the face and upper body with lukewarm water.
- Drink plenty of fluids.
- Try cough medicine to relieve cough symptoms.
- Take pain relievers for headache, fever and general discomfort. **NEVER give aspirin to children/teenagers unless your healthcare provider orders it. It can cause Reye's syndrome, a rare but often fatal condition.** Acetaminophen (Tylenol) or ibuprofen (Advil, Motrin) are safe alternatives.

Final Notes

Most people experience a smooth recovery from measles, but complications can develop. They include respiratory tract diseases such as pneumonia, bronchitis and croup. Bacterial infections in the eyes, lungs, ears and other areas can occur also. (See index.) *Encephalitis* (inflammation of the brain) is a rare but life-threatening complication.

See ***Decision helper,*** p. 84.

Measles

Do these apply:

- Measles is accompanied by a change in mental status (such as confusion, severe irritability, memory loss, etc.); *lethargy* (fatigue); severe headache; stiff neck; vomiting or convulsions
- Measles is present with bleeding from the nose, mouth or rectum, or beneath the skin
- Symptoms of pneumonia develop following measles (severe breathing difficulty; high fever; shaking chills or bluish color to the skin or lips)

no   **yes**

Seek Emergency Care

- Measles occurs along with earache, rapid breathing or sore throat
- Someone who has not been vaccinated for measles is exposed to the illness

no   **yes**

Call Doctor

See **What You Can Do,** p. 83.

Apply Self-Care

Mumps

Mumps is a viral disease that usually causes painful swelling of the salivary glands. The virus is spread through coughing, sneezing or direct contact with saliva-contaminated materials. Infected persons can transmit the disease from about two days before symptoms develop to nine days afterward. A person who has had mumps or been vaccinated usually is immune for life.

Note the Symptoms

Almost one-third of those infected do not develop symptoms. Others will start noticing symptoms 14 to 21 days after exposure. These may include chills, earache, loss of appetite, *malaise* (feeling lousy) or a low- to moderate-grade fever.

The salivary glands between the ear and the angle of the jaw (the *parotids*) typically swell and become tender, as does the face. The combination creates the chipmunk-cheek look. The first sign of swelling may be pain while chewing or swallowing, especially when consuming anything acidic, like pickles or lemon juice.

A fever of 103° to 104° F (39.4° to 40° C) is common in adults but not typical in young children. Symptoms usually last two weeks or less.

Prevention

All babies should be immunized against mumps with the measles, mumps and rubella (MMR) vaccine between 12 and 15 months. A second dose should be given between ages 4 and 6. If the second dose has not been given as scheduled, have your doctor give it during any office visit by the child's 11th or 12th birthday. Babies up to 1 year of age are usually immune because they carry antibodies from their mother. The vaccine shouldn't be given to pregnant women or those with weakened immune systems.

What You Can Do

To speed recuperation and prevent spreading the infection:
- Stay home until the swelling goes down or your doctor recommends returning to work or school.
- Bed rest is helpful until the fever subsides, but shouldn't be forced on a child who is happy playing quietly.

- Drink plenty of fluids but avoid acidic ones like orange juice.
- Take pain relievers for headache and general discomfort. **NEVER give aspirin to children/teenagers unless your healthcare provider orders it. It can cause Reye's syndrome, a rare but often fatal condition.** Acetaminophen (Tylenol) or ibuprofen (Advil, Motrin) are safe alternatives.

Final Notes

Complications of mumps, although rare in an otherwise healthy individual, are more common in adults than in children. These include deafness; an inflammation of the testes (*orchitis*) in males past puberty; an inflammation of the ovaries (*oophoritis*) in females past puberty; an inflammation of the pancreas (*pancreatitis*); and an inflammation of the membranes of the brain or spinal cord (*meningitis*). (See *Meningitis*, p. 245.)

Decision *helper*

Mumps
Do these apply:

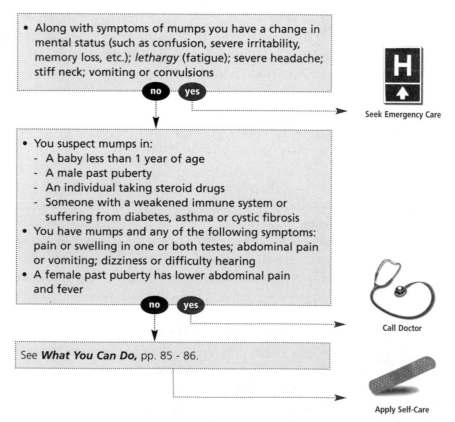

- Along with symptoms of mumps you have a change in mental status (such as confusion, severe irritability, memory loss, etc.); *lethargy* (fatigue); severe headache; stiff neck; vomiting or convulsions

no — yes

Seek Emergency Care

- You suspect mumps in:
  - A baby less than 1 year of age
  - A male past puberty
  - An individual taking steroid drugs
  - Someone with a weakened immune system or suffering from diabetes, asthma or cystic fibrosis
- You have mumps and any of the following symptoms: pain or swelling in one or both testes; abdominal pain or vomiting; dizziness or difficulty hearing
- A female past puberty has lower abdominal pain and fever

no — yes

Call Doctor

See **What You Can Do,** pp. 85 - 86.

Apply Self-Care

Roseola

Roseola is a virus that mainly affects children under the age of 4, most commonly those younger than 2, causing a rash and high fever. These symptoms are usually more alarming to parents than they are threatening to a young child's health. The virus is spread through the air when infected children cough, sneeze or share drinking cups or glasses. Hand-to-hand contact (after rubbing the nose or mouth) also spreads the virus. Once children have had it, they won't get it again.

 Note the Symptoms

Roseola develops after a seven- to 17-day incubation period. Symptoms may include:

- Fever and irritability which occur suddenly. The fever may be as high as 105° F (40.5° C) and last three to seven days. Even with this high fever, a child may remain alert and active.
- A mild sore throat, runny nose or cough
- Slight swelling of the lymph glands in the neck and behind the ears
- Sudden drop in fever to normal or below around the fourth or fifth day
- A mild rash that may appear on the torso and extend to the neck, arms or thighs as the temperature falls. These pink, well-defined patches turn white when touched with light pressure and may be slightly bumpy. The rash may last from a few hours to a few days and may be so mild that it goes unnoticed.

The sudden high fever of roseola may cause a febrile seizure. (See *Fever*, p. 100.) Although frightening, these seizures seldom cause problems.

What You Can Do

There is no medication for treating roseola, but you can make your child more comfortable by:

- Dressing him or her lightly and encouraging fluids

- Keeping a fever down with ibuprofen (Advil, Motrin) or acetaminophen (Tylenol); use as directed. **NEVER give aspirin to children/teenagers unless your healthcare provider orders it. It can cause Reye's syndrome, a rare but often fatal condition.**

Decision *helper*

Roseola
Do these apply:

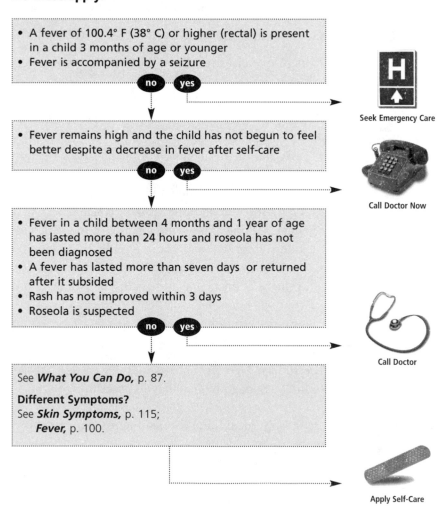

- A fever of 100.4° F (38° C) or higher (rectal) is present in a child 3 months of age or younger
- Fever is accompanied by a seizure

no   yes

Seek Emergency Care

- Fever remains high and the child has not begun to feel better despite a decrease in fever after self-care

no   yes

Call Doctor Now

- Fever in a child between 4 months and 1 year of age has lasted more than 24 hours and roseola has not been diagnosed
- A fever has lasted more than seven days or returned after it subsided
- Rash has not improved within 3 days
- Roseola is suspected

no   yes

Call Doctor

See *What You Can Do,* p. 87.

Different Symptoms?
See *Skin Symptoms,* p. 115;
    Fever, p. 100.

Apply Self-Care

Scarlet Fever

Scarlet fever is caused by a streptococcal infection, usually of the throat (see *Sore Throat*, p. 156) and gets its name from its characteristic red rash.

Scarlet fever requires a trip to the doctor for a rapid strep test or throat culture and antibiotics.

- A high fever is sometimes accompanied by a headache or stomachache, vomiting and/or a red, sore throat.
- The rash is red and fine, and sometimes described as feeling like sandpaper. It appears 12 to 48 hours after the illness begins and often covers the entire body within 24 hours. It is most prominent on the cheeks, chest, abdomen and groin. The area around the mouth is pale. Little bumps on the tongue get progressively bigger and redder, until the tongue looks like a strawberry. The tongue and glands in the neck may also become swollen.
- After the rash subsides, the skin may peel for several weeks, especially on the palms of the hands.

Antibiotics are particularly important in treating scarlet fever because they can prevent *rheumatic fever*, a complication caused by the streptococcal infection that can result in heart damage.

Scarlet Fever
Do these apply:

- A rash accompanies a sore throat
- You suspect scarlet fever or have been exposed to it

no   yes

Call Doctor

Different Symptoms? See *Skin Symptoms*, p. 115.

Fifth Disease

Fifth disease gets its name from being one of the top five illnesses to which children are prone. Its mosts common symptom is its "slapped cheek" rash.

The rash is fine and red and usually begins on the cheeks, sometimes spreading to the back of the arms and legs as well. It is usually gone within four or five days but can reappear and disappear again over the course of several weeks before it goes away entirely. This rash, which often is the only symptom a child may have, usually gets brighter in response to heat.

While highly contagious, Fifth disease rarely causes problems in children and most children who have it tend to feel generally well. Fever is not a symptom and few children describe feeling sick. If a rash and fever occur together in a child, the illness is probably not Fifth disease.

Symptoms can be more serious in adults. The rash, which is pink rather than red in adults, is often accompanied by joint pain, which can last from one to three months. Over-the-counter anti-inflammatory medications such as ibuprofen (Advil, Motrin) usually work well to relive symptoms.

Pregnant women should avoid exposure to Fifth disease, if possible, as it poses some risk to a developing fetus. See your doctor if you are pregnant and think you may have been exposed to Fifth disease.

Other Common Concerns

Croup

Croup is a viral infection of the respiratory tract characterized by difficulty breathing and a hoarse night-time cough (seal-like "bark") that usually subsides during the day. In addition, there may be a low-grade fever and hoarseness sometimes preceded by a cold or mild upper-respiratory infection.

Because it usually occurs in children under 3 or 4 years of age, and often at night, croup can be an alarming experience for parents. Fortunately, croup can frequently be treated at home and symptoms generally improve within a week or so.

Open Air Passages for Easier Breathing

- Expose the child to humidity. Bathroom steam is a good source of warm, moist air. Let the shower run with hot water, then bring the child into the bathroom with you. Shut the door and hold the child on your lap for several minutes in the steamy room.
- Moisten the air with a cool-mist vaporizer. Cool-mist vaporizers eliminate the danger of scalding associated with vaporizers that heat water for steam.
- Take your child into the cool night air or a cool garage or basement.

If one of these approaches does not bring relief in 10 to 15 minutes and the child is not worsening, try another approach.

Monitor Your Child's Improvement

Croup is usually relieved with simple home remedies. A more serious, but less common illness with similar symptoms, called *epiglottitis*, does not respond to these self-care techniques. The child should receive medical attention immediately if epiglottitis is suspected. It is caused by a bacterial infection and generally affects children 2 months to 3 years of age. Children with epiglottitis have extreme difficulty breathing. They drool and often assume a position with their head tilted forward and chin jutted out, while gasping for air.

Final Notes

Due to the alarming cough and the late hour croup often strikes, many parents panic when faced with the child's first case. Try to stay calm and begin the self-care steps suggested under *What You Can Do* (pp. 91 - 92).

Decision *helper*

Croup
Do these apply:

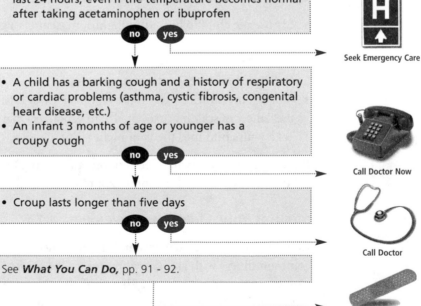

- There is a seal-like bark and: significant respiratory distress, bluish color to the lips or skin, drooling, chin jutting with mouth open, *retractions* (sucking in of the skin between the ribs and collarbone when inhaling), acute agitation or exhaustion
- There is no improvement in *stridor* (a high pitched sound heard with breathing in and/or out) within 15 minutes of self-care
- An infant 3 months of age or younger has had a rectal temperature of 100.4° F (38° C) or higher within the last 24 hours, even if the temperature becomes normal after taking acetaminophen or ibuprofen

no   yes

H ↑
Seek Emergency Care

- A child has a barking cough and a history of respiratory or cardiac problems (asthma, cystic fibrosis, congenital heart disease, etc.)
- An infant 3 months of age or younger has a croupy cough

no   yes

Call Doctor Now

- Croup lasts longer than five days

no   yes

Call Doctor

See **What You Can Do,** pp. 91 - 92.

Apply Self-Care

Ear Infections

Most children get a middle ear infection (*otitis media*) at least once, if not several times, by the time they are 3 years of age. Of course, ear infections can occur at any age. (For adults, see *Middle Ear Infection*, p. 173.)

Ear infections usually strike after an upper respiratory infection, when the tubes between the ear and the throat (*eustachian tubes*) swell and close. As a result, fluid and mucus gather in the middle ear and viruses or bacteria breed. Infants and young children are most susceptible to ear infections because their eustachian tubes are narrow and not fully developed.

Infants and young children who cannot yet talk may tug on an ear as a sign of ear pain. Other symptoms may include fever, decreased hearing, diarrhea, feeding problems, difficulty sleeping and fussiness.

Prevention

- Breast-feed your baby. This will pass on a natural resistance to infection.
- Feed infants in an upright or semi-upright position to prevent milk from getting into the eustachian tubes. Don't allow babies to fall asleep with a bottle.
- Teach children to blow the nose gently, with the mouth open.
- Avoid exposing children to cigarette smoke. Irritation and inflammation caused by smoke can narrow the eustachian tubes and contribute to ear problems.

What You Can Do

- See your doctor for evaluation. If the ear seems infected, often a "watch and wait" period will be recommended, to see if it will clear on its own. Pain medication may be given and, if symptoms do not improve, an antibiotic may be prescribed. (Make sure the child takes all the prescribed medication.) Follow up in three 3 months with the doctor.
- Acetaminophen (Tylenol) or ibuprofen (Advil, Motrin) may help relieve discomfort. **NEVER give aspirin to children/teenagers unless your healthcare provider orders it. It can cause Reye's syndrome, a rare but often fatal condition.**

- Encourage the child to get as much rest as possible and drink plenty of clear fluids.
- Place a warm washcloth, warm water bottle or heating pad (set on low) directly on the affected ear. Do not leave a child alone with a heating pad.
- Use a cool-mist vaporizer to moisturize the air, which helps control levels of mucus.
- Do not insert **any** type of object into the ear to relieve itching or pain.

If your child suffers from recurrent ear infections, you and your doctor may want to discuss the possibility of surgical insertion of tiny tubes (*tympanostomy tubes*) through the eardrum to improve drainage and ventilation of the middle ear.

> **Worried about hearing loss?** While children may suffer temporary and minor hearing loss during and immediately following an ear infection, there is seldom any permanent hearing loss if prompt medical treatment is provided.
>
> Pressure caused by an ear infection can also rupture the eardrum. (See *Ruptured Eardrum,* p. 174.) A single rupture is not serious, but repeated ruptures may cause hearing loss.

Ear Infections
Do these apply:

• An infant younger than 3 months has had a rectal temperature of 100.4° F (38° C) or higher within the past 24 hours, even if the temperature normalizes after acetaminophen or ibuprofen is given

Seek Emergency Care

• An infant or young child has a cold or any of the following: fussiness, difficulty sleeping, tugging or pulling at an ear, vomiting, diarrhea or feeding problems
• There is ear pain and any of the following: fever, bloody or other discharge, decreased hearing, dizziness, ringing or a sense of fullness in the ears
• Ear infection is suspected
• Ear pain lasts more than 12 hours
• Symptoms increase—or fail to improve—after two or three days of antibiotic treatment
• Stuffy ears or hearing loss persists, without other symptoms, more than 10 days after a cold clears up

Call Doctor

See **What You Can Do,** pp. 93 - 94.
For adults, see **Middle Ear Infection,** p. 173; **Fever,** p. 100.

Apply Self-Care

Object in the Nose

Young children place nearly everything they touch in their mouths, but sometimes strange objects find their way into young noses, too.

- Foul-smelling yellow or gray-green nasal discharge, often from one nostril
- Swelling or obstruction of the nose
- Nasal tenderness

- Use a nasal decongestant spray or drops in the affected nostril to reduce swelling.
- Pinch the opposite nostril and let the child try to blow the object out.
- If you can see the object, carefully use tweezers to remove it while holding the child's head still. Be sure you don't push the object further inside the nose.
- An alternate technique involves blowing into the child's mouth while he or she is positioned on the back. Sometimes this propels the object out from behind; several tries may be necessary. Make sure the child is comfortable and not upset with this technique.
- Call the doctor if you're unable to retrieve the object or if there are any signs of infection present, such as significant redness in the nasal area, red streaks radiating from the nose, tender or swollen lymph nodes, or fever.
- Also call your doctor if any discharge, swelling or tenderness does not clear up within a day or so.

Colic

Babies with colic seem to have an internal alarm—and when it goes off you can be assured of hours of seemingly endless crying. This nerve-fraying condition is quite common among infants; about 25 percent of newborns become "colicky" between 2 and 3 weeks of age.

It's not clear what causes colic. Current evidence indicates gastrointestinal problems are not to blame and it's unlikely that milk allergies are the cause, either. If your child is allergic to milk, other symptoms will appear, such as vomiting, diarrhea or eczema. (See index for these topics.)

While lengthy periods of crying are the most prominent symptom of colic, excessive crying can signal other problems, too. If your baby cries frequently or for long periods and has a fever or diarrhea, something other than colic is responsible and your baby should be seen by a doctor.

Colicky babies may have gas or an enlarged stomach right after feeding. When they cry, they may pull their legs up to their stomachs or stiffen and extend them. Colicky babies are usually healthy and are considered to have colic only when all other causes for prolonged crying have been ruled out. Your pediatrician can help you decide if colic is the culprit.

What You Can Do

For Your Baby

- If you breast-feed, talk with your doctor about eliminating milk, eggs, wheat and nuts from your diet.
- If you bottle-feed, make sure the nipples are large enough to drip one drop of formula per second. Ask about hypoallergenic formulas.
- Burp the baby often. Crying often stops after the infant burps or passes gas.
- Be sure your baby is getting enough to eat. It takes about two hours for a baby to digest a feeding. If crying occurs less than two hours after feeding, the baby probably is not really hungry. Try steps other than feeding to calm your infant.
- Use a pacifier to soothe the infant between feedings.

- Place the infant on its stomach over your knees or forearm to ease discomfort.
- Use motion, such as walking, rocking or strolling, to comfort your baby.

For You

- Find a reliable sitter and enjoy an evening away once a week.
- It's OK occasionally to let the baby cry while you try to relax. However, don't let a newborn cry alone for more than 15 minutes.
- Know that colic is not the result of something you have done—it simply happens.

Final Notes

Colic seems to last forever, but take heart; most infants suddenly end their crying bouts when they reach 3 to 4 months of age.

Decision *helper*

Colic

Do these apply:

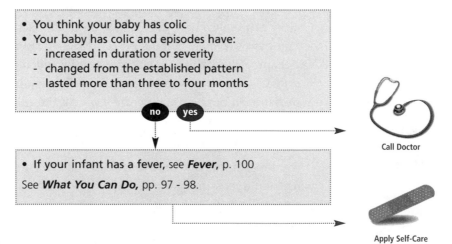

- You think your baby has colic
- Your baby has colic and episodes have:
  - increased in duration or severity
  - changed from the established pattern
  - lasted more than three to four months

no   yes

Call Doctor

- If your infant has a fever, see *Fever*, p. 100

See *What You Can Do,* pp. 97 - 98.

Apply Self-Care

SECTION 4
Health Concerns

Neurological

Fever

Fever is a symptom—not an illness—that indicates the body is fighting an infection. It is an elevation in body temperature above "normal" that varies in individuals.

Under healthy circumstances, your temperature varies throughout the day. It is lowest in the morning and highest in late afternoon. It is also normal for temperatures to rise due to anxiety, food consumption, wearing heavy clothing and hormonal changes during a woman's monthly menstrual cycle.

People are considered to have a fever if their oral temperature is higher than 99.5° F (37.5° C) or if their rectal temperature is higher than 100.4° F (38° C).

Note Your Symptoms

Generally, fever is caused by viruses, bacterial infections, fungi or parasites. Fever can also result from inflammatory diseases (like lupus and rheumatoid arthritis) and from cancers, such as Hodgkin's disease and kidney cancer. Other physical signs of fever include:

- Feeling hot or cold
- Shivering
- Headache
- Muscle aches
- Joint pains
- General *malaise* (feeling lousy)

Since it is difficult for a young child to tell you about a fever, look for symptoms that may indicate fever or a more serious illness:

- Unusual or high-pitched cry
- Irritability or inability to be comforted
- Difficulty being roused
- Pale and/or bluish skin
- Symptoms of dehydration (see *Dehydration,* p. 236)

- Diminished activity
- Lethargy in newborns, which may be accompanied by blotchy skin and altered eating patterns

Studies suggest that fever probably plays a role in combating infection. In other words, it's not always a bad thing. But it can be very uncomfortable, so most people prefer to minimize discomfort with remedies such as acetaminophen (Tylenol), aspirin and ibuprofen (Advil, Motrin).

- **NEVER give aspirin to children/teenagers unless your healthcare provider orders it. It can cause Reye's syndrome, a rare but often fatal condition.** Children and teenagers who take aspirin when they have chickenpox or flu are at higher risk of developing Reye's syndrome. Since these illnesses, in the early stages, can often be mistaken for some other ailment, it is recommended that parents always give children and teenagers acetaminophen or ibuprofen rather than aspirin.
- Read all package instructions carefully to determine the proper dosage of medications for children. Dosage is based on both weight and age.
- Keep clothing, such as cotton pajamas, to a minimum.
- Do not bundle infants because they cannot undress themselves if they overheat.
- Keep room temperature cool; use a fan if it's stuffy.
- Encourage fluids; offer children their favorite beverages in a favorite container.
- Try warm (but never cold) baths or showers to help lower a fever. If the fever is 104° F (40° C) or higher, remove clothes and apply cool cloths to the head and chest. Sponging with lukewarm (not cold) water can also be effective. **Never sponge with alcohol for a fever.**
- Practice good hygiene, particularly handwashing, which is important in preventing infectious illnesses that cause fever.
- Generally, keep children with contagious illnesses home from school or day care.
- Immunize your children according to your doctor's recommendations to prevent fever-related illnesses.

Febrile Seizures

A child with a high fever may experience a *febrile seizure* (also called a convulsion). Signs include sudden loss of consciousness and rigidity of the arms and legs followed by rhytmic twitching a few seconds later. These seizures are relatively common and generally stop on their own within five minutes. However, while they rarely cause long-term problems, febrile seizures should be treated like emergencies, just in case something more serious is involved.

Cooling the child very quickly will NOT stop the seizure or prevent further convulsions. NEVER leave an infant or child unattended in a bathtub, especially if there is a history of seizures.

If an infant has a seizure:
- Time the convulsion. Do not move the baby or restrain movement.
- Breathing may stop momentarily; the baby should start breathing again independently in 30 to 60 seconds.
- Keep your fingers, pacifiers and other objects out of the mouth. Infants may bite their tongue, but will not swallow it.
- If vomiting occurs, place the baby on its stomach or side; never place an infant on its back.
- If breathing becomes labored, gently pull the jaw and chin forward by placing two fingers behind each corner of the jaw.
- After the seizure, **seek emergency care**.

If a child older than 1 year has a seizure:
- Time the convulsion. Lay the child down, removing any nearby objects that could cause injury. Do not restrain movement.
- Roll the child on its side to prevent the tongue from blocking the airway and to prevent choking.
- After the seizure, **seek emergency care**.

Fever in Adults
Do these apply:

- A fever is accompanied by a severe headache, stiff neck, lethargy, confusion, lack of responsiveness, limpness or floppiness of the limbs or body, or a *petechial rash* (widespread bruising or little blood spots under the skin) (see *Meningitis,* p. 245)
- Fever is accompanied by a seizure
- A diabetic adult has a blood glucose level higher than 200 mg/dL and experiences a fever.

no **yes**

Seek Emergency Care

- A fever is higher than 103° F (39.4° C) oral or 104° F (40° C) rectal, and 50 minutes of self-care measures fail to bring it down (even briefly)
- A fever subsides following self-care, but the person continues to feel ill
- A person with diabetes or an immune system disorder has a fever
- A pregnant woman has a fever higher than 102° F (38.9° C), taken orally

no **yes**

Call Doctor Now

- A fever shows no improvement (steady decrease) after 72 hours
- A fever has lasted more than 5 days
- A person who has had surgery within the past 4 weeks has a fever
- A fever worsens within 48 hours or fails to improve within 72 hours of beginning antibiotic therapy
- A pregnant woman has a fever higher than 100.4° F (38° C)

no **yes**

Call Doctor

See *What You Can Do,* pp. 101 - 102.
See *Fever* in the index.

Apply Self-Care

For children, see *Decision helper,* pp. 104 - 105.

Fever in Children

Do these apply:

- An infant younger than 3 months has had a rectal temperature of 100.4° F (38° C) or higher in the past 24 hours, even if the temperature has returned to normal
- A newborn, infant or child too young to verbalize has a fever or a bulging soft spot or cries in a unusual way (e.g., high-pitched, weak, continual or inconsolable)
- A child younger than age 3 has a fever and looks dehydrated
- An infant or child has a fever along with:
  - Seizure
  - A severe or increasing headache
  - A stiff neck or increasing pain when the neck is flexed or extended
  - Sensitivity to light
  - Confusion or pronounced irritability
  - A lack of responsiveness or inability to be roused
  - Limpness or floppiness of the limbs or body
  - Bruises or little red spots under the skin (petechial rash)
- A diabetic child has a blood glucose level higher than 200 mg/dL, as well as unusually flushed skin that is not relieved one hour after the fever is reduced

no   yes

See next page.

H
↑
Seek Emergency Care

Do these apply: See previous page.

- Anyone over the age of 3 has a fever and shows signs of dehydration
- A child with an immune system problem has a fever
- A child with diabetes has a fever and a blood glucose level higher than 350 mg/dL
- A fever is higher than 103° F (39.4° C) oral or 104° F (40° C) rectal and an hour of self-care measures has failed to bring it down
- A high fever has come down recently but the child continues to feel ill

no   yes

Call Doctor Now

- A child less than 1 year of age has had a fever for more than 24 hours
- A child who has had surgery within the last 4 weeks has a fever
- A fever has not begun to drop steadily (from its highest peak) within 72 hours, or has lasted longer than 5 days
- A fever worsens within 48 hours or fails to improve within 72 hours of begining antibiotic therapy

no   yes

Call Doctor

See **What You Can Do,** pp. 101 - 102.
See **Fever** in the index.

Apply Self-Care

Tension-type Headaches

Tension-type headaches are extremely common. Almost everyone has had one at some point. They can range in intensity from a dull ache to an unbearable pain, and last from hours to days. For some, they occur just a few times a year; for others, they recur more frequently. Tension-type headaches apparently are caused by reactions of the pain pathways in the head and may be triggered by a number of factors, including stress. The pain of a tension-type headache may feel like a band around your head and is generally dull and continuous, with fluctuations in intensity.

Tension-type headaches are frequently triggered by emotional or physical factors. Figuring out what triggers your headaches may help you reduce or avoid them in the future. Situations that make you grit your teeth, tighten your shoulders or clench your fist, for example, may cause them. Other causes could include commuting, loud noises, dealing with a difficult person, sitting in an uncomfortable desk chair, or getting too much or too little sleep.

What You Can Do

- Aspirin, ibuprofen (Advil, Motrin) or acetaminophen (Tylenol) can blunt or eliminate pain. **NEVER give aspirin to children/teenagers unless your healthcare provider orders it. It can cause Reye's syndrome, a rare but often fatal condition**.
- Soak in a hot bath or lie down in a darkened room with an ice bag on your forehead. For protection, place a washcloth between bare skin and ice.
- Get a massage.
- Take a nap.
- Exercise regularly and consider yoga, meditation or muscle-relaxation techniques.

See *Decision helper,* p. 109.

Migraine Headaches

Migraine headaches can cause excruciating pain and prevent sufferers from carrying out daily activities. Migraines account for 2 to 7 percent of all headaches, affect more women than men and usually start to appear between the ages of 7 and 30. Some people experience fewer episodes as they grow older and may even enjoy a complete remission after age 50. Migraines often run in families.

Migraines are believed to occur when pain pathways to the brain are triggered easily, resulting in inflammation and blood vessel changes in the head. Researchers have found that *serotonin*, a chemical that transmits messages in the brain, is involved in migraines. Migraine medications can bind to serotonin sites, called *receptors*, and relieve headache symptoms. Migraine symptoms include pain (which can be one-sided), sensitivity to light or noise, nausea, vomiting, or visual changes.

Factors that trigger migraines include glare from harsh light, stress, hunger, climatic changes, certain foods and beverages, oral contraceptives and medications, the menstrual cycle, physical or mental exhaustion, or too much or too little sleep.

If you are susceptible to migraines, you will generally experience several headaches a year (each lasting one to three days). If your headaches increase in severity or frequency, you may want to call your doctor. Many medications are now available to prevent headaches or control pain.

The good news is that with the right combination of self-care techniques and appropriate medication, you can make a significant difference in your ability to manage, and possibly eliminate, this painful disorder.

The key is to identify your triggers. Keeping a diary of your symptoms, possible triggers and which self-care techniques work and which don't provides helpful information for both you and your doctor.

You may be able to relieve or control migraine pain by:

- Lying down in a cool, dark, quiet room
- Putting an ice bag on your head. For protection, place a washcloth between bare skin and ice.
- Taking over-the-counter (OTC) painkillers such as aspirin, acetaminophen (Tylenol) or ibuprofen (Advil, Motrin). **NEVER give aspirin to children/ teenagers unless your healthcare provider orders it. It can cause Reye's syndrome, a rare but often fatal condition**. Avoid taking OTC pain medications more than twice a week and limit the amount of caffeine found in food or beverages. Both can cause rebound headaches. (See *Medication Precautions*, p. 324.)
- Practicing yoga, meditation or muscle-relaxation techniques

See ***Decision helper,*** p. 109.

Cluster Headaches

Cluster headaches are similar to migraines with a few differences. They occur mostly in men and are not necessarily inherited. They are usually one-sided like a migraine, but the throbbing, burning pain behind or above the eye intensifies rapidly and lasts from 10 minutes to several hours. One to three attacks can occur within a 24-hour period, and nasal stuffiness also may occur. Nausea and vomiting are rare. Treatment requires prescription medication, which may include oxygen. Studies indicate that cluster headaches originate from the hypothalamic area of the brain, which governs many *autonomic* (involuntary) activities, such as body temperature and hormone regulation.

See ***Decision helper,*** p. 109.

Headaches

Do these apply:

- A headache is associated with:
  - Sudden confusion, trouble speaking or understanding speech
  - Sudden trouble seeing in one or both eyes
  - Sudden trouble walking or loss of balance or coordination
  - Sudden severe pain with no known cause
  - Sudden numbness on one side of the face or body
  - Rash, stiff neck or drowsiness (see *Meningitis,* p. 245)
- Headache is the "worst ever," occurs after an injury, or accompanies marked irritability

Seek Emergency Care

- A migraine is severe and does not respond to prescribed measures or vomiting makes you unable to retain oral medications

Call Doctor Now

- A child's headaches persist or recur several times a week
- Headache without an obvious cause persists or doesn't improve with self-care
- Headaches increase in severity and frequency and interfere with daily activities
- Pain relievers are needed several times a week
- Previously effective measures no longer provide the same level of relief
- You suspect a migraine or cluster headache

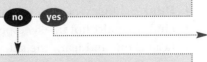

Call Doctor

See *What You Can Do, Tension-type Headaches,* p. 106; *What You Can Do, Migraine Headaches,* pp. 107 - 108.

Apply Self-Care

Dizziness/Fainting

Most of us have felt faint or dizzy at some time. There are many causes for these sensations—some minor and a few more serious. Most of these problems can be eased or eliminated with self-care.

Although many of these sensations seem similar, the differences in symptoms are important to help determine the cause and treatment. *Dizziness* is a sensation of spinning inside your head and can cause a loss of balance. *Fainting (syncope)* is the temporary decrease or loss of consciousness due to a momentary inadequate supply of blood to your brain. *Light-headedness* is a very mild faint or "woozy" feeling.

All of these sensations can be brought on by hunger, exhaustion, emotional upsets, severe pain, hot stuffy environments, laughing, drugs, alcohol, dehydration, variations in heart rhythm, a drop in blood pressure, standing up suddenly, or anything that momentarily decreases blood flow to your brain. *Vertigo* is when the room seems to move or spin around you, and is often caused by a problem in the inner ear. (See *Middle Ear Infection,* p. 173.)

- Eat well-balanced meals at regular intervals and snacks between meals if you are hungry.
- Work and exercise in moderate amounts. Stop and rest at intervals to avoid becoming exhausted.
- Drink eight glasses of water daily. Drink more in hot conditions.
- Limit your alcohol intake, especially in warm weather.
- Read about and learn the side effects of all medications and drugs you are taking.
- Get up slowly after sitting or lying in one position for a long time.
- Treat motion sickness with appropriate medications such as Dramamine or Bonine.
- Try to identify the cause of dizziness and avoid that activity in the future.

What You Can Do

Dizziness/Fainting

- If you feel faint or dizzy, sit or lie down. Raise your legs above the level of your heart.
- Rest until the feeling passes.
- Loosen restrictive clothing.
- Don't drive.
- Drink small amounts of liquid frequently if you are dehydrated. (See *Dehydration*, p. 236.)
- Move to a cool area if you're in a warm, stuffy environment.
- Check with your doctor about the possible side effects of medication.

Vertigo (feeling the room around you spinning)

- Move away from stairs, glass and other potential hazards.
- Lie quietly in a darkened room or assume the position of most comfort.
- Avoid sudden head movements.
- Focus on one object or keep your eyes closed to help ease the spinning sensation.
- Don't drive.

See **Decision helper,** p. 114.

Weakness/Fatigue

Although they are often discussed together, weakness and fatigue are two distinctly different problems.

Weakness is a decrease in your physical ability or an increase in difficulty moving one or more muscles. It is usually the more serious symptom, especially when it involves a large group of muscles such as an arm or a leg, or one whole side of the body. Temporary or prolonged weakness in one part of the body may be a warning of injury to the nervous system or a stroke.

Fatigue is a feeling of weariness, exhaustion or a decrease in energy. Causes may include stress, a sudden change in one's physical activity level, a change in medication, limited or altered sleep, exposure to toxic chemicals, recovery from a major health or emotional event, depression, poor nutrition or excessive alcohol drinking. In many cases, symptoms can be treated and relieved through self-care within two months.

Chronic Fatigue Syndrome

If other conditions are ruled out, a diagnosis of *Chronic Fatigue Syndrome* (CFS) may be made. CFS is a flu-like illness, with the main symptom being prolonged and extreme fatigue. Other symptoms include a sore throat, swollen lymph nodes, muscle and joint pain, weakness, headache and problems with concentration or memory.

There are no definitive tests for CFS and no cure has been found. Treatment is focused on relieving the symptoms. Support is an important part of therapy, and many support groups are available.

Prevention and self-care for problems related to weakness and fatigue include:
- Exercising regularly; include exercises that strengthen and tone muscle and improve aerobic endurance (see *Staying Active*, p. 330)
- Eating a well-balanced diet that is high in fiber and low in fat (see *Eating Right*, p. 331)
- Improving your sleeping habits (see *Insomnia*, p. 318)

- Dealing with any feelings of depression (see *Depression*, p. 320)
- Limiting your consumption of alcohol, caffeine and nicotine
- Providing variety in your activities and interests
- Avoiding exhaustion by scheduling time for rest and relaxation

What You Can Do

- Follow the prevention guidelines above.
- You can help your doctor diagnose the cause of your fatigue by keeping track of when the feeling started, when it occurs or is most intense, what seems to make it worse or better, whether others in your home or work setting have similar problems, and any other changes or symptoms you notice.
- Listen to your body. Notice the effect drugs, activities, emotions and stress have on you.
- Be patient. It may take six to eight weeks of practicing prevention and self-care guidelines regularly before you feel strong and energetic again.

Final Notes

Prolonged or extreme fatigue that does not respond to self-care may be a sign of a more serious problem. Chronic fatigue is a symptom often found in diseases such as diabetes, hypothyroidism, anemia, mononucleosis, lupus, heart disease and rheumatoid arthritis, to name a few.

Decision *helper*

Dizziness/Fainting/ Weakness/Fatigue

Do these apply:

- There is a complete loss of consciousness (see *Unconsciousness,* p. 37)
  - Lay the person down in a safe place. Check for response (see p. 19). Start CPR if needed.
- Any of the following have occurred:
  - Sudden confusion, trouble talking or understanding speech
  - Sudden trouble seeing in one or both eyes
  - Sudden trouble walking or loss of balance or coordination
  - Sudden severe headache with no known cause
  - Sudden numbness on one side of the face or body
- Symptoms follow a head injury (see *Head/Spinal Injury,* p. 56)

no   yes

Seek Emergency Care

Apply Emergency First Aid

- Sudden dizziness or vertigo with no known cause
- Irregular heartbeat accompanied by dizziness or light-headedness (see *Palpitations,* p. 197)
- Fainting has occurred but the person is now awake and alert

  The patient should not drive him- or herself to the doctor appointment.

no   yes

Call Doctor Now

- Dizziness or vertigo persists after three days
- You think your symptoms are caused by a medication
- Weakness or fatigue is persistent or progressive

no   yes

Call Doctor

See *What You Can Do, Dizziness/Fainting,* p. 111; *What You Can Do, Weakness/Fatigue,* p. 113.

Apply Self-Care

Skin Concerns

Skin Symptoms

General Skin Conditions

Condition	Appearance/Location	Itching	Fever	Other Symptoms/Comments
Acne p. 124	Red pimples, cysts, blackheads; on face, back, chest	No	No	Pimples may become whiteheads, may include general skin redness
Bedbugs p. 141	Firm lump(s) in lines or clusters, found anywhere on skin	Intense	No	For itching, see p. 126 and follow advice given for itching with hives
Boils p. 128	Red, swollen, painful bump (like a large pimple); common on buttocks, groin, waist, armpits, neck, face	No	No	Occurs in infected hair follicles that are under pressure or chafed
Dandruff p. 121	White to yellow to red, some crusting on scalp, eyebrows, groin	Occasional	No	Fine, oily scales and flaking
Eczema p. 118	Red; cracking and thickening of dry areas on elbows, wrists, knees, cheeks	Moderate to intense	No	Moist, oozing, water-filled blisters
Impetigo p. 130	Shallow sores that have gold crusty surface color; often at site of a scrape or injury	Occasional	Maybe	Weepy blisters form crust that spreads infection
Lice p. 140	Tiny white eggs (nits) attached to hair shaft; tiny insects (very difficult to see) close to the scalp	Intense	No	Swollen glands in back of neck, scratch marks around hairline
Psoriasis p. 118	Thick, silvery skin patches; often on knees, elbows, scalp	Moderate to intense	No	Symptoms come and go over weeks to months
Scabies p. 138	Small red, raised dots, commonly on finger webs, wrists, armpits, genitalia or breasts	Intense	No	Track marks; open sores from scratching
Shingles p. 77	Small, fluid-filled blisters usually on one side of body (most often the torso), accompanied by sharp nerve pain	Intense	Maybe	Blisters rupture, forming yellow, crusty scabs

chart continues next page

General Skin Conditions *continued from previous page*

Condition	Appearance/Location	Itching	Fever	Other Symptoms/Comments
Skin Cancer p. 147	Change in size or shape of a mole	Occasional	No	Skin irregularity that is smooth, shiny or waxy; mole that scales, oozes or bleeds
Warts p. 136	Raised, grainy, lump anywhere on body	No	No	Can be flat in areas of pressure, like soles of feet
Fungal Rashes				
Athlete's Foot p. 134	Colorless to red; between toes	Mild to intense	No	Cracks, scaling, oozing blisters
Jock Itch p. 133	Patches of redness, scaling and raised areas that ooze; on groin	Mild to intense	No	Penis and scrotum usually not involved
Ringworm p. 132	Red, slightly raised rings; located anywhere, including scalp	Occasional	No	Fungus can cause hair loss and patchy bald spots; nails can be infected, too
Allergic and Contact Reactions				
Hives p. 126	Welt-like elevations, surrounded by redness; located anywhere	Intense	No	Reaction to an allergen; many possible causes
Poison Ivy/ Poison Oak	Red, elevated blisters on any exposed area; oozing; some swelling; rash begins 12 - 48 hrs. after contact with plant and may persist for up to two weeks	Intense	No	Also spread by pets, contaminated clothing, smoke from burning plants; to treat, clean affected skin area with soap and water, bathe with Aveeno powder; an OTC product, Ivy Block, can be used for prevention
Rashes caused by chemicals p. 118	Red, possible blisters on any exposed area	Moderate to intense	No	Oozing and/or swelling
Childhood Rashes/Illnesses				
Infant Rashes p. 76	See *Infant Rashes* chart			
Chickenpox p. 77	Red rash progresses from flat to raised, then blisters form crusts; may start anywhere, most prominent on torso and face	Intense	Yes	Mild, generalized ill feeling
Fifth Disease p. 90	Red and flat, lacy appearance; first on face, then arms, legs and rest of body	No	No	Slapped-cheek appearance, rash can come and go

Childhood Rashes/Illnesses

Condition	Appearance/Location	Itching	Fever	Other Symptoms/Comments
Measles p. 82	Pink, then red, flat; first on face, then chest and abdomen, then arms and legs	None to mild	Yes	Preceded by fever, cough, red eyes
Roseola p. 87	Pink and flat, with occasional bumps; first on torso, then arms and neck; slight on face and legs	No	Yes	High fever for about three days, then rash appears
Rubella (German Measles) p. 80	Light red; flat or slightly raised; first on face, then torso, then extremities	No	Yes	Swollen glands behind ears; occasional joint pain
Scarlet Fever p. 89	Red, flat, like sandpaper; first on face, then elbows; spreads in 24 hours to entire body	No	Yes	Sore throat; skin peeling afterwards, especially on palms of hands

Eczema and Psoriasis

Eczema, also known as *dermatitis,* is commonly found on the face, neck, hands, elbows, wrists and/or knees. It is characterized by dry, scaly, irritated, itchy skin patches or rashes. Causes range from contact with detergents or other harsh substances (also called *contact dermatitis*) to emotional stress. The cause of eczema often is unknown, however.

A common form of eczema is called *atopic dermatitis.* You're a likely candidate if you have a personal or family history of asthma, hay fever or some other allergy. Recent studies suggest that certain foods—such as citrus fruits, wheat, eggs and nuts—may also be responsible for some cases of eczema.

Eczema is rare in infants under 2 months of age, but if it does develop it can be severe. Although infants can't scratch themselves with their fingers, they can rub itchy areas against their bed sheets, causing redness.

What You Can Do

- Avoid drying out the skin. Limit the use of soap and bathe or shower in cool or lukewarm water. Follow with an unscented moisturizer.
- Use hypoallergenic makeup or none at all. Wear rubber gloves for dishwashing and other household chores. Sweat aggravates eczema, so wear lightweight, loose-fitting cotton clothing, especially during exercise. (Wool and synthetic materials may be irritating.)
- Swim in salt water, if possible; fresh or chlorinated pool water can aggravate eczema.
- Most complications result from scratching or rubbing. Trim nails to minimize the effects of scratching.
- Do not apply anesthetic lotions or antihistamine creams unless your doctor prescribes them; they can actually increase irritation. For the worst areas, try using a cool gauze dressing soaked in diluted aluminum acetate solution (Domeboro, Bluboro, Burow's). Follow package directions.

Psoriasis

Eczema can be confused with other skin conditions, such as *psoriasis,* another chronic skin condition. Psoriasis appears as silvery skin patches or *plaques,* often located on the knees, elbows and scalp. Normally, skin cells mature and are shed once a month. With psoriasis this occurs at a much faster rate—every three to four days. Because the *dermis* (lower layer of skin cells) is dividing so rapidly, dead cells accumulate in thicker-than-normal patches on the *epidermis* (skin's outermost layer). The symptoms of this chronic disease typically come and go over weeks or months and then may disappear altogether.

As many as 4 to 5 million Americans cope with psoriasis. Although there is no cure, the right therapy can help control symptoms. Care is individualized and based on the severity of symptoms. Treatment may consist of self-care, *phototherapy* (exposure to ultraviolet or infrared light) and a variety of medications to help relieve the scaling.

- Bathe daily to help soak off the scales.
- Avoid hot water or harsh soap. Anything that is drying to your skin will worsen psoriasis.
- Use an unscented moisturizer that does not contain lanolin.
- Treat small patches with occasional use of hydrocortisone cream.
- Try medicated shampoos (such as Head & Shoulders, Selsun Blue and Capitrol) for scalp psoriasis.

If you think you have psoriasis, consult your doctor for a treatment plan that is best for your symptoms. If you've been diagnosed with psoriasis and your current treatment is no longer working, call your doctor. New products are being developed that may help.

Eczema and Psoriasis

Do these apply:

- Signs of infection are present:
  - Redness around the area or red streaks leading away from it
  - Swelling
  - Warmth or tenderness
  - Pus
  - Fever of 101° F (38.3° C) or higher
  - Tender or swollen lymph nodes

Call Doctor Now

- The whole body, or the eyelids, face or genitals, are involved
- Eczema sores become crusty or develop a weepy discharge
- No improvement occurs or symptoms worsen after one week of treatment
- Itching makes sleeping difficult despite self-care
- Eczema or psoriasis interferes with daily functions or causes emotional stress

Call Doctor

See **What You Can Do,** pp. 118, 119.
History of allergies? See **Allergies,** p. 189.

Apply Self-Care

Different Symptoms?
See **Skin Symptoms,** p. 115.

Dandruff

Dandruff, or *seborrhea*, is a common condition characterized by flaky scaling of the scalp. Genetic factors play a role in who gets dandruff and climate can affect symptoms. (Dandruff is more severe in winter when indoor air is dry.) A yeast normally found in hair follicles may be responsible for many cases.

Symptoms similar to dandruff can be caused by psoriasis, poison ivy, poison oak, lice, eczema and ringworm. (See index for these topics.)

- Use a dandruff shampoo (such as Head & Shoulders, Sebutone, Denorex, or brands containing salicylic acid) daily or every other day until symptoms improve.
- Once your symptoms improve, continue using dandruff shampoo twice a week to keep dandruff under control.
- For severe scaling and redness, ask your doctor about prescribed corticosteroid medication, such as fluocinolone or triamcinolone.
- Try antifungal medications to treat severe dandruff.

Dandruff
Do these apply:

- You have an immune system disorder and severe symptoms occur and/or dandruff is spreading to other areas of the body
- Symptoms become more severe, or over-the-counter (OTC) medications fail to relieve them
- Symptoms spread to the face, along the hairline, behind and in the ears, or on the chest

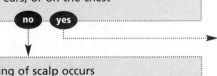

no   yes

Call Doctor

- Dry or greasy scaling of scalp occurs
See **What You Can Do,** this page.

Apply Self-Care

Hair Loss

Hair is constantly lost and replaced by your body. By far the most common reason for hair loss, or *alopecia*, is male-pattern baldness, in which hair replacement fails to keep up with hair loss.

Causes

The cause of hair loss is often indicated by the way it falls out and the condition of the scalp. In *male-pattern baldness*, typically the hair loss starts with a receding hairline, continuing until only a horseshoe-shaped area of hair remains around the head. The scalp looks healthy. Both aging and genetics play a part in balding, with as many as 60 percent of men over age 50 affected. *Female-pattern baldness*, which is a general thinning of hair at the crown or hairline, is also genetic and influenced by hormonal changes during or after menopause.

Sudden loss of hair in patches is called *alopecia areata*. The hair generally grows back normally within several months.

Hair that falls out in large clumps and uncovers a normal-looking scalp may be due to a rare condition called *generalized alopecia*. It can be alarming to see clumps of hair in the shower drain or on a pillow. Causes usually involve physical or emotional stress such as surgery, trauma, pregnancy, high fever or burns. The hair usually falls out three to four months after the stressful event and eventually grows back.

Chemotherapy can cause complete or partial hair loss on the body, with hair almost always growing back when treatment ends. Some common medications that can cause significant hair loss include heparin, oral contraceptives, amphetamines and beta blockers.

Hair loss that develops over weeks, months or even years can be due to autoimmune disease (such as *systemic lupus*), infectious diseases (such as *syphilis*) or endocrine disorders (such as *thyroid disease*).

Hair loss that is accompanied by an inflamed or scaly scalp may be caused by psoriasis (see *Psoriasis*, p. 119) or dandruff (see *Dandruff*, p. 121). The hair usually thins because of intense scratching or applied treatment. If hair loss leaves bald spots with a gray-green scale, *ringworm* (a fungal infection) should be suspected. (See *Ringworm*, p. 132.)

Some people, especially children, may develop a nervous hair-pulling habit that can also lead to hair loss.

Male- and female-pattern baldness can't be prevented, but the over-the-counter (OTC) drug minoxidil (Rogaine) has been used with mixed results. When rubbed on the scalp, this expensive lotion has sometimes slowed hair loss and generated new hair growth, but many people have been disappointed with the results.

Other alternatives include a variety of hair restoration surgeries and the oral prescription medications Finasteride and Propecia.

Hair Loss
Do these apply:

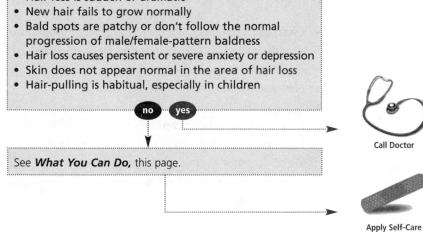

* Bald areas have a grayish-green scale (see **Ringworm,** p. 132)
* Hair loss is sudden or dramatic
* New hair fails to grow normally
* Bald spots are patchy or don't follow the normal progression of male/female-pattern baldness
* Hair loss causes persistent or severe anxiety or depression
* Skin does not appear normal in the area of hair loss
* Hair-pulling is habitual, especially in children

no   yes

See **What You Can Do,** this page.

Call Doctor

Apply Self-Care

Acne

Acne vulgaris refers to a spectrum of skin eruptions—blackheads, whiteheads, pimples, cysts and nodules—that can be sore, painful or itchy. Few people escape adolescence without a pimple or two.

Acne begins when a fatty oil (*sebum*) and dead cells clog the pores around small hair follicles. The results can range from whiteheads to blackheads and pimples.

Acne tends to occur in areas where there are high concentrations of these *sebaceous glands*—the face, neck, shoulders, and upper and central back. In both genders, elevated secretion of *androgen* (male) hormones during puberty stimulates these glands to produce extra sebum, increasing the likelihood of acne.

Practice Smart Personal Hygiene

- Use a cleansing agent or soap that dries the skin enough to cause minor shedding; avoid too much drying since this can cause further irritation.
- Use a clean washcloth—gently.
- Never scrub the skin.
- Always rinse thoroughly.
- Give yourself an occasional mini-steam bath by placing a warm, wet towel on your skin for 10 to 15 minutes. This will help open pores and allow deeper cleaning.
- Use oil-free cosmetics, loose powder, gel-based sunscreens and avoid getting hairspray on your skin.

Skin Medications

Acne medications unblock pores by drying up oil and promoting peeling. Many are available without a prescription and come in solutions that help cover up redness and scarring. Sunlight may temporarily clear up skin, but it can have other damaging effects—especially if drying agents or antibiotics are being used.

A doctor can prescribe stronger topical skin medications or a special formulation of vitamin A, called retinoic acid (Retin-A), and antibiotics. An oral form of vitamin A, called Accutane, also may be prescribed for severe cases and should be taken only as directed by your doctor—too much vitamin A can be toxic.

Final Notes

Carefully follow the directions, warnings and precautions on any drugs you use. Call your doctor if you have questions. And be patient—it may take two to six weeks or more to see progress with any of these self-care treatments or medications.

Decision *helper*

Acne
Do these apply:

- Signs of infection occur, such as:
  - Increasing redness or red streaks leading away from it
  - Excessive swelling, warmth or tenderness
  - More pus than is usual with pimples
  - Fever of 101° F (38.3° C) or higher
  - Tender or swollen lymph nodes

no **yes**

Call Doctor Now

- Acne seems to be caused or worsened by a medication
- Acne cysts are large and painful
- Acne is extremely irritating or embarrassing
- A post-adolescent woman develops severe acne and facial hair
- Acne does not improve after four to six weeks of self-care
- Symptoms worsen despite self-care

no **yes**

Call Doctor

See *What You Can Do,* pp. 124 - 125.

Apply Self-Care

Hives

Hives are red, itchy, raised welts on the skin that may vary in size from less than a quarter-inch (.64 cm) to more than an inch (2.54 cm). Usually caused by allergies, they tend to occur after exposure to something that causes the body's cells to react. This prompts the release of *histamines,* one of the body's chemical defense mechanisms, resulting in symptoms of allergy, such as hives. (Wheezing, runny nose and watery eyes are among other allergic symptoms caused by histamines.)

The most common causes of hives are things like insect stings and bites, medication reactions, and many foods (including peanuts, eggs, milk and shellfish). Hives can also be of non-allergic origin, triggered by a heightened bodily sensitivity to such things as cold temperatures, sunlight, hot showers, exercise, or even anxiety.

It is often difficult to determine the underlying cause of hives. Because of this, symptom relief is the major goal of treatment for mild cases. If hives are frequent and/or severe, allergy testing may be performed to try to determine the cause(s) and prevent future episodes.

Prevention

- Avoid foods, medications or contacts that may have caused hives in the past.
- Use insect repellent and extra caution when you are in areas that have insects that may trigger your allergies.
- Inform all your doctors and dentists about your allergies.
- Learn stress-management techniques if stress appears to be a trigger for your hives. (See *Stress,* p. 314.)

What You Can Do

- Relieve itching skin by applying cool, wet compresses soaked in cold water or aluminum acetate solution (Domeboro, Bluboro, Burow's).
- Bathe in lukewarm water containing one-half to one cup of Aveeno powder, or one cup of baking soda or finely ground oatmeal to ease itching in large areas.
- Try over-the-counter (OTC) oral antihistamines. Read the precautions on the label regarding drowsiness.

- Do not use creams, lotions or ointments unless your doctor recommends them.
- Cut nails short or wear cotton gloves at night to prevent the harmful effects of scratching.
- Avoid substances that cause your hives.

Hives

Do these apply:

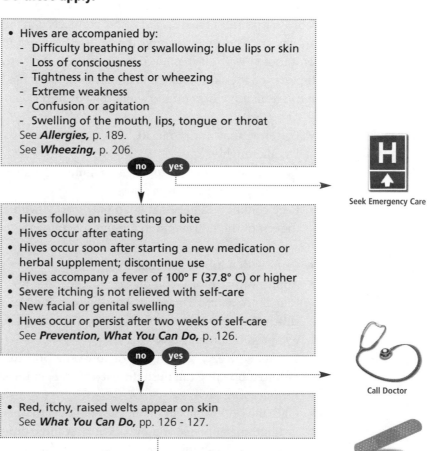

- Hives are accompanied by:
  - Difficulty breathing or swallowing; blue lips or skin
  - Loss of consciousness
  - Tightness in the chest or wheezing
  - Extreme weakness
  - Confusion or agitation
  - Swelling of the mouth, lips, tongue or throat

  See *Allergies,* p. 189.
  See *Wheezing,* p. 206.

no / yes

H ↑
Seek Emergency Care

- Hives follow an insect sting or bite
- Hives occur after eating
- Hives occur soon after starting a new medication or herbal supplement; discontinue use
- Hives accompany a fever of 100° F (37.8° C) or higher
- Severe itching is not relieved with self-care
- New facial or genital swelling
- Hives occur or persist after two weeks of self-care

  See *Prevention, What You Can Do,* p. 126.

no / yes

Call Doctor

- Red, itchy, raised welts appear on skin

  See *What You Can Do,* pp. 126 - 127.

Apply Self-Care

Different Symptoms?
See *Skin Symptoms,* p. 115.

Boils

A boil is a red, swollen, painful bump that looks like a large pimple. It is usually caused by an infected hair follicle in an area of your body that is under pressure or chafed.

Common sites for boils are the buttocks, groin, waistline, armpits, neck and face. Bacteria, most often *Staphylococcus,* get blocked in the follicle and develop an abscess. The tissue around the follicle becomes tender and inflamed as it tries to wall off the infection. This forces the abscess outward until it ruptures on the skin surface and drains. If the wound is left open and clean, it can heal; if it closes off too soon, the pus pocket can form again.

Prevention

- For areas that are prone to boils, wash well with antibacterial soap. Dry thoroughly.
- Avoid clothing that is too tight. Eliminate chafing and ease pressure against your skin whenever possible.
- Keep clothes and personal linen of someone with a boil separate from the rest of the household to prevent spreading the infection.

What You Can Do

- Bathe with antibacterial soap to prevent boils from spreading.
- Apply warm, moist compresses to the boil for 15 to 20 minutes, four times a day. The moist heat helps bring the boil to a head and soften the skin to ease the rupture. This may take up to a week of compress treatments.
- **Do not squeeze, scratch, cut or force the boil to drain.** Any pressure or forced opening can push the bacteria deeper into the skin and spread the infection.
- Once the boil begins to drain, keep the wound open and clean, and:
  - Continue applying compresses at least three times a day.
  - Wash the area thoroughly with soap and water twice a day or as needed.
  - Apply antibacterial ointment and a sterile bandage after each compress treatment or whenever the old dressing becomes moist.

- Take aspirin or ibuprofen (Advil, Motrin) to ease pain and inflammation (follow the directions on the package). **NEVER give aspirin to children/ teenagers unless your healthcare provider orders it. It can cause Reye's syndrome, a rare but often fatal condition.**
- Watch for signs of infection moving beyond a simple boil:
  - Increasing redness or swelling extending beyond the border of the boil or red streaks leading away from it; fever of 101°F (38.3°C) or higher; tender or swollen lymph nodes

Boils

Do these apply:

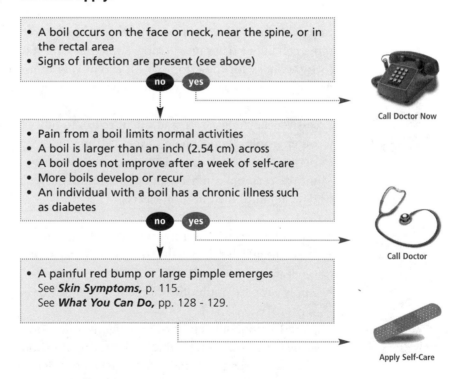

- A boil occurs on the face or neck, near the spine, or in the rectal area
- Signs of infection are present (see above)

no   yes

Call Doctor Now

- Pain from a boil limits normal activities
- A boil is larger than an inch (2.54 cm) across
- A boil does not improve after a week of self-care
- More boils develop or recur
- An individual with a boil has a chronic illness such as diabetes

no   yes

Call Doctor

- A painful red bump or large pimple emerges
  See *Skin Symptoms,* p. 115.
  See *What You Can Do,* pp. 128 - 129.

Apply Self-Care

Different Symptoms?
See *Skin Symptoms,* p. 115.

Impetigo

Impetigo is a highly contagious bacterial infection that frequently occurs around the mouth and nose and is most common among children. It is characterized by itchy red sores on the face, legs or arms. Symptoms begin with red, blistering sores that ooze for several days, later forming a sticky, honey-colored crust. *Ecthyma* is a form of impetigo that causes deeper sores.

Impetigo often follows minor scrapes and fungal infections, scabies, lice or other conditions that cause itching. Sometimes insect bites cause impetigo. (See the index for these topics.) All except very minor infections require prescription medication to ensure complete and rapid healing.

Prevention

Excessive scratching can spread the infection to other parts of the body or to other people. Do not share towels, clothing or razors with anyone until impetigo is completely gone. Keep fingernails short to minimize scratching. Minimize personal contact with others (children should stay out of school or daycare) until the infection clears.

What You Can Do

- Soak off crusts with warm water and a washcloth.
- Wash the affected area gently several times a day with antibacterial soap or cleanser.
- Apply a topical antibiotic ointment if your doctor advises it.

Final Notes

The most serious side effect of impetigo is a rare kidney condition called *glomerulonephritis*. It turns urine dark brown and is often accompanied by headaches and elevated blood pressure. If you have these symptoms, see your doctor. Most people recover completely.

Impetigo
Do these apply:

- Impetigo is worsening or not responding to treatment and you develop symptoms of a systemic infection (fever, malaise, fatigue, nausea)
- An infant under 6 months of age has symptoms of impetigo
- Signs of infection develop:
  - Increasing redness around the area or red streaks leading away from it
  - Swelling, warmth or tenderness
  - Pus
  - Fever of 101° F (38.3° C) or higher
  - Tender or swollen lymph nodes
- Facial areas (nostrils, lips, etc.) swell and become tender

Call Doctor Now

- You have symptoms of impetigo
- Impetigo doesn't begin to heal or worsens after two to three days of antibiotic treatment
- Impetigo covers two inches (5.08 cm) or more in diameter
- Anyone in your family or neighborhood has had glomerulonephritis recently (see p. 130)

Call Doctor

See **What You Can Do,** p. 130.

Apply Self-Care

Different Symptoms?
See **Skin Symptoms,** p. 115.

Ringworm

Oddly enough, ringworm has nothing to do with worms. It is a fungal infection of the nails, skin or scalp, caused by the same group of fungi responsible for athlete's foot (see *Athlete's Foot*, p. 134) and jock itch (see *Jock Itch*, p. 133). Ringworm gets its name from its characteristic red rings.

The infection can be spread from one person to another, from an animal to a person, or acquired by contact with contaminated soil, shoes, shower stalls or carpeting.

Ringworm typically begins as a small, pink, round patch which eventually turns red and grows into a ring shape. The center clears as the ring enlarges. Within a week or two, more patches may appear.

Prevention

Have all pets checked for ringworm before bringing them into your home and teach children not to touch stray dogs or cats. Launder secondhand clothing. Always use your own towels and wear sandals in public showers or locker rooms.

What You Can Do

Over-the-counter (OTC) medications applied to the skin are effective treatments for ringworm. Popular medications include tolnaftate (Tinactin), miconazole (Micatin), terbinafine (Lamisil cream) and clotrimazole (Lotrimin). Follow directions on the container.

Ringworm thrives in warmth and moisture, so keep the infected area clean and dry. Wear loose, cotton clothing and clean all clothes in hot water and detergent.

See *Decision helper*, p. 135.

Jock Itch

Jock itch most often affects men and sometimes, boys. Symptoms include minor to intense itching in the groin area and, in more serious cases, patches of redness, scaling and raised areas that ooze. The penis and scrotum are usually not involved.

Since this fungus thrives in warmth and moisture, your goal is to eliminate both. That means changing sweaty or soiled clothes as soon as possible and washing underwear, jock straps and exercise clothes in hot water and detergent. Loose, cotton boxer shorts are better than tight shorts or briefs. Use a powder, such as cornstarch, two to three times a day to dust the groin area, especially after showering.

Nonprescription medications can be used, such as tolnaftate (Tinactin), terbinafine (Lamisil cream), miconazole (Micatin), or clotrimazole (Lotrimin). Be sure to follow directions on the container. You may need to continue use after symptoms are gone to prevent recurrence.

See *Decision helper,* p. 135.

Athlete's Foot

Athlete's foot, which can make your feet red and feel itchy and irritated, is really ringworm, and affects one in five Americans. These fungi typically spread from person to person in public areas such as locker rooms, gyms and swimming pools.

Once it infects the feet, athlete's foot thrives in the warmth and moisture of shoes and socks. Other symptoms may include tenderness, soreness, scaling and a burning sensation. In severe cases, the skin between the toes or even the soles of the feet may become unnaturally soft, peel and crack.

Prevention

Keep your feet well-ventilated and dry by wearing sandals, canvas shoes and moisture-absorbent socks that wick water away from your feet. Cotton used to be the material of choice and is still appropriate. However, there are several new, more breathable socks available on the market. Examples are DuPont CoolMax and the new acrylics. Read sock labels for moisture absorbency qualities.

What You Can Do

Keep your feet clean and dry. Wash them twice a day with soap and water, drying them completely, especially between the toes. After drying, sprinkle an over-the-counter (OTC) antifungal powder on them, such as Desenex or Zeasorb-AF. Change your socks twice a day to keep feet dry.

If athlete's foot persists, try a nonprescription antifungal medication such as miconazole (Micatin), clotrimazole (Lotrimin), tolnaftate (Tinactin) or undecylemic acid (Cruex).

See *Decision helper,* p. 135.

Ringworm/Jock Itch/ Athlete's Foot

Do these apply:

- Signs of infection develop:
  - Redness around the area or red streaks leading away from it
  - Swelling
  - Warmth or tenderness
  - Pus
  - Fever of 101° F (38.3° C) or higher
  - Tender or swollen lymph nodes

Call Doctor Now

- Symptoms of athlete's foot or other foot problems occur in a person with diabetes and/or peripheral vascular disease
- Toenails are thickened, distorted, yellowish or crumbly *(possible fungal infection of nails)*
- Symptoms of ringworm occur on the scalp or on large areas of the chest or abdomen
- Jock itch seems to spread to the anal area
- Symptoms of any fungal problems persist or worsen after self-care
- Ringworm is not completely gone after four weeks of treatment

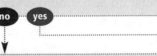

Call Doctor

- The rash begins as small, round, pink patches
- Patches turn red and grow into a ring shape
- The center of the ring clears as it enlarges
  See *What You Can Do, Ringworm,* p. 132.
- Groin itching is mild to intense
  See *What You Can Do, Jock Itch,* p. 133.
- Feet are red, itchy and irritated
  See *What You Can Do, Athlete's Foot,* p. 134.

Apply Self-Care

Warts

Warts are small lumps (caused by a virus) that appear on the skin. They are very common, especially among young people. Warts are usually harmless and often disappear by themselves or with minimal treatment. However, in some cases they persist for years. Very rarely, a wart may become cancerous.

The appearance and size of a wart depends on its location and whether it is subjected to pressure, irritation or trauma. *Plantar warts* (flattened growths on the soles of the feet), for example, can be very painful because of the pressure of standing on them.

What You Can Do

Repeated applications of topical over-the-counter (OTC) medications clear up many types of warts. For painful plantar warts, applying a donut-shaped pad to the area may provide temporary relief. Do not attempt to treat plantar warts yourself—see your doctor. Persistent warts may require acid treatment or surgical removal by your doctor. Most warts disappear spontaneously within two years. **Diabetics and people with peripheral vascular disease should never use OTC treatments unless advised to do so by a doctor.**

Final Notes

For warts that do not respond to treatment with OTC medications, your doctor may remove them using various methods (which may cause scarring):

- Freezing with liquid nitrogen
- Topical medicines
- Electrical burning
- Laser surgery

Warts

Do these apply:

- Warts look infected after being irritated or knocked off
- Warts occur in the anal or genital area (see *STD Chart,* pp. 306 - 307)
- You have an abnormal skin growth and you don't know what it is
- Warts occur on the face or feet
- Warts are painful
- Warts are cosmetically bothersome
- Warts continue to be a concern and do not respond to self-care
- You have diabetes or PVD

no   **yes**

See *What You Can Do,* p. 136.

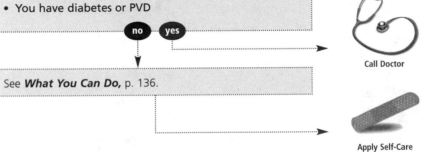

Call Doctor

Apply Self-Care

Scabies

Scabies is a highly contagious condition caused by tiny parasitic creatures called *mites*. They are usually transmitted through skin-to-skin contact and spread easily through households and schools.

Mites burrow into the skin and lay eggs just below its surface. The skin reacts with a rash and intense itching which is usually worse at night. Red track marks may be noted. These symptoms are most common between the fingers or on the inside of wrists, armpits, genitalia and on the breasts.

Scratching may transmit bacteria already present on the skin into the open sores, resulting in a secondary bacterial infection.

What You Can Do

Five percent permethrin (Elimite Cream), available by prescription, is the recommended treatment for scabies. Crotamiton (Eurax) also is effective but is not approved for use by children or pregnant women.

Following your doctor's or the package instructions, apply medication all over the body from the neck down, except the vaginal or urethral openings. Infants may need treatment of the scalp, sides of the face and neck (avoid the eyes and mucous membranes). Itching may be relieved by cool baths, cortisone cream or ointment, or calamine lotion. Itching may persist for one or two weeks after treatment.

Scabies
Do these apply:

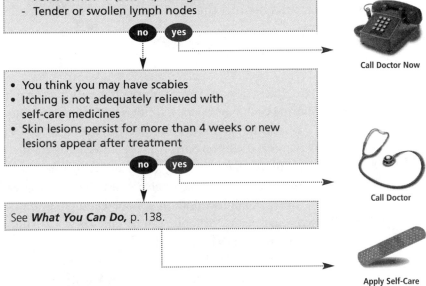

- Signs of infection develop:
  - Redness around the area or red streaks leading away from it
  - Swelling
  - Warmth or tenderness
  - Pus
  - Fever of 101° F (38.3° C) or higher
  - Tender or swollen lymph nodes

no   yes → **Call Doctor Now**

- You think you may have scabies
- Itching is not adequately relieved with self-care medicines
- Skin lesions persist for more than 4 weeks or new lesions appear after treatment

no   yes → **Call Doctor**

See **What You Can Do,** p. 138.

→ **Apply Self-Care**

Different Symptoms?
See **Skin Symptoms,** p. 115.

Lice

Pediculosis is a highly communicable infestation of small, white, blood-sucking insects called lice. The eggs are called *nits*; lice lay them on hair shafts close to the scalp or on the body. Pediculosis may result in swollen glands in the back of the neck and scratch marks behind the ears, along the hairline and on the neck. Lice are hard to see without a magnifying glass.

Lice infestation is spread through direct personal contact or through sharing clothing or personal items with someone who is infested.

Infestation is most common on the head or genital area but also sometimes occurs on body hair, eyebrows and eyelashes. Overcrowded living conditions where clothing and bedding may be shared or stored close to items used by an infested person raise the risk of spreading lice.

Head lice infestation in school children is unrelated to hygiene or economic status. Schools, camps and anywhere children share common space can be sites of outbreak.

Genital lice (*crabs*) are frequently transmitted through sexual contact, but may also be acquired from infested toilet seats, towels, bedding or clothes.

Lice bites usually leave a tiny red spot but scratching can cause larger sores to develop.

What You Can Do

- Over-the-counter (OTC) pesticides such as permethrin (Nix Creme Rinse) or pyrethrins (A-200, RID, Triple X, R&C) are recommended for head and pubic lice. Follow package directions.
- Use a nit-picking comb to remove nits as thoroughly as possible.
- Treat lice in the eyelashes with a thick layer of petroleum jelly made especially for the eye area, twice daily for eight days. If any nits are left, they can be removed with tweezers.
- Treat all exposed people at the same time to avoid reinfestations.

- Wash combs, brushes, hats, barrettes and other sources of contamination in prescription-grade lice shampoo or very hot soapy water.
- Wash all clothing and bedding in hot (130° F [54.4° C]) water and hang out to dry or dry on the hot cycle for 20 minutes.
- Vacuum carpets and upholstered furniture.

See *Decision helper,* p. 142.

Bedbugs

As you may have guessed, bedbugs spend most of their time in bed, living in the darkness of sheets and blankets. Although related to lice, bedbugs are entirely different creatures. They are wingless, red, oval bugs about one-quarter inch (.64 cm) in length. They feed for 10 to 15 minutes a day, hate light and have a strong sense of when a warm body is nearby. They are very difficult to catch.

A bedbug bite is a firm lump or cluster of lumps which can be found anywhere on the skin.

Treat the infested bed and room to get rid of bedbugs (they do not hide on the body or in clothing) by washing your bedding in hot, soapy water. Follow the advice of your local health department for preventing future infestations.

See *Decision helper,* p. 142.

Lice/Bedbugs

Do these apply:

- Signs of infection develop:
  - Redness around the area or red streaks leading away from it
  - Swelling
  - Warmth or tenderness
  - Pus
  - Fever of 101° F (38.3° C) or higher
  - Tender or swollen lymph nodes

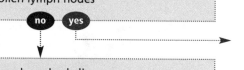

Call Doctor Now

- You think you may have body lice
- Your skin is severely irritated or lice infestation recurs after treatment
- A pregnant or breastfeeding woman or child younger than two years of age has lice

Call Doctor

- You have symptoms of head or pubic lice or bedbugs
  See **What You Can Do,** pp. 140, 141

Apply Self-Care

Different Symptoms?
See **Skin Symptoms,** p. 115.

Tick Bites

Ticks are small parasites related to spiders that embed themselves in the skin. Although tick bites are rarely harmful, ticks may transmit serious diseases such as *Rocky Mountain spotted fever* and *Lyme disease*.

Ticks are common in all outdoor areas of the United States and may be passed to people by their pets. Ticks frequently lodge in the scalp, nape of the neck, ankles, genital area or skin folds. Although small, ticks embedded in the skin are usually visible.

Tick bites often go unnoticed. They are characterized by itching, a small, hard lump on the skin, and redness surrounding the bite.

- Avoid tick-infested areas, such as thickly wooded brush, whenever possible.
- Use an insect repellent on your skin and clothing whenever you plan to be outdoors for any length of time, especially in the warm months of spring and summer.
- Wear light-colored clothing; long-sleeved shirts and long pants. Make sure your shirt is tucked inside your pants, and tuck your pants inside your boots or socks.
- After being in a known tick-infested area, check your body thoroughly and remove any ticks you find.

Never Scratch a Tick Bite

The body of the tick may break off, leaving the head embedded in the skin.

Removal of Ticks

Ticks should be removed carefully and promptly to help prevent the diseases they carry.
- With small tweezers, grip the tick as close to the surface of the skin as possible. Pull straight up and out using gentle, steady pressure. Do not squeeze the body of a tick, since this can increase the chance of getting a tick-borne disease.

- Extract the tick slowly and firmly to assure complete removal.
- Clean the area of the tick bite with soap and water, then apply antiseptic.

Lyme disease is usually transmitted by small deer ticks, common in summer and early fall. Symptoms develop up to three weeks after a bite.

Rocky Mountain spotted fever is usually transmitted by wood ticks in the West and by dog ticks and lone star ticks in the East and Southeast. This disease generally occurs in warm weather and symptoms begin suddenly, two to 14 days after the bite.

Tick Bites
Do these apply:

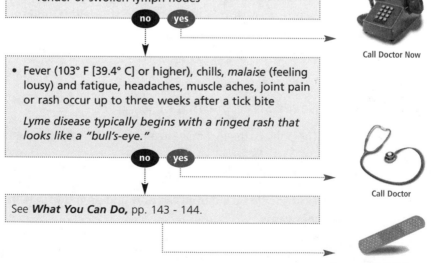

- You are unable to remove a tick or think part of the tick is still embedded
- Signs of infection develop:
  - Redness around the area or red streaks leading away from the bite
  - Swelling
  - Warmth or tenderness
  - Pus
  - Fever of 101° F (38.3° C) or higher
  - Tender or swollen lymph nodes

no   yes → Call Doctor Now

- Fever (103° F [39.4° C] or higher), chills, *malaise* (feeling lousy) and fatigue, headaches, muscle aches, joint pain or rash occur up to three weeks after a tick bite

Lyme disease typically begins with a ringed rash that looks like a "bull's-eye."

no   yes → Call Doctor

See **What You Can Do,** pp. 143 - 144.

→ Apply Self-Care

Sunburn

A sunburn is a true burn of the outer layer of the skin. A *first-degree* burn causes skin redness and moderate discomfort. Severe sunburns with blisters, pain and swelling are *second-degree* burns and involve the deeper skin layer. Repeated sunburning and tanning speed the skin's aging process and increase the risk of some cancers. (See *Burns*, p. 28 and *Skin Cancer*, p. 147.)

Prevention

- Use sunscreen on all skin surfaces, even under your clothing, with a sun protection factor (SPF) of at least 15. Apply sunscreen 15 minutes before exposure and reapply it every two hours. Use a sunscreen that protects against both UVA and UVB light. Ask your pharmacist for recommendations.
- Wear long sleeves and a hat with a broad brim or visor while you are in the sun.
- Avoid the sun between 10 a.m. and 3 p.m., when the sun's rays are strongest. Cloudy conditions do not screen out the rays that can burn your skin.
- Check with your doctor or pharmacist to find out if any of your medications increase your skin's sensitivity to sunlight. If they do, use extra caution in the sun.
- Take sunburn precautions at high altitudes, in tropical climates, and around snow or water.
- Drink extra fluids on sunny days, even if the temperature is not hot.

What You Can Do

- Try cool compresses or baths to ease sunburn discomfort. Adding one cup (230 mL) of baking soda or finely ground oatmeal to the bath water may increase the soothing effects.
- Take aspirin or ibuprofen (Advil, Motrin) to ease the pain and decrease inflammation. **NEVER give aspirin to children/teenagers unless your healthcare provider orders it. It can cause Reye's syndrome, a rare but often fatal condition.**

- Apply aloe vera gel or lotion to make your skin more comfortable.
- Avoid oil-based products, such as petroleum jelly, for 24 hours after a sunburn. They may actually retain the heat.
- Avoid products that contain anesthetic "caines" such as benzocaine. They may cause an allergic reaction in sensitive skin.
- Drink extra water and watch for signs of dehydration. (See *Dehydration*, p. 236.)
- Get extra rest and avoid exertion for 24 hours.

Sunburn
Do these apply:

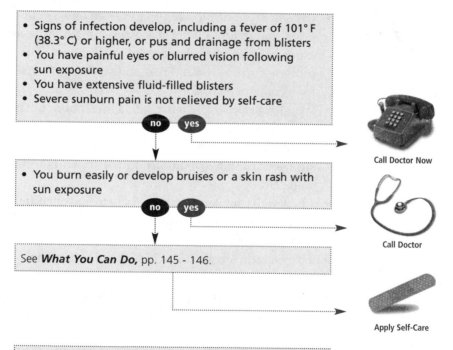

- Signs of infection develop, including a fever of 101° F (38.3° C) or higher, or pus and drainage from blisters
- You have painful eyes or blurred vision following sun exposure
- You have extensive fluid-filled blisters
- Severe sunburn pain is not relieved by self-care

no   yes

Call Doctor Now

- You burn easily or develop bruises or a skin rash with sun exposure

no   yes

Call Doctor

See *What You Can Do,* pp. 145 - 146.

Apply Self-Care

Different Symptoms?
See *Skin Symptoms,* p. 115.

Skin Cancer

There are many types of skin cancer, but the three most common types are basal cell carcinoma, squamous cell carcinoma and malignant melanoma.

Basal cell carcinoma: the most common type. It is a slow-growing cancer that forms in the outermost layer of the skin. If treated early, it is usually completely curable. If untreated, it can spread (*metastasize*) and cause extensive skin damage.

Squamous cell carcinoma: the second most frequent type. It can grow more quickly than basal cell carcinoma and can spread to other parts of the body.

Malignant melanoma: the most agressive and deadliest type of skin cancer is cancer of the *melanocyte* (pigment cells of the skin). Malignant melanoma can spread quickly through the lymph system and the bloodstream. That's why it is very important that it be detected in the earliest possible stage. More than 70 percent of cases of early melanoma can be cured. However, the outcome is not as favorable for cases that are treated in later stages. A patient's age and general health also influence the success of treatment.

Some Causes

The primary known cause of all types of skin cancer is exposure to ultraviolet (UV) radiation from sunlight. People who live in sunny climates and those with fair skin, freckles, blond or red hair, or blue eyes are at greatest risk. However, people with dark skin also can develop skin cancer. Some people with many moles (*nevi*) that contain abnormal (*dysplastic*) cells have an increased risk of developing melanoma.

A variety of other factors can increase the risk of skin cancer, including exposure to artificial light sources (such as tanning beds), certain medications and a variety of chemicals.

Skin cancer forms without causing any symptoms of illness. Therefore, it's extremely important to be aware of the signs, especially in people with known risk factors.

Check your skin once a month for any irregularities. If you have any suspicious growths on your skin, have them checked by your doctor. A skin *biopsy*, in which part or all of the tissue from a mole or suspicious growth is removed for analysis, may be required. Biopsy is the only definitive test for melanoma and other skin cancers.

Melanoma

The "hallmark" sign of melanoma is a change in the size or shape of a mole. "ABCD" is an abbreviation used to make it easy to remember the four basic signs of possible melanoma:

- Asymmetry—The shape of one half of a mole doesn't match the other.
- Border—The edges are ragged, notched or blurred.
- Color—The color is uneven and shades of black, brown or tan are present. Areas of white, red or blue may also be seen.
- Diameter—There is a change in size. The mole may be raised or flat, round or oval.

Other signs include a mole that scales, oozes, bleeds or changes in the way it feels. Some moles will become hard, lumpy, itchy, swollen or tender. Melanoma may also appear as a new mole.

Other Skin Cancers

Watch for any new growths or skin irregularities that:

- Have a smooth, shiny or waxy surface
- Are rough, scaly or crusty
- Bleed
- Are flat or lumpy, red or pale

The best approach to skin cancer is preventing it in the first place:

- Stay out of the sun as much as possible, especially if you have fair skin, a history of sunburns or a current diagnosis of skin cancer.
- If you can't avoid sun exposure, wear protective clothing, such as hats, long sleeves, and UV-protective sunglasses.
- Avoid or limit sunlight exposure between 10 a.m. and 3 p.m., when the sun's rays are the most direct.
- Check all prescription and over-the-counter (OTC) medications for precautions about sun exposure. Some medications can greatly increase the likelihood of sunburn.
- ALWAYS use sun block, even on overcast, cloudy days. Sunscreens are rated by a sun protection factor (SPF); the higher the SPF number, the greater the protection.
- Make sure children are adequately protected from the sun; exposure during childhood is a significant risk factor for developing skin cancer later in life.
- Check your skin regularly.

Skin Cancer
Do these apply:

- You are concerned about a skin lesion or growth
- There is a change in the size, shape or feel of a mole

 yes

Call Doctor

Eye Concerns

Red, Irritated Eyes

Eye discomfort ranges from simple itching, which can be caused by a common cold or an allergic reaction, to pain that may signify a much more serious eye disease.

Conjunctivitis (pinkeye) refers to an inflammation of the *conjunctiva*—the outermost membrane that covers the eye and inner part of the eyelid—and is the most common eye disease. Pinkeye can be caused by viruses, bacteria, allergies, pollution or other irritants such as cigarette smoke. The most common symptoms are redness of the whites of the eyes, gritty or itchy eyes, tearing, swelling, eye discharge that is matted in the morning, and sensitivity to light.

Newborns are susceptible to bacteria in the birth canal that can cause a type of conjunctivitis that must be treated immediately to prevent blindness.

It's best not to rub your eyes, which may aggravate symptoms and increase the risk of spreading infection to the other eye or to other people. Most forms of eye discomfort respond well to self-care.

Prevention

Some preventive measures can reduce your risk of eye problems:
- Don't share washcloths or towels.
- Never use anyone else's makeup.
- Discard your mascara after a couple of months.
- Wear goggles to protect your eyes when you use tools and when you swim in chlorinated swimming pools.
- Use vacuum cleaners and heating and air systems with HEPA filters, which reduce airborne allergens. Be sure to change filters regularly.

What You Can Do

Conjunctivitis

- Avoid rubbing or touching your eyes.
- Wash your hands frequently with soap and water, especially if you're around a child who has pinkeye.
- Don't share washcloths or towels.

- Change bed linens and pillowcases daily.
- Apply warm or cool compresses.
- If you wear contact lenses, remove them until the infection subsides.
- Try over-the-counter (OTC) eye drops to relieve itchiness.
- Try antihistamines to help relieve allergic eye discomfort. Read the precautions on the label regarding drowsiness.

Final Notes

Eye pain sometimes is caused by injury, infection or some other disease. Sensitivity to bright light is common with viral infections such as flu and disappears once the infection clears up. Injury to the eye by a foreign object also can cause pain. This type of eye pain should be treated by your doctor. (See *Object In Eye*, p. 154.)

Decision *helper*

Red, Irritated Eyes
Do these apply:

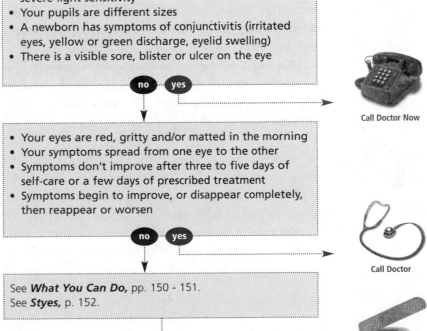

- You have persistent eye pain, tearing or blinking or severe light sensitivity
- Your pupils are different sizes
- A newborn has symptoms of conjunctivitis (irritated eyes, yellow or green discharge, eyelid swelling)
- There is a visible sore, blister or ulcer on the eye

no   yes

Call Doctor Now

- Your eyes are red, gritty and/or matted in the morning
- Your symptoms spread from one eye to the other
- Symptoms don't improve after three to five days of self-care or a few days of prescribed treatment
- Symptoms begin to improve, or disappear completely, then reappear or worsen

no   yes

Call Doctor

See **What You Can Do,** pp. 150 - 151.
See **Styes,** p. 152.

Apply Self-Care

Styes

Styes are caused by a bacterial infection of the tiny glands near the base of the eyelashes. They almost never result in damage to the eye or sight, and should not be confused with blocked tear ducts—which appear most commonly in infants as a bump along the side of the nose just below the inner corner of the eye.

A stye typically starts out looking like a pimple on the eyelid—a small, red, tender and swollen bump—and grows to full size over a day or so. The stye then fills with pus and ruptures within a few days. If the bacteria spread, more than one stye may occur. Styes can also form inside the eyelid, but this is less common.

What You Can Do

Wring out a clean cloth soaked in warm or hot water. Place it directly on the affected (closed) eye. For best results, do this three or four times a day for about 10 to 15 minutes each time. The stye should rupture and drain, which usually occurs after about two days. Sometimes a stye may fade away without ever coming to a head and draining.

Since styes can be spread from one eye to another, and from one person to another through close contact, wash your hands frequently. Never pinch the stye to try to remove the pus, since this may spread infection deeper into the tissue.

Final Notes

Styes are common enough that many people can identify them on their own. Occasionally, they are confused with a *chalazion*, a swelling caused by a blocked gland within the eyelid. Unlike a stye, a chalazion is painless and is not helped by self-care. It may require minor surgery.

For a stye, a doctor may prescribe an antibiotic solution applied directly to the eyelid. Oral antibiotics are usually reserved for styes that do not respond to other treatment or are very large or located inside the eyelid.

A particularly stubborn stye may need to be lanced and drained by a surgeon. Never try to do this on your own.

A stye can be extremely unpleasant because of its pain and appearance. Properly treated, it will disappear soon after it comes to a head and drains.

Styes
Do these apply:

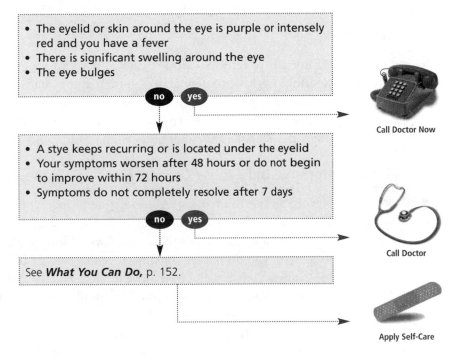

- The eyelid or skin around the eye is purple or intensely red and you have a fever
- There is significant swelling around the eye
- The eye bulges

no **yes**

Call Doctor Now

- A stye keeps recurring or is located under the eyelid
- Your symptoms worsen after 48 hours or do not begin to improve within 72 hours
- Symptoms do not completely resolve after 7 days

no **yes**

Call Doctor

See *What You Can Do,* p. 152.

Apply Self-Care

Object in Eye

Tears and blinking are your natural defenses against sand, dust and other particles that enter the eye. But when something larger injures the eye, other steps are necessary to protect your vision and speed recovery.

Nearly all eye injuries reported each year could have been prevented by wearing goggles or safety glasses during sports activities or while using tools (drills, hammers, grinders and saws) and heavy machinery. Other injuries could have been avoided by using common sense when handling fireworks, BB guns and other potential hazards.

Remove Only Those Objects Floating on the Eye's Surface

Never rub the injured eye. Ask someone to help you remove the object from your eye, or use a mirror to locate it yourself. Sit in a well-lighted room, and use clean hands to pull the lower eyelid gently down while you look up. If you do not see the object, gently pull the upper lid out as you look down. Only attempt to remove foreign material if it is "floating." **Do not try to remove anything embedded in the eye. Seek emergency care.**

- If you cannot readily see the object, grasp the lashes of your upper lid and pull down. Blink several times. This sometimes removes small particles.
- Flush the eye with clean water by pressing the rim of a small glass against the eye socket and tilting your head back. Open and close the eye.
- If flushing with water is unsuccessful, moisten a cotton swab and gently lift off the object. Flush the eye with water afterward.
- Do not use ointments or anesthetic drops on the eye.

Handling Possible Complications

- If a trip to the doctor is necessary (see next page, *Decision helper*), cover the eye with a sterile pad or clean cloth and keep it still. Close both eyes to prevent involuntary movement.
- If you can't close your eye, tape a paper cup over it.

Final Notes

An object in the eye can scratch the *cornea* (the covering of the eye) and may cause significant vision loss. Your recovery depends on how deep the object penetrates the eye, how quickly the injury is treated and whether an infection develops.

Decision *helper*

Object in Eye
Do these apply:

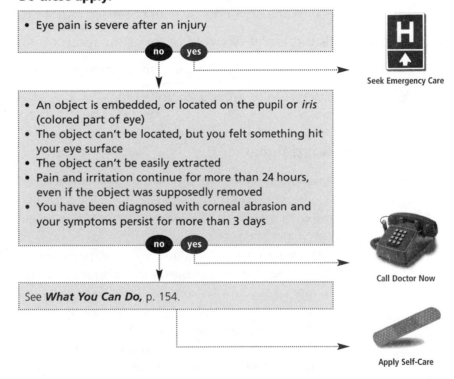

• Eye pain is severe after an injury

no   yes

Seek Emergency Care

• An object is embedded, or located on the pupil or *iris* (colored part of eye)
• The object can't be located, but you felt something hit your eye surface
• The object can't be easily extracted
• Pain and irritation continue for more than 24 hours, even if the object was supposedly removed
• You have been diagnosed with corneal abrasion and your symptoms persist for more than 3 days

no   yes

Call Doctor Now

See **What You Can Do,** p. 154.

Apply Self-Care

Ear/Nose/Throat

Sore Throat

A sore throat, or *pharyngitis,* is most often the result of a virus, although bacteria can also cause infection and dry or polluted air or tobacco smoke can cause irritation. Typically, a sore throat is part of a cold or flu or the result of postnasal drip from allergies, but in some cases it can be the symptom of a more serious condition, such as strep throat, which requires a doctor's care.

Strep Throat

Strep throat is caused by an infection with streptococcal bacteria; untreated it can cause serious complications. Symptoms usually include severe sore throat that is bright red, swollen tonsils and glands, and a fever higher than 101° F (38.3° C).

Strep usually targets children and may compound sore throat symptoms by making it difficult to open the mouth and causing the child to drool. It can spread rapidly; some children may show no symptoms yet be carriers. When one child has strep, it's not uncommon for others in the family to come down with it as well.

Complications from strep may include ear infection, sinusitis, inflammation of the kidneys and *rheumatic fever,* a painful joint disease that can also damage the heart. When a sore throat is prolonged, severe or coupled with other symptoms, a throat culture or rapid strep test is often performed to determine the cause. Antibiotics are the treatment for bacterial infections.

Mononucleosis

If an older child or adolescent has a severe sore throat combined with fatigue and a feeling of weakness, *infectious mononucleosis* (or mono) may be the cause. Mono is a viral infection which may cause enlargement of the spleen but few other complications. It rarely occurs in adults. A blood test is used to confirm the diagnosis and treatment is limited to rest and plenty of fluids.

Tonsillitis

Symptoms of *tonsillitis*, an inflammation and swelling of the *tonsils* (lymph tissues located on either side at the back of the throat) are similar to those of mononucleosis. Lymph nodes on the side of the neck may be tender and swollen and your child may have foul-smelling breath. Tonsillitis normally occurs in children and is usually caused by a viral infection. However, a bacterial infection may be the culprit.

If repeated infections persist, tonsils may be removed.

Inflamed Adenoids

Inflamed *adenoids* may trigger sore throats as well, and they are common among children. Like the tonsils, the adenoids are lymph tissues in the back of the throat; however, adenoids are hard to see. Swollen adenoids can cause difficulty breathing, ear infections and sleep disturbances.

What You Can Do

Time and patience are the greatest healers if the sore throat is viral in origin; antibiotics are not effective. Other tips:

- Use over-the-counter (OTC) pain relievers, such as aspirin, ibuprofen (Advil, Motrin) and acetaminophen (Tylenol), to ease the soreness. **NEVER give aspirin to children/teenagers unless your healthcare provider orders it. It can cause Reye's syndrome, a rare but often fatal condition.**
- Gargle with warm salt water (one-fourth teaspoon [600 mg] of salt added to eight ounces [230 mL] of water) several times a day.
- Use throat lozenges to soothe inflamed mucous membranes.
- Eat a soft or liquid diet to avoid irritating the throat.
- Drink plenty of liquids.
- Get plenty of rest.
- If you smoke, stop.

Final Notes

While many adults suffer from an occasional sore throat while battling colds or the flu, children between the ages of 5 and 10 are very susceptible to the ailment. Fortunately, in most cases, the condition disappears by itself within a week or so.

Sore Throat
Do these apply:

- A child younger than age 6 is unable to swallow saliva
- There is a bluish appearance to the skin or lips
- Fatigue from rapid breathing occurs, along with an inability to catch the breath

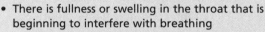

Seek Emergency Care

- There is fullness or swelling in the throat that is beginning to interfere with breathing
- A child age 6 or older has a sore throat and is unable to swallow
- The person is unable to touch the chin to the chest or holds the head tilted to one side
- There is visible swelling or distortion of the *uvula* (the soft hanging structure at the back of the throat)
- There is trauma to the mouth, throat or neck
- A pregnant woman has a sore throat and a fever of 102° F (38.9° C) or higher

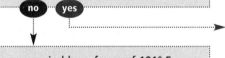

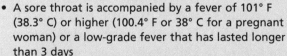

Call Doctor Now

- A sore throat is accompanied by a fever of 101° F (38.3° C) or higher (100.4° F or 38° C for a pregnant woman) or a low-grade fever that has lasted longer than 3 days
- A red rash or strawberry-colored tongue accompanies a sore throat
- Pus or blisters are visible at the back of the throat
- Exposure to strep throat or scarlet fever has occured
- Sore throat persists for more than 5 days
- Symptoms increase or fail to improve after 2 or 3 days of antibiotic treatment

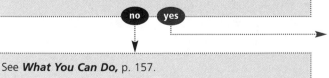

Call Doctor

See **What You Can Do,** p. 157.

Apply Self-Care

Laryngitis/Hoarseness

Laryngitis is an inflammation of the *larynx* (voice box), which is located at the top of the windpipe. When the vocal cords, which are part of the larynx, become inflamed, they swell and cause hoarseness and other distortions of the voice.

Laryngitis may be caused by allergies or illnesses such as the common cold, bronchitis or the flu, or by:

- Excessive talking, singing or shouting
- Reflux of irritating stomach contents into the throat (GERD)
- Inhalation of irritating chemicals
- Paralysis of or benign polyps or tumors on the vocal cords
- Heavy smoking or excessive alcohol intake

Note Your Symptoms

Laryngitis is usually identified by its primary symptom, hoarseness. Other symptoms can include loss of the voice, tickling, rawness or pain in the throat, or a constant need to clear the throat.

What You Can Do

You may be able to relieve symptoms of laryngitis by:

- Resting your voice (but don't whisper; write notes instead)
- Inhaling steam (sit in the bathroom with the shower turned on hot to make steam) or cool mist from a vaporizer
- Drinking lots of liquids, especially warm, soothing ones
- Not smoking
- Gargling with warm salt water (one-fourth teaspoon [600 mg] of salt added to eight ounces [230 mL] of water) to soothe the throat
- Taking antihistamines to relieve symptoms if they are caused by allergies (read the precautions on the label regarding drowsiness)

If laryngitis is caused by GERD, polyps, exposure to irritants, or excessive alcohol consumption, the cause must be dealt with before the symptoms can be eliminated. (See *Getting And Staying Healthy*, p. 330.)

See **Decision helper,** p. 160.

Laryngitis/Hoarseness

Do these apply:

• You have laryngitis and severe difficulty breathing

no   yes

Seek Emergency Care

• Symptoms of laryngitis begin suddenly and you suspect a child or adult has food or another foreign object stuck in the throat (see *Choking,* p. 22)

no   yes

Apply Emergency First Aid

• You begin to develop breathing difficulty
• Laryngitis occurs in an infant or young child with a history of (or recurring) croup or respiratory disease
See *Croup,* p. 91.
See *Allergic Reaction, Wheezing,* p. 206.

no   yes

Call Doctor Now

• Symptoms of laryngitis are accompanied by a fever that doesn't improve in two to three days
• Chronic laryngitis or symptoms have lasted for two weeks or more

no   yes

Call Doctor

See *What You Can Do,* p. 159.

Apply Self-Care

Swollen Glands

Lymph nodes (glands) swell to help the body fight infection. Frequently, swollen glands mean there's an infection in the area of the body where the glands are located. For example, swollen neck glands frequently accompany sore throats and earaches. Lymph glands in the groin area sometimes swell when there is an infection in the feet, legs or genital region.

Swollen glands in the neck can be a sign of a viral or bacterial throat infection (see *Sore Throat*, p. 156). Swollen glands behind the ears can be a sign of a scalp infection. If there is no scalp infection (see *Skin Symptoms*, p. 115), *German measles* (see *Rubella*, p. 80) or *infectious mononucleosis* (see *Sore Throat*, p. 156) could be the cause.

Glands become painful as a result of their rapid enlargement when they first begin to fight an infection. The pain usually goes away in a couple of days, but the lymph glands may stay enlarged for quite a while, sometimes several weeks.

On rare occasions, glands that have been enlarging over several weeks are a symptom of a serious underlying cause.

What You Can Do

If you have discomfort from swollen glands, you can:

- Rest and drink plenty of fluids.
- Take acetaminophen (Tylenol), ibuprofen (Advil, Motrin) or aspirin to relieve discomfort. **NEVER give aspirin to children/teenagers unless your healthcare provider orders it. It can cause Reye's syndrome, a rare but often fatal condition**.
- Place a warm washcloth, water bottle or heating pad (set on low) directly on the affected area. (Do not leave a child alone with a heating pad.)

Most swollen glands don't require any treatment because they are fighting an infection somewhere else in the body. An exception to this is if the gland itself develops a bacterial infection, making it red and tender. Sometimes a doctor will prescribe antibiotics to get rid of the bacteria causing the infection.

Swollen Glands
Do these apply:

• Swollen glands and signs of infection are present: redness around the area or red streaks leading away from it, swelling, warmth or tenderness, pus, or fever of 101° F (38.3° C)
• You have swollen glands and immune system problems

Call Doctor Now

• You have swollen glands and a sore throat
• Swollen glands are present in multiple locations
• Swollen glands persist or have increased in size for 2 to 3 weeks
• Swollen glands follow a cat scratch or tick bite
• Swollen glands and a fever of 100.5° F (38.1° C) are present for 2 days or more
• You have enlarged glands just above the collar bone
• A gland is larger than one-half inch (1.0 cm) in diameter
• Swollen glands are present for 3 to 4 weeks or longer
• Swollen glands accompany unintentional weight loss, excessive fatigue or night sweats

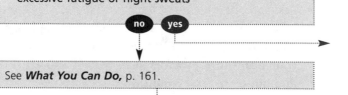

Call Doctor

See **What You Can Do,** p. 161.

Apply Self-Care

Different Symptoms?
See **Rubella,** p. 80; **Mumps,** p. 85; **Roseola,** p. 87;
    Children's Ear Infections, p. 93; **Sore Throat,** p. 156;
    Middle Ear Infection, p. 173.

The Common Cold

A cold is a viral illness that can cause a sore throat, runny nose and other symptoms. Most colds are caused by *rhinoviruses* ("rhino" refers to the nose), which are transmitted through sneezes, coughs or handling virus-contaminated objects.

Since there's no cure, avoiding the cold virus is the best way to beat the bug.

- Wash your hands frequently, especially after coughing or sneezing, and teach your children to do the same. Use soap and water or an alcohol-based hand cleaner.
- Avoid touching your eyes, nose or mouth after touching objects that could be contaminated with the cold virus, such as doorknobs or stair railings.
- Cover your mouth and nose with a tissue when coughing or sneezing.
- If you don't have a tissue, cough or sneeze into your upper sleeve, not your hands.
- Avoid close contact and kissing when illness is present.

Cold symptoms develop suddenly within two to six days of exposure. A runny, stuffy nose is a very common symptom. However, runny noses are also caused by hay fever or *allergic rhinitis*. (See *Hay Fever*, p. 191.)

The excess mucus produced by a runny nose can cause postnasal drip, which triggers a nighttime cough and can lead to a sore throat. Ear or sinus infections also may develop if mucus plugs the sinuses or *eustachian* tube between the nose and ear. (See *Sinusitis*, p. 169; *Middle Ear Infection*, p. 173.)

Other cold symptoms include:

- Scratchy or sore throat
- Sneezing
- Watery eyes
- Headache
- Swollen glands
- Cough
- Fever, usually below 101° F (38.3° C) in adults, but which can climb to 103° F (39.4° C) or 104° F (40° C) in children (see *Fever*, p. 100)

A cold usually runs its course in five to seven days.

What You Can Do

Simple Steps to Relief

- Get plenty of rest.
- ~~Drink lots of fluids.~~
- Use a cool-mist vaporizer to relieve congestion. Change the water daily and rinse the vaporizer with a vinegar and water solution.
- Ease nasal congestion in infants with a bulb syringe. Avoid excessive use to prevent damage inside the nose.

Medication Considerations

Over-the-counter (OTC) medications will not shorten the course of a cold, but they may offer temporary relief from some symptoms. All have minor side effects. (See *Using Medications*, p. 324; *Home Pharmacy*, p. 325.)

- Nose drops or nasal sprays are effective decongestants, but they can increase stuffiness if they are used for more than three days in a row. Instead, substitute an OTC or homemade saline solution of one-fourth teaspoon (600 mg) of salt to eight ounces (230 mL) of water. Discard any unused homemade saline daily.
- Oral decongestants may act as stimulants and make you restless or unable to sleep. Often they are combined with antihistamines (which tend to cause drowsiness) to lessen this side effect.
- Antihistamines appear to be more effective against allergy symptoms than cold-related complaints. Some of them cause drowsiness, which can help you sleep, but are dangerous to use while driving or operating heavy machinery.
- Pain relievers, such as aspirin, ibuprofen (Advil, Motrin) and acetaminophen (Tylenol), can lessen aches, pains and fevers. **NEVER give aspirin to children/teenagers unless your healthcare provider orders it. It can cause Reye's syndrome, a rare but often fatal condition.**
- Do not give antihistamines, nose drops, nasal spray or oral decongestants to children younger than 12 months without speaking to a pediatrician first. Relieve congestion with homemade saline solution (see above) or a nasal syringe.

Final Notes

In some cases, the common cold can lead to ear or sinus infections, laryngitis, bronchitis or pneumonia. Other conditions—such as strep throat, allergies and measles—produce symptoms which mimic a cold. Monitor the cold's progress—especially with children—and watch for high fevers, rashes, ear pain or breathing difficulty that can signal a more serious illness. (See index.)

Common Cold

Do these apply:

- An infant younger than 3 months has a rectal temperature of 100.4° F (38° C) or higher, even if the temperature becomes normal

no · · · yes

Seek Emergency Care

- An infant between 3 months and 1 year has a fever for more than 24 hours
- An infant or young child has symptoms of an ear infection (see *Ear Infections,* p. 93)
- You have symptoms of sinusitis (see *Sinusitis,* p. 169) or an earache (see *Middle Ear Infection,* p. 173)
- Cold symptoms do not worsen or do not improve after 5 to 7 days
- A cough lingers for more that 7 to 10 days after other cold symptoms have cleared

no · · · yes

Call Doctor

See *What You Can Do,* p. 164.

Apply Self-Care

Coughs

A cough is a natural reflex designed to clear your breathing tubes of mucus and foreign particles.

Note Your Symptoms

Coughs are usually referred to as "productive" or "nonproductive." A productive cough jars loose phlegm and helps expel it from the body. You'll probably be advised to let a productive cough do its work and avoid cough suppressants. Productive coughs may signal viral or bacterial infections. Mucus is usually yellow or white with a viral infection, but it may be yellow, gray-green or rust-colored and contain pus with a bacterial infection. Bacterial infections usually require antibiotics.

A nonproductive cough is dry or hacking and you may need to take steps to quiet it. Learning to spot a cough's characteristics can help you pinpoint the appropriate steps for relief. Some common causes for dry, nonproductive coughs are dry air, some medications, gastroesophogeal reflux disease (GERD), smoking and postnasal drip.

Coughs in infants are very unusual and can suggest a serious problem. In older infants and young children, a cough may signal a foreign object lodged in the throat. A youngster's barking cough may mean croup. (See *Croup*, p. 91.)

What You Can Do

- Drink lots of water to loosen phlegm and soothe your irritated throat.
- Use a cool-mist vaporizer to increase humidity.
- Use throat lozenges or hard candies to relieve the "tickle" and throat irritation.
- If postnasal drip is causing the dry, hacking cough, try an over-the-counter (OTC) decongestant. Avoid medications with antihistamines, which thicken the secretions you are trying to dislodge.
- Try a nonprescription cough medication containing guaifenesin, which can thin secretions. OTC cough suppressants with dextromethorphan may help quiet the cough at night so you can get some rest. Use cough suppressants only as directed. (See *Home Pharmacy*, p. 325.)
- Use pillows to elevate your head at night.
- If you smoke, stop.

Final Notes

Another cause of cough that is again becoming more common is whooping cough, or *pertussis*. Prior to the 1940s, whooping cough was one of the most common childhood diseases, and a major cause of death in children. After introduction of the pertussis vaccine, the number of cases dropped dramatically. However, immunity gained from immunization fades in late adolesence, and in recent years the number of cases has increased, especially among adolescents and young adults. It is very important to treat people with whooping cough and those exposed to it. This is especially true for infants too young to be immunized and young children, who are at the greatest risk of serious complications. Call your doctor if after a week or so of cold-like symptoms, bouts of violent coughing develop (making it hard to catch the breath) that are followed by a "whooping" sound during inhalation.

See *Decision helper,* p. 168.

Coughs

Do these apply:

- A hard cough begins suddenly and without other symptoms, especially in a child who might have inhaled an object
- There is significant respiratory distress, such as:
  - A feeling of suffocation
  - Gasping or straining to get a breath
  - Bluish color to the lips or skin

 no · yes

Seek Emergency Care

- A child with a cough is younger than 3 months
- You have difficulty breathing, such as shortness of breath or rapid respirations
- You cough up bright red blood

no · yes

Call Doctor Now

- A cough ends with a whooping sound
- A cough is persistent or unexplained
- A cough lingers more than 7 to 10 days after other symptoms have cleared
- Coughing interferes with your sleep despite self-care measures
- A cough is associated with chest pain or produces yellow, gray-green or rust-colored sputum

no · yes

Call Doctor

See **What You Can Do,** p. 166.

Apply Self-Care

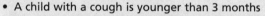

Sinusitis

Sinusitis is an inflammation of the *sinuses*, the four pairs of empty chambers in the facial bones surrounding the nose and eyes. These chambers are located near the cheekbones, above the eyebrows, behind or between the eyes and near the temples. Inflammation can be caused by viral, bacterial or fungal infection, or by allergies.

The condition is usually brought on by an upper respiratory tract infection, hay fever (see *Hay Fever,* p. 191) or a *deviated septum* (a deformity in the structure between the nostrils that divides the inside of the nose into right and left sides). About 25 percent of chronic sinusitis cases that occur in the area near the cheekbones are related to dental infections. (See *Dental Care,* p. 184.)

Note Your Symptoms

- Tenderness and swelling over the area involved
- Pain around the eyes or cheeks
- Difficulty breathing through the nose
- Redness and swelling inside the nose
- Yellow or gray-green nasal discharge
- General feeling of illness and fatigue
- Fever (may or may not be present)

What You Can Do

- Inhale steam to promote nasal drainage. Try sitting in a steamy bathroom or using a cool mist vaporizer.
- Stay indoors and keep rooms at an even temperature.
- Drink plenty of fluids (a glass of water or juice every one to two hours), which may help open the nasal passages and promote sinus drainage.
- Try decongestant nasal sprays, but do not use them for more than three days in a row.
- Apply hot and cold compresses to the forehead and cheeks (alternately, one minute each, for 10 minutes) to aid sinus drainage.
- Increase home humidity.

Anyone with a history of recurring sinusitis should begin self-care treatment at the first sign of a cold, other respiratory tract infection or allergy symptoms.

A doctor may prescribe antibiotics to treat chronic sinusitis or sinusitis caused by a bacterial infection. On rare occasions, surgical repair of the sinuses may be necessary.

Sinusitis
Do these apply:

- You suspect sinusitis and have diabetes or an immune system condition
- You have severe sinusitis symptoms or a fever of 102° F (39° C) or higher after 3 days of illness
- You have tooth pain
- You have had an episode of diagnosed sinusitis within the past year and have new symptoms now
- Symptoms of nasal congestion, sinus pain, headache and/or colored nasal discharge have failed to improve or have worsened after 7 days

no   yes

See **What You Can Do,** pp. 169 - 170.
See **The Common Cold,** p. 163;
    Hay Fever, p. 191.

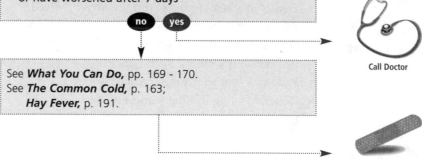

Call Doctor

Apply Self-Care

Nosebleeds

Nosebleeds are usually messier and more embarrassing than they are serious, and can almost always be stopped with self-care. They are usually caused by trauma or by things that irritate nasal tissues, such as dry air, allergies or blowing the nose too forcefully.

Prevention

Frequently, nosebleeds are related to the common cold, when blood vessels in the nose are irritated by a virus or by constant nose blowing. Treating cold symptoms may reduce these nosebleeds.

Nosebleeds tend to occur more often in the winter when people spend more time indoors where the air is dry and heated. Turning the heat down and using a cool-mist vaporizer to put moisture back into the air sometimes brings relief.

Finding the cause of recurrent nosebleeds is, of course, the first step in preventing them.

What You Can Do

When you have a nosebleed:

- Sit in a chair, keeping your head level rather than tilted back. This prevents the blood from running down your throat.
- Blow the nose to remove any remaining blood or clots.
- Squeeze the nostrils shut between your thumb and forefinger.
- Breathe through your mouth and apply pressure for 15 full minutes without letting go of your nose.
- If the bleeding doesn't stop, repeat these measures, but before applying pressure, gently insert a dry gauze pad; do not use facial tissue. An alternate method is to use one or two sprays of nasal decongestant in each nostril before pinching the nose again for 15 minutes.

When the bleeding stops, try to remain quiet for a few hours. Don't blow your nose, laugh or talk loudly.

See **Decision helper,** p. 172.

Nosebleeds

Do these apply:

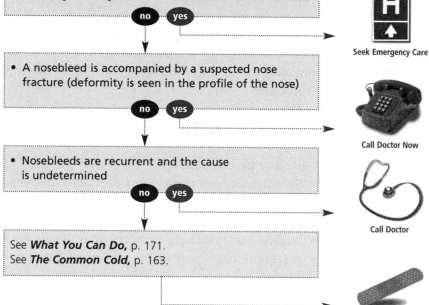

- Symptoms of shock are present: cool, pale clammy skin; weak, rapid pulse; shallow, rapid breathing; confusion, anxiety or restlessness; faintness, weakness, dizziness or loss of consciousness; dilated pupils; nausea, vomiting or thirst
- You have a nosebleed and:
  - You are on an anticoagulant, take aspirin frequently or have a bleeding disorder
  - Blood is flowing heavily down the back of your throat
- Bleeding is heavy and has lasted more than 30 minutes

no   yes

Seek Emergency Care

- A nosebleed is accompanied by a suspected nose fracture (deformity is seen in the profile of the nose)

no   yes

Call Doctor Now

- Nosebleeds are recurrent and the cause is undetermined

no   yes

Call Doctor

See **What You Can Do,** p. 171.
See **The Common Cold,** p. 163.

Apply Self-Care

Middle Ear Infection

Middle ear infections (*otitis media*) usually occur as a complication of an upper respiratory infection or allergy (see index for *Colds, Sinusitis* and *Hay Fever*), when the *eustachian* tubes between the ear and the throat swell and close. As a result, fluid gathers in the middle ear and bacteria breed.

The hallmark symptom of otitis media—persistent ear pain—may be accompanied by decreased hearing, a ringing or sense of fullness in the ear, fever, ear discharge, dizziness and a runny nose.

Otitis media requires a visit to your doctor, who may prescribe an antibiotic or suggest a "watch and wait" period since many ear infections clear up on their own.

Self-care includes:
- Getting plenty of rest
- Increasing your consumption of clear fluids
- Placing a warm washcloth, water bottle or heating pad (set on low) directly on the affected ear (do not leave a child alone with a heating pad)
- Blowing your nose gently, with your mouth open
- Using a cool-mist vaporizer to moisturize the air and help control mucus levels
- Taking acetaminophen (Tylenol), ibuprofen (Advil, Motrin) or aspirin to relieve discomfort. **NEVER give aspirin to children/teenagers unless your healthcare provider orders it. It can cause Reye's syndrome, a rare but often fatal condition.**

NOTE: Do not insert any object in the ear to relieve itching or pain.

See *Decision helper,* p. 176.

Ruptured Eardrum

Pressure building up in the middle ear, blows to the ear, or sharp objects can rupture the eardrum. Symptoms may include mild to severe ear pain, partial temporary hearing loss, and a bloody or white to yellowish discharge from the ear.

See a doctor promptly; antibiotics may be prescribed to prevent or treat an infection in the middle ear.

A one-time rupture is not serious. The eardrum usually heals within two months. However, repeated eardrum ruptures may cause hearing loss.

Pain can be relieved by using over-the-counter (OTC) pain relievers and a heating pad set on low. Hearing almost always returns to normal after the eardrum heals.

See **Decision helper,** p. 176.

Fluid in Middle Ear

Serous otitis media results when fluid collects in the middle ear, either from a previous infection or ongoing irritations such as allergies. An infection is not necessarily associated with this condition but can occur if bacteria build up. Symptoms may include temporary hearing loss and a feeling of stuffiness or sensitivity in the ear.

Most cases of serous otitis media clear up in about a week. Chewing gum and swallowing may help open the *eustachian* tube (connecting the ear and throat), and decongestants or pain relievers may provide additional relief.

If the problem does not clear up with self-care, a doctor may prescribe a higher dose of decongestant or suggest inserting a small tube through the eardrum to drain the middle ear. If a bacterial infection is involved, antibiotics may be prescribed.

See *Decision helper,* p. 176.

Barotitis

"Airplane ears" (or *barotitis*) usually occurs as a result of air pressure changes—driving in the mountains, flying in an airplane—when you have a cold or stuffy nose. This results in a blocked-up feeling in the ears.

- Yawning, swallowing, chewing gum or gently blowing through your nose while holding your nose shut and closing your mouth to "pop" the ears, may solve the problem. Using an oral decongestant or decongestant nasal sprays 30 minutes before an airplane descends can also help.
- An infant with barotitis may bat at the ears or fuss more than usual; offering the baby a bottle or letting him or her nurse may help.
- Contact your doctor for preventive measures if you or your child has a cold or stuffiness and you are planning on flying or driving over a high mountain pass within the next two days.

See *Decision helper,* p. 176.

Middle Ear Infection/ Ruptured Eardrum/Fluid in Middle Ear/Barotitis

Do these apply:

• Ear pain is accompanied by a severe headache, a change in mental status or stiff neck (see *Meningitis,* p. 245)

no   yes

Seek Emergency Care

• The person looks very ill and there is swelling, redness and pain around the ear

no   yes

Call Doctor Now

• Ear infection is suspected
• Ear pain occurs with the following:
  - Fever
  - Bloody or other discharge
  - Decreased hearing
  - Dizziness or vertigo
  - Ringing or a sense of fullness in the ears
• Ear pain lasts longer than 12 hours
• Symptoms of barotitis persist for more than 10 days
• Symptoms increase—or fail to improve—after two or three days of antibiotic treatment
• Stuffy ears or hearing loss persists, without other symptoms, more than 10 days after a cold clears up
• Airplane travel is planned

no   yes

Call Doctor

See *What You Can Do,* pp. 173, 174, 175.
See *Children's Ear Infections,* p. 93.

Apply Self-Care

Ear Wax

The purpose of ear wax is to protect the ear and keep it clean. The wax normally exists in liquid form and drains by itself. Ear wax almost never causes problems unless you try to "clean" your ears using a cotton swab or some other instrument, which can pack the ear wax down tightly. If compacted ear wax builds up, it can block the ear canal, sometimes causing a stuffy feeling and hearing loss.

Ear wax usually doesn't cause pain or a fever. If you experience these symptoms, suspect an ear infection. (See *Middle Ear Infection*, p. 173.)

Prevention

In most cases, taking warm showers or washing the outside of the ears with a washcloth and warm water provides enough vapor to prevent the buildup of wax.

Children normally have more ear wax than adults. The ears should be left alone unless the ear wax is causing problems, like a ringing in the ears or hearing loss.

What You Can Do

Normally, packed-down ear wax can be removed by gently flushing the ear with warm water using a bulb syringe (available at drugstores). Always use water that is as close to body temperature as possible. Using cold water can cause dizziness and vomiting. Wax softeners such as hydrogen peroxide (3 percent), Debrox or Cerumenex, also can be used. Follow instructions carefully for commercial softening products.

Never put anything into the ear if you have an earache, ear discharge or think the eardrum might be ruptured. Do not attempt ear wax removal if you have an ear tube.

See *Decision helper,* p. 179.

Swimmer's Ear

Swimmer's ear (*otitis externa*) is a persistent irritation and inflammation of the outer ear canal that occurs after swimming or following repeated attempts to clean wax from the ear.

Symptoms include tenderness and a feeling of fullness (as though the ear is full of water), itching, burning and pain when the outer ear is tugged. More serious cases involve redness of the ear canal; a crusty, pus-filled discharge; and possibly some hearing loss.

Prevention

The key to removing water from the ears immediately after swimming or showering is to shake the head to remove trapped water. Use the twisted corners of a facial tissue to dry each ear. Tip your head to the left as you dry the left ear, and repeat the process on your right ear.

Swim-team members or others who spend a lot of time in the water can use over-the-counter (OTC) or prescription ear drops to change the acid/alkali level in the ear canal and potentially prevent swimmer's ear.

What You Can Do

- Look in the ear with a light to make sure there isn't an object or insect in the ear.
- Try rinsing the affected ear with a homemade solution (half warm water, half white vinegar). Gently fill the ear using a bulb syringe with the solution.
- Use swimmer's ear drops. Have the affected person lie on his or her side. Drip the fluid (or a few drops of rubbing alcohol mixed with white vinegar) into the ear in small quantities, so air can escape. If air gets trapped, it will keep the solution from penetrating. Wiggle the ear to prevent this problem.
- Use a heating pad set on low and OTC pain relievers to ease discomfort. **NEVER give aspirin to children/teenagers unless your healthcare provider orders it. It can cause Reye's syndrome, a rare but often fatal condition.**
- Try to keep the ear as dry as possible until the infection subsides.

As the old saying goes, don't put anything smaller than your elbow in your ear. Inserting hairpins or other instruments can be dangerous because eardrum damage can result. Cotton swabs generally pack down ear wax instead of getting it out and can push foreign bodies farther into the ear. Learn how to safely remove ear wax. (See *What You Can Do,* p. 177.)

Ear Wax/Swimmer's Ear
Do these apply:

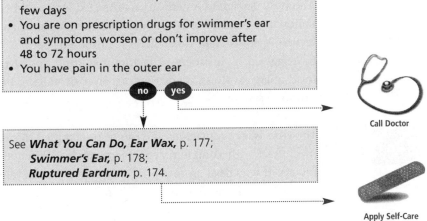

- You suspect a ruptured eardrum
- You have drainage from the ear
- You are not successful at ear wax removal
- Swimmer's ear doesn't respond to self-care within a few days
- You are on prescription drugs for swimmer's ear and symptoms worsen or don't improve after 48 to 72 hours
- You have pain in the outer ear

no   yes

See **What You Can Do, Ear Wax,** p. 177;
     Swimmer's Ear, p. 178;
     Ruptured Eardrum, p. 174.

Call Doctor

Apply Self-Care

Mouth Concerns

Oral Herpes

Oral herpes is a common viral infection characterized by small, fluid-filled sores on the skin and mucous membranes of the mouth. This herpes simplex type 1 virus is not the same as—but is related to—herpes simplex type 2, which causes *genital herpes*.

About 90 percent of Americans are infected with oral herpes by the age of 5. Following the initial infection, the virus remains dormant with new episodes recurring at different frequencies for different people. New outbreaks can be triggered by a variety of factors including dental treatment, sunburn, food allergies, stress, menstruation, fever-producing illness or a damaged immune system.

Prevention

The virus is very contagious and can be transmitted through personal contact or contact with contaminated objects such as kitchen utensils, razors or towels. If you have an active infection, avoid close physical contact with others and do not share personal items.

What You Can Do

- Salves can relieve pain, but are not effective in all cases. Try various methods, such as over-the-counter (OTC) oral and topical *analgesics* (pain relievers). Use what works best for you.
- Acyclovir (Zovirax) and other antiviral agents can be applied to the skin to speed healing if they are applied during the initial outbreak. Oral acyclovir is sometimes prescribed for frequent or severe outbreaks.

Attacks of oral herpes usually go away, with or without treatment, within seven to 10 days and have no lasting complications.

See **Decision helper,** p. 183.

Canker Sores

A canker sore is a painful ulcer that develops on the gums, tongue or inside the mouth. The cause is unknown but any of the following increase the likelihood of getting one: viruses, allergies, gastrointestinal problems, immune reactions, deficiencies of iron, B12 or folic acid, trauma to the inside of the mouth, and stress.

There's no known way to prevent canker sores, but nonprescription topical anesthetic gels or rinses will lessen the pain. A dental protective paste, such as Orabase, prevents irritation of the sores. Acetaminophen (Tylenol) and nonsteroidal anti-inflammatory drugs may help, too.

See *Decision helper,* p. 183.

Coxsackie Virus

Coxsackie virus, or hand-foot-mouth disease, can also cause mouth sores in children. The virus, which usually includes spots on the hands and feet, goes away by itself. The symptoms are mild and the child generally feels well.

See *Decision helper,* p. 183.

Thrush

Thrush, or *oral candidiasis,* is a fungal yeast infection that causes painful, creamy-white sore patches in the mouth or throat. Eating or brushing your teeth can scrape off the patches, making the sores bleed.

Thrush is common in infants and children and often disappears eventually without treatment. In infants, obvious discomfort while feeding or an unwillingness to eat may indicate thrush.

Some people develop thrush when they are on antibiotics. Conditions such as diabetes, AIDS or immunosuppressive therapy can make people more susceptible to the infection as well.

What You Can Do

Although thrush often disappears on its own, an antifungal medication usually speeds healing. Various antifungal medications may be recommended by your doctor. With treatment, symptoms usually disappear within seven to 10 days.

A diet of soft foods may lessen discomfort until the symptoms are gone.

The goals for treatment of mouth sores are to relieve pain and maintain an adequate fluid intake—mouth sores can often interfere with eating or drinking. A child can go several days without taking a full meal, but it is very important to give a child enough liquid. Try offering drinks that soothe a tender mouth, such as cold liquids, Popsicles or frozen juices.

Decision *helper*

Mouth Sores
Do these apply:

- Fever and mouth sores appear after starting any medication

Call Doctor Now

- An undiagnosed mouth sore persists for two weeks
- You suspect that medication may be causing mouth sores
- You are pregnant and have mouth sores
- Painful ulcers occur on the gums, tongue or inside the mouth, especially with large or multiple lesions (suggestive of canker sores)
- You have frequent or severe cold sores
- Creamy-white sore patches appear inside the mouth, on the tongue or in the throat (suggestive of thrush)
- You are being treated for thrush and your symptoms persist for more than 10 days

Call Doctor

See *What You Can Do, Oral Herpes,* p. 180;
    What You Can Do, Canker Sores, p. 181;
    What You Can Do, Thrush, p. 182.
See *Coxsackie Virus,* p. 181.

Apply Self-Care

Dental Care

Prevention. That's the key word in dental care—taking care of your teeth now to avoid future problems. Since teeth are living organisms, they are subject to damage from the foods we eat, especially those containing sugar. Bacteria that are not removed from the teeth by brushing or flossing become a sticky, colorless film called *plaque*. Food particles, especially sugar, stick to plaque and produce acid. This acid damages tooth enamel. When this damage, or decay, spreads down the root canal to the nerve, it causes pain and inflammation. In other words: a toothache.

Another problem caused by an accumulation of plaque is gum disease, or *gingivitis*. It is an inflammation of the gums that can cause redness, discomfort, swelling, watery discharge and bleeding when you brush or chew. Gingivitis also distorts the gums, with the crevice between the gums and teeth deepening and forming pockets. In severe cases, this can result in tooth loss.

Most dental problems can be prevented by good self-care and regular visits to the dentist. With proper care and injury prevention, we can expect to keep our teeth for life, unlike previous generations. The following methods help keep teeth and gums healthy.

Regular Checkups

Have teeth professionally cleaned every six to 12 months, beginning at about age 3. Regular dental checkups can provide early detection of gingivitis, cavities and other problems, making treatment easier. The American Academy of Pediatrics recommends the first visit to a dentist by 12 months of age.

Brushing

Brush your teeth thoroughly twice a day, especially after eating (if possible). The goal is to remove plaque from all surfaces of the teeth. Children over 3 years of age and adults should use a soft-bristle toothbrush with rounded tips, and replace it every three to four months. Use a small amount (pea size) of fluoride toothpaste.

Infant gum care should start before teeth erupt. Wipe the gums with a soft, clean cloth after feeding and before bedtime. After teeth appear, use a soft, small child's toothbrush. Do not use toothpaste until a child can rinse and spit.

Electric toothbrushes or water piks may help some people clean hard-to-reach areas. Check with your dentist regarding what's best for you.

The formation of *tartar*, mineral deposits that get trapped on the teeth by plaque, can be slowed by tartar-control toothpastes.

Be sure to brush the tongue as well as the teeth. Plaque on the tongue can cause bad breath. Also, since you can actually harm your gums by brushing too hard or in the wrong direction, consult your dentist on the best brushing procedures.

Flossing

Daily flossing is the best way to prevent gum disease between teeth. The purpose is to scrape off the plaque that forms between the teeth and just under the gum line.

The various types of dental floss (waxed, unwaxed, extra fine, flossing tape and flossing ribbons) each have advantages. Select the type that works best on your teeth.

The most important aspect of flossing is to curve the floss around the tooth being cleaned and slide it under the gum line. With both fingers holding the floss against the tooth, move the floss up and down several times to scrape off the plaque.

Flossing should be started with children as soon as they have teeth that touch each other. A child usually can't floss until about age 8. Using a flossing tool can be helpful in doing a good job in a small mouth.

Fluoride

Fluoride is a mineral found in most food and water supplies that strengthens tooth enamel and lowers the risk of tooth decay. In many areas of the country, fluoride is added to the water because the natural levels of fluoride are too low to protect teeth.

Infants and children in low-fluoride areas can be given fluoride supplements in the form of tablets or drops. Fluoride toothpastes, rinses or topical applications also are beneficial.

Sealants

A sealant is a plastic coating usually applied to a child's back teeth. It protects the *molars* from developing decay. By using sealants and fluoride, it is possible for children to grow up without cavities.

What You Can Do

If you have a toothache, taking aspirin, ibuprofen (Advil, Motrin) or acetaminophen (Tylenol) may lessen the pain while a dental appointment is being made. **NEVER give aspirin to children/teenagers unless your healthcare provider orders it. It can cause Reye's syndrome, a rare but often fatal condition**.

Final Notes

Do not put infants or young children to bed with a bottle. Liquids pool around teeth and can cause serious tooth decay called *bottle mouth*.

See *Decision helper,* p. 188.
See *Accidental Tooth Loss,* p. 59.

Temporomandibular Joint Syndrome (TMJ)

This is a condition in which jaw movement is abnormal. The *temporomandibular joint* attaches the jaw to the skull. Abnormalities and inflammation of this joint can produce pain, difficulty in opening and closing your mouth, clicking or grinding sounds while chewing, ringing in the ears and, occasionally, hearing loss.

Causes of TMJ include failure of the jaw to close properly, poorly fitting dentures, arthritis, trauma from fractures or dislocations of the jaw, stress-induced muscle tension and repetitive tooth grinding.

Note Your Symptoms

Depending on the underlying cause, symptoms can vary with each individual. Common symptoms include:
- Pain over the TMJ area (on either side of the face, in front of the ears)
- Dull ear pain without fever
- Dull headaches
- Grinding, clicking or popping sounds
- Ringing in the ears
- Limited mouth opening

Some sufferers of TMJ may suddenly dislocate their jaw, causing pain and making it impossible to close the mouth after yawning or while chewing.

Other causes of jaw pain include *angina pectoris* (pain from coronary artery disease) and sinus and ear infections. (See index for these topics.)

What You Can Do

- Try over-the-counter (OTC) anti-inflammatory medications to relieve pain. (See *Home Pharmacy*, p. 326.)
- Rest the jaw, keeping the teeth apart and the lips closed.
- Avoid foods that are hard to chew.
- Avoid chewing gum, tooth grinding and other activities that cause repetitive movements of the jaw.

- For most TMJ, use heat or ice (depending on what feels better) to relieve pain. Ice can be applied to the joint for 15 to 20 minutes at a time, with 20 minutes between applications. (For protection, place a washcloth between bare skin and ice.) Moist heat can be applied to the jaw for 20 minutes at a time, three times a day.
- If TMJ is the result of injury, follow the RICE and MSA pain relief guidelines on pages 67 and 68.
- When the pain has stopped, open and close the mouth gently and repeatedly to improve jaw strength and flexibility.

Decision *helper*

Dental Care/TMJ
Do these apply:

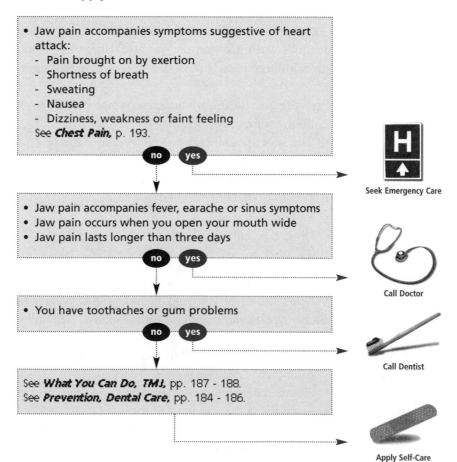

- Jaw pain accompanies symptoms suggestive of heart attack:
  - Pain brought on by exertion
  - Shortness of breath
  - Sweating
  - Nausea
  - Dizziness, weakness or faint feeling
  See *Chest Pain*, p. 193.

no   yes

H ↑

Seek Emergency Care

- Jaw pain accompanies fever, earache or sinus symptoms
- Jaw pain occurs when you open your mouth wide
- Jaw pain lasts longer than three days

no   yes

Call Doctor

- You have toothaches or gum problems

no   yes

Call Dentist

See *What You Can Do, TMJ*, pp. 187 - 188.
See *Prevention, Dental Care*, pp. 184 - 186.

Apply Self-Care

Allergies

Food Allergies

Food allergies may cause adverse physical reactions after certain foods are eaten. If you suffer from other allergies, such as hay fever, you are more likely to be affected. (See *Hay Fever*, p. 191.) Nearly any food can trigger an allergic reaction, but the most common culprits are seafood, eggs, peanuts and other nuts, and cow's milk.

Note Your Symptoms

Food allergies can prompt a wide range of reactions, in some cases life-threatening. Symptoms appear soon after eating and may include:

- Hives and eczema (especially in children)
- Runny nose, sneezing
- Vomiting and stomach cramps or diarrhea
- Wheezing (see *Asthma*, p. 206)
- Itching, tingling or swelling in the mouth, nose, ears or throat
- Extreme breathing difficulty, constriction of the chest, swelling of the mouth, lips, tongue or throat, erratic pulse, severe hives and itching, or violent coughing. This is very likely a severe anaphylactic reaction and can quickly lead to death. Seek emergency care.

What You Can Do

If You Know What Foods Produce Reactions

- Avoid foods that produce allergic symptoms. Make sure friends and relatives know of your allergies so you are not exposed to these foods without knowing it when dining.
- Ask about the ingredients in foods when you eat out.
- Be aware that foods can contain unexpected ingredients.
- If you are at risk for anaphylactic reactions, carry an anaphylactic kit to use if necessary. Your doctor can provide you with a prescription.
- Wear a medical-alert bracelet to inform others of your allergy.

If You Don't Know What Causes Your Reactions

- Keep a food diary and list symptoms you experience after eating.
- Try eliminating foods from your diet one at a time, and note any reactions.
- Introduce new foods to young children one at a time.

Final Notes   Food allergy reactions generally become more acute each time the food is eaten, making it even more important to identify foods that cause severe reactions.

Food Allergies
Do these apply:

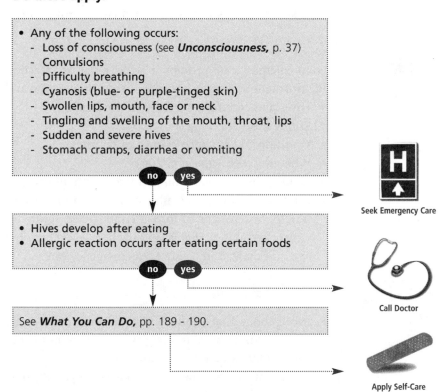

- Any of the following occurs:
  - Loss of consciousness (see *Unconsciousness,* p. 37)
  - Convulsions
  - Difficulty breathing
  - Cyanosis (blue- or purple-tinged skin)
  - Swollen lips, mouth, face or neck
  - Tingling and swelling of the mouth, throat, lips
  - Sudden and severe hives
  - Stomach cramps, diarrhea or vomiting

no   yes

Seek Emergency Care

- Hives develop after eating
- Allergic reaction occurs after eating certain foods

no   yes

Call Doctor

See *What You Can Do,* pp. 189 - 190.

Apply Self-Care

Hay Fever

Hay fever sufferers can blame pollen for the sneezing, watery, itchy eyes and runny nose that mark this common allergy. Some form of pollen is almost always in the air, whether from trees in the spring, summer grass or fall ragweed. The severity of your symptoms can depend on the time of year and the airborne pollen present on a particular day.

Note Your Symptoms

Hay fever (*allergic rhinitis*) occurs when antibodies in your system react to pollen and prompt the release of chemicals called *histamines*. Histamines inflame the lining of nasal passages and eyes and cause sneezing, itching, runny nose and watery eyes. Wheezing, headaches, hives and a cough are possible, too.

Hay fever can be confused with the common cold, but you can suspect you have allergies if your symptoms last for long periods and return during the same season each year. If hay fever runs in your family, chances are your sneezes are based on allergies, too. If necessary, your doctor can test your nasal secretions to confirm whether you have hay fever. Allergy testing can identify which pollens cause the most problems for you.

What You Can Do

- Stay indoors on dry, windy days or when pollen counts are high. Pollen counts are often reported daily in the media. Exercise indoors at a gym or walk in a mall.
- Rid your home of pollen traps, such as carpeting or dirty air filters.
- Try over-the-counter (OTC) antihistamines to relieve mild symptoms. If your antihistamines make you drowsy, never use them when driving or using heavy machinery. Nasal decongestant sprays will help dry up your runny nose, but overuse can cause the symptoms to worsen so you should never use them for more than three days in a row. (See *Home Pharmacy*, p. 325.)

Final Notes

Hay fever can develop at any age. While irritating, hay fever symptoms will go away when the offending pollen disappears at the end of the season.

Decision
helper

Hay Fever

Do these apply:

- Symptoms interfere with your daily routine
- Symptoms are not relieved with over-the-counter (OTC) medications
- You have hay fever and develop symptoms of sinusitis
- You have hay fever and develop symptoms of an ear infection

no   yes

Call Doctor

See **What You Can Do,** p. 191.
See **The Common Cold,** p. 163;
    Sinusitis, p. 169;
    Middle Ear Infection, p. 173;
    Home Pharmacy, p. 325.

Apply Self-Care

Chest/Respiratory

Chest Pain

Chest pain is often associated with the heart and can be a frightening symptom. Although this discomfort may be a warning from your heart and must be handled correctly, there are many other causes of chest pain that are less serious and easier to treat. Knowing the different types of chest pain can help you make safer decisions and get faster relief. **All chest pain should be taken seriously.**

Heart Pain

Sharp pain from the heart may be caused by an infection in the outer lining (*pericarditis*), or inner lining and its valves (*endocarditis*). This often follows an infection in another part of the body. Palpitations can cause sudden, brief jabs of pain, usually in the left side of the chest. (See *Palpitations*, p. 197.)

Angina pectoris is a warning that the heart muscle is not getting enough oxygen. Anginal pain is a tightness, squeezing, heaviness or feeling of pressure over the front of the chest. It may also be felt in the throat, neck, jaws, upper back, shoulders or both arms. It usually comes on with exertion, stress or overeating and lasts less than 15 minutes. It is relieved by rest or medication. **Any angina means that the heart is in trouble; the pain does not have to be severe to be serious.**

Heart Attack

Chest pain that is crushing, squeezing or increasing in pressure may be a warning of heart attack, known as *myocardial infarction*. The pain is like angina, and may not be severe, but continues for more than 15 minutes and is not eased with rest. It is often accompanied by nausea, sweating, dizziness, shortness of breath, rapid or irregular pulse and a feeling of doom or danger. The symptoms are caused by a blocked coronary artery, which stops blood flow to part of the heart muscle.

Chest Wall Pain

The chest wall includes skin, muscles, ligaments, ribs and rib cartilage. Pain can be caused by infection, inflammation, bruises, strains, sprains and broken ribs. Chest wall pain is usually sharp, burning or itching and is limited to a small area. It often comes and goes for days; touching, bending, stretching, coughing or taking a deep breath may prompt or increase pain.

Other Non-Heart Pain

Anxiety is a common cause of chest pain. It may be a sharp jab or dull pressure and is often located in the left chest area. Pain from *hyperventilation* (excessive rapid breathing) often causes or comes with anxiety. (See *Hyperventilation Syndrome,* p. 316.)

Chest pain can be from the lungs, *pleura* (the thin membranes that cover the lungs), esophagus, diaphragm or several of the organs in the upper abdomen. Pain from the lungs and pleura is similar to chest wall pain and frequently follows a cold or flu-like illness. Lung problems like pneumonia, blood clots and asthma may produce chest pain.

If the discomfort is caused by the esophagus or the stomach, there may be an acid taste in the mouth and a burning feeling in the chest that improves with eating.

Prevention

There are many causes of chest pain, and prevention is not possible for all of them. However, good health habits decrease your risk of illness and improve your chances of quick, full recovery.

- Maintain a normal body weight. (See *Eating Right,* p. 331.)
- Follow a low saturated-fat, well-balanced diet. (See *Eating Right,* p. 331.)
- Exercise regularly. (See *Staying Active,* p. 330.)
- If you smoke, start taking steps to kick the habit. (See *Quit Smoking,* p. 334.)
- Have regular checkups to help detect any health problems early. (See *Screening Guidelines,* p. 337.)
- Learn about any chronic illnesses you have and follow your doctor's advice. (See *Becoming Partners With Your Doctor,* p. 343.)
- Learn about stress and stress management. (See *Stress,* p. 314.)

What You Can Do

- Learn CPR (see *CPR*, p. 18) and know what to do for emergencies. (See *Emergencies Introduction*, p. 16.)
- Try to identify what may be causing your pain and avoid that activity or food.
- If chest wall pain is from an injury, treat with the **RICE** process (see *Strains and Sprains*, p. 67) and take aspirin or ibuprofen (Advil, Motrin) for pain and inflammation. **NEVER give aspirin to children/teenagers unless your healthcare provider orders it. It can cause Reye's syndrome, a rare but often fatal condition**.
- If pain is from stress or hyperventilation, follow stress-reduction methods. (See *Stress*, p. 314.)
- Pain from stomach or esophagus may be relieved by:
  - Eating smaller meals and eating slowly
  - Not smoking
  - Avoiding foods and drugs that seem to trigger pain
  - Raising the head of your bed on 4- to 6-inch (10 to 15 cm) blocks and not eating for at least three hours before bedtime
  - Taking antacids (follow directions on the package)

See *Decision helper,* p. 196.
See *Abdominal/Gastrointestinal,* p. 214.

Decision *helper*

Chest Pain
Do these apply:

- There is crushing, squeezing or increasing pressure in the chest
- Chest, jaw, neck, shoulder, mid-to-upper back or arm discomfort occurs with:
  - Shortness of breath
  - Confusion, dizziness, weakness or a faint feeling
  - Sweating
  - Nausea or vomiting
  - Rapid or irregular pulse
- Chronic heart disease exists and chest pain is not relieved with nitroglycerin medication or is different from the usual pain
- Sudden chest pain occurs with coughing up blood or a feeling of suffocation

Rest quietly with your head elevated on pillows; keep warm. Wait for emergency transport or advice from the emergency system. Chew an aspirin while you wait (adults).

Seek Emergency Care

 (FIRST AID)
Apply Emergency First Aid

- Chest wall pain occurs after trauma or with weakness or dizziness
- You have chronic heart disease and chest pain is more frequent, more intense or present during times of rest

Call Doctor Now

- Chest wall pain occurs with a fever or blistery rash
- There is chest pain and cough with yellow, gray-green or rust-colored sputum (phlegm)
- There is no diagnosis of angina and you have episodes of chest pain with exertion, heavy eating or stress that subside within 15 minutes
- Your symptoms worsen or have not improved after 48 hours of self-care

Call Doctor

See **What You Can Do,** p. 195.

Apply Self-Care

Palpitations

Everyone feels a skip, flutter, flip-flop, thump or pounding in the chest at times. These feelings are *palpitations* and are caused by a change in your normal heart rhythm; they can involve very strong, rapid or irregular beats.

Causes of palpitations include *hyperventilation* (rapid breathing), anxiety, fever, excess thyroid, stimulants such as caffeine and nicotine, alcohol and many drugs and medicines. Palpitations, or *arrhythmias*, can occur in some types of heart disease. In most cases, palpitations are brief, harmless and go away without treatment.

- Exercise regularly. (See *Staying Active*, p. 330.)
- If you smoke, start taking steps to kick the habit. (See *Quit Smoking*, p. 334.)
- Limit the amount of alcohol (see *Alcohol And Drugs*, p. 334) and caffeine you drink.
- Read warnings on packages and labels of all the drugs you take.
- Do what you can to control your stress. (See *Stress*, p. 314.)
- Have regular checkups to help detect and treat health problems early. (See *Screening Guidelines*, p. 337.)

- Look for the cause of your palpitations. Do they come after consuming certain foods or beverages? At a specific time of day? During or following a certain activity? Eliminate the possible cause and see if it takes care of the problem.
- Ask your doctor or pharmacist about possible medication side effects.
- Follow the prevention guidelines listed above.
- Relax and remember that most palpitations are harmless.

See **Decision helper,** p. 198.

Palpitations

Do these apply:

- You have palpitations and:
  - Shortness of breath
  - Crushing, squeezing or increasing pressure in the chest or pain in jaw, neck, shoulders, mid-to-upper back or arms
  - Fainting
  - Confusion
- Your heart rate is too fast to count

While waiting, rest quietly with your head elevated on pillows unless you feel faint. If you do, lie flat with your feet elevated higher than your heart.

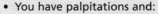

Seek Emergency Care

Apply Emergency First Aid

- You have palpitations and:
  - Fatigue
  - Weakness or a faint feeling
  - Light-headedness or dizziness
  - Temporary blindspots
- New swelling (edema) of the legs or arms

Call Doctor Now

- Palpitations are increasing in severity or lasting longer
- You take medications for palpitations and experience:
  - New or recurring symptoms
  - More severe symptoms
  - Unpleasant side effects
- There are frequent skipped heartbeats, feelings of fluttering, flip flops, thumping or pounding in your chest

Call Doctor

See *What You Can Do,* p. 197.

Apply Self-Care

Hypertension

Hypertension, or high blood pressure, is known as "the silent killer." Although it is very common and can lead to serious health problems—such as heart attack, heart failure and stroke—it often goes undetected. The best way to detect hypertension is to have your blood pressure checked regularly.

Your blood pressure normally goes up and down, depending on your activities and emotions. A normal blood pressure reading can vary, but for an adult, it is lower than 120/80. The first number refers to *systolic* pressure, when the heart contracts; the second to *diastolic* pressure, when the heart rests between beats.

Hypertension is usually defined as consistent readings of 140 systolic, or 90 diastolic, or higher. Most hypertension is called "primary," which means that the exact cause is unknown. However, it may also be caused by other conditions—such as diabetes, coronary artery disease, kidney disease, smoking, or side effects from certain medications.

What You Can Do

Detecting Hypertension

- Have your blood pressure checked regularly—at least every two years for adults, and preferably more often.
- If you are at higher risk of developing hypertension or heart disease because of high cholesterol, obesity, diabetes or family history, have your blood pressure checked at least once a year. *(Screening clinics and pharmacies can provide easy access to blood pressure information.)*

Lifestyle Changes

Studies indicate that many people with slightly elevated blood pressure can bring about significant reductions in hypertension through lifestyle changes:
- Get regular exercise. (See *Staying Active*, p. 330.) Regular, consistent physical activity can have a significant effect on lowering blood pressure—as much as some medications! Check with your doctor before beginning an exercise program.

- Lose weight if you are overweight and maintain a healthy weight.
- Restrict dietary sodium intake to no more than 2,400 mg (about one teaspoon of salt) per day and reduce dietary fats, especially saturated fats. (See *Eating Right*, p. 331.)
- Eliminate or restrict alcohol consumption. (See *Alcohol And Drugs*, p. 334.)
- If you smoke, start taking steps to kick the habit. (See *Quit Smoking*, p. 334.)
- The National Heart, Lung and Blood Institute (NHLBI) recommends the Dietary Approaches to Stop Hypertension or "DASH" diet:
  - Eat 7 to 8 servings of grains and grain products (whole wheat bread and pastas, brown rice, etc.) each day.
  - Eat 8 to 10 servings of fruits and vegetables per day. One serving is equal to 1 medium apple, $1/2$ cup (115 mL) of fruit, $3/4$ cup (173 mL) of juice, 1 cup (230 mL) of leafy vegetables or $1/2$ cup (115 mL) of other vegetables.
  - Eat 4 to 5 servings a week of nuts, seeds and dried beans.
  - Get adequate potassium each day (3.5 mg). Good sources are orange juice, bananas, potatoes and winter squash.
  - Get 2 to 3 servings of low-fat or nonfat dairy products daily. One serving is 1 cup (230 mL) of milk or yogurt, 1 to $1 1/2$ ounces (30 to 45 grams) of low-fat cheese, or 2 ounces (60 grams) of processed cheese.
  - Eat two servings or fewer of lean meats, poultry or fish each day.
  - Get 2 to 3 servings of fats each day. Concentrate on polyunsaturated fats, olive oil, olives, avocados and peanuts.

Medications

If you are diagnosed with high blood pressure, your doctor may use the "stepped approach" to treatment, beginning with *diuretics* (medications known as water pills that increase fluid loss) and adding drugs that act directly on the blood vessels, heart and blood chemistry.

The goal of medical treatment is to control hypertension while creating as few side effects as possible.

Final Notes

It's crucial that you comply with the treatment program your doctor prescribes if you are diagnosed with hypertension. If you have problems with any part of the program, discuss them with your doctor. Your doctor will decide how often to have follow-up visits, based on the severity of your hypertension, treatment response and other factors.

Hypertension

Do these apply:

- Your blood pressure reading is over 210 systolic or 120 diastolic along with any of the following:
  - Headache
  - Drowsiness or confusion
  - Visual changes
  - Nausea
  - Profound sweating
  - Shortness of breath
  - Chest pain
  - Weakness or numbness of any area of the body

Seek Emergency Care

- Your blood pressure reading is over 210 systolic or 120 diastolic with no other symptoms

Call Doctor Now

- Your blood pressure reading is over 180 systolic or 110 diastolic
- Drug side effects or unpleasant changes occur while taking medication
- You stop taking or forget to take your antihypertensive medication
- Your blood pressure continues to be elevated in spite of taking your antihypertensive medicine
- You consistently have blood pressure readings of 120 systolic or 80 diastolic or higher

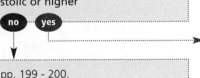

Call Doctor

See **What You Can Do,** pp. 199 - 200.

Apply Self-Care

Bronchitis

Bronchitis is usually characterized by a cough accompanied by soreness and tightness in the chest. The cough is often dry at first, but becomes productive after a few days. The presence of yellow, gray-green or rust-colored sputum (phlegm) may indicate a serious bacterial infection.

Acute bronchitis is an inflammation of the airways that results from irritation or infection. It frequently follows a bout with the flu or a cold and may last up to two weeks.

Chronic bronchitis is a more serious condition that involves a permanent thickening of the passageways to the lungs. In both types, the cells lining the inside of the breathing passages that normally sweep away mucus and debris stop working. The cough response is the body's way of ridding itself of these irritants. (See *Emphysema, Wheezing,* p. 206.)

What You Can Do

- If you smoke, start taking steps to kick the habit. (See *Quit Smoking,* p. 334.)
- Avoid exposure to second-hand smoke and lung irritants.
- Drink plenty of liquids—about six to eight glasses per day.
- Use a cool-mist vaporizer to help keep your lungs clear.
- Avoid respiratory irritants. If you must work around them, use a respirator or other protective gear.
- Get plenty of rest to enable your lungs to heal.
- Unless your doctor instructs otherwise, avoid around-the-clock usage of cough suppressants containing dextromethorphan (DM) or codeine. Coughing can actually help eliminate secretions from your airways. Old-fashioned home remedies (tea with honey) may be soothing. (Do NOT give honey to children under 1 year of age).
- An over-the-counter (OTC) expectorant containing guaifenesin may help liquify secretions so they are easier to cough up.
- Don't use medicines containing antihistamines if you will be driving or operating machinery, since these preparations can make you drowsy.

Decision *helper*

Bronchitis
Do these apply:

- You have signs of significant respiratory distress, such as a feeling of suffocation, gasping or straining to get a breath
- Bluish color to the lips or skin

no   yes

Seek Emergency Care

- You have difficulty breathing, such as shortness of breath or rapid respirations
- You have bronchitis symptoms and a history of chronic heart or lung disease

no   yes

Call Doctor Now

- Your symptoms worsen or don't improve and:
  - Your cough often awakens you
  - Your chest is sore from coughing
  - You have a cough with a fever that doesn't improve after four or five days
- Your *sputum* (phlegm) is yellow, gray-green or rust-colored
- Your cough is accompanied by wheezing
- Your cough lingers for 7 to 10 days after other symptoms have cleared
- You have a relapse or second rise of fever
- Chest pain is associated with breathing or coughing

no   yes

Call Doctor

See *What You Can Do,* p. 202.

Apply Self-Care

See *Home Pharmacy,* p. 325.

Influenza

Influenza, also known as *flu*, is a highly contagious respiratory infection caused by viruses. Symptoms are similar to those of a common cold, but more severe and include sudden onset of fever above 101° F (38.3° C), chills, headache, sore throat, cough, stuffy nose, watery eyes, exhaustion and muscular aches. Children can experience nausea, vomiting and diarrhea along with these symptoms, but they are not typical.

Influenza often occurs in epidemics during the "flu season," which generally lasts from late fall to early spring. Flu is spread by inhaling virus-laden droplets when an infected person sneezes, coughs or even talks.

Prevention

Getting vaccinated against the flu reduces the incidence of infection and is recommended for anyone over the age of 6 months. For adults over age 50, people with chronic diseases or impaired immune systems, and women in the last three months of pregnancy, vaccination is especially important. Call your doctor early in the fall to discuss preventive treatment. Also, wash your hands frequently.

What You Can Do

- Take aspirin, acetaminophen (Tylenol) or ibuprofen (Advil, Motrin) to relieve aches and pains. **NEVER give aspirin to children/teenagers unless your healthcare provider orders it. It can cause Reye's syndrome, a rare but often fatal condition.**
- Drink plenty of clear liquids—water, juice, ginger ale—to restore fluids.
- Drink salty liquids like chicken soup and bouillon to help combat dizziness.
- Gargle with warm salt water (one-fourth teaspoon [600 mg] of salt added to eight ounces [230 mL] of water), drink tea with honey or lemon, or use lozenges to soothe sore throat pain. (Do NOT give honey to children under 1 year of age.)
- Get plenty of rest.
- Try decongestants to help relieve runny nose and watery eyes.

Final Notes

Antiviral medications are available to either prevent influenza or shorten its course, but must be given soon after exposure or as soon as symptoms develop.

Decision *helper*

Influenza
Do these apply:

- You have signs of significant respiratory distress, such as a feeling of suffocation, gasping or straining to get a breath
- There is a bluish color to the lips or skin

no   yes

Seek Emergency Care

- You have difficulty breathing, such as shortness of breath or rapid respirations
- You are at high risk for complications and develop a productive cough with yellow, gray-green or rust-colored sputum; chest pain; shaking, chills or high fever; or you look very ill.

no   yes

Call Doctor Now

- You have been exposed to influenza or have just started to have symptoms (*call to discuss use of a prescription anti-influenza medication*)
- You develop any of the following symptoms of pneumonia:
  - A relapse or second rise of fever
  - Chest pain associated with breathing or coughing
  - Coughing of yellow, gray-green or rust-colored sputum (phlegm)
- You suspect influenza and may be at risk for complications
- Symptoms persist or worsen for more than 7 days

no   yes

Call Doctor

See **What You Can Do,** p. 204.
See **Coughs,** p. 166; **Pneumonia,** p. 212.

Apply Self-Care

Wheezing

The respiratory system resembles an upside-down tree with the "trunk" at the throat and the "limbs" (*bronchi*), smaller "branches" (*bronchioles*), and "leaves" (*alveoli* or air sacs) in the lungs. Wheezing is a high-pitched whistle caused by the obstruction of air as it moves through the bronchi and bronchioles. The restriction may be due to narrowing of the airway walls or a blockage in the passage. It can be localized in a small area or spread throughout the lungs.

Wheezing is heard in lung infections such as pneumonia or bronchitis, or when a foreign body or mucus blocks an airway. It is the most prominent symptom of asthma (see *Asthma*, p. 209) and is also common in allergic reactions and chronic obstructive pulmonary disease (COPD). Wheezing needs professional evaluation when it first occurs.

Chronic Obstructive Pulmonary Disease (COPD)

Emphysema and chronic bronchitis are diseases that cause permanent lung damage. They share symptoms such as cough, *sputum* (phlegm) production, shortness of breath, limited airflow and poor oxygen exchange in the lungs.

Emphysema involves damage to the air sacs, which become brittle and enlarged, decreasing their ability to exchange oxygen and carbon dioxide. Chronic bronchitis is an inflammation of the lower breathing passages (*bronchi*). These diseases commonly occur together and are almost always the result of smoking.

Unfortunately, there is no cure for COPD. The goal of treatment is to enhance breathing capacity and ease the struggle to breathe.

Allergic Reaction

Allergic reactions occur when the body's immune system reacts and goes on the defensive against an element that, under most circumstances, is harmless. Allergens trigger your body's antibodies to counterattack and release chemicals, called *histamines*, directly into various body tissues. Your symptoms are the result of tissues reacting to these chemicals. Allergic wheezing is common in people who have asthma.

Wheezing can be created by spasms in bronchial and bronchiolar walls, swelling in the wall lining and production of excess mucus. *This can be a serious allergic reaction which can quickly become life-threatening.*

- If you smoke, start taking steps to kick the habit. (See *Quit Smoking*, p. 334.)
- Avoid respiratory irritants such as secondary smoke or exposure to fumes.
- Avoid anything that has triggered an allergic attack in the past. (See *Allergies*, p. 189.)
- Wear or carry medical-alert identification related to your allergies and any chronic disease.
- Inform all doctors, dentists and pharmacists about your allergies.
- Ask your doctor about pneumonia and flu vaccinations.
- Exercise regularly. (See *Staying Active*, p. 330.) Swimming and water aerobics are especially good for building up your respiratory strength.
- Learn stress-management techniques if stress is a factor in your wheezing. (See *Stress*, p. 314.)
- Maintain a normal weight to prevent additional stress on your respiratory system.
- Contact your doctor for information about further prevention and treatment of your specific wheezing problems.

- Drink at least two quarts (1.9 L) of water daily to thin bronchial mucus.
- Maintain a humid environment with a cool-mist vaporizer.
- Learn and use relaxation techniques. (See *Stress*, p. 314.) Anxiety and panic increase breathing distress and waste energy.
- If you have asthma, make sure you have, and follow, an asthma treatment plan, including which medications to take and when, how often to use your peak flow meter, and when to contact your doctor or go to the emergency room if symptoms worsen.

See **Decision helper,** p. 208.

Wheezing
Do these apply:

- You have symptoms of significant respiratory distress, such as a feeling of suffocation, gasping or straining to get a breath
- There is a bluish color to the lips or skin
- You have signs of a severe allergic reaction with the sudden onset of any of the following:
  - Loss of consciousness, confusion or agitation
  - Tightness in the chest, wheezing, hives or itching
  - Swelling of the lips, tongue, mouth or throat

Seek Emergency Care

- You have difficulty breathing, such as shortness of breath or rapid respirations
- An acute episode of wheezing occurs for the first time
- Wheezing is more severe or not responding to the usual treatment
- Wheezing is accompanied by a chronic health problem such as heart disease
- Wheezing begins soon after a dose of new medication (discontinue use until you contact a doctor)
- Chest pain is associated with breathing or coughing
- Sputum is yellow, gray-green or rust-colored

Call Doctor Now

- Wheezing requires additional medication and treatment to control or prevent
- You need more information and education to understand and control wheezing

Call Doctor

See **What You Can Do,** p. 207.
See **Hives,** p. 126; **Asthma,** p. 209; **Hay Fever,** p. 191; **Chest Wall Pain,** p. 194; **Bronchitis,** p. 202; **Pneumonia,** p. 212.

Apply Self-Care

Asthma

Asthma is a chronic lung disease that inflames, swells and constricts lung airways and causes coughing, wheezing, chest pain and an increased production of mucus. Frequently, an asthma attack involves a feeling of suffocation or even panic.

Asthma is a growing health problem throughout the world. It is the most common chronic disease of childhood and its prevalence is increasing in adults between 18 and 44 years of age. About 30 percent of all asthmatics are under 18 years of age.

If you have allergies, you're particularly susceptible to asthma. Many people with asthma are sensitive to dust, animal dander, pollen, mold and other common allergens. If you're like most people with asthma, appropriate care and drug therapy can help you lead a normal, active life. There is no routine screening to detect the likelihood of developing asthma.

Your doctor will diagnose asthma by taking your medical history and performing a physical examination. In some cases, tests of lung function and chest x-rays also may be used to confirm the diagnosis.

Asthma drugs are often administered using a *metered dose inhaler* (MDI). This tubular device propels small particles of drug through the mouth into the lungs. If you have difficulty using an MDI, your doctor may recommend modifications for proper drug treatment.

Prevention

If you have asthma, these are some steps you can take to reduce the number and severity of attacks:

- If your doctor has given you an acute-care regimen and you begin to have an attack, implement the measures immediately. The key to managing an asthma attack is to prevent it from getting out of control.
- Eliminate or reduce exposure to "triggers" that cause attacks, such as cigarette smoke, pollen, dust and other irritants.
- If pollen triggers attacks, stay inside as much as possible during periods of high pollen count—preferably an inside environment with filtered air.
- Remove the carpets in your home, and at work if possible, to decrease attacks. Dust mites, which often trigger attacks, thrive in carpeting.

- Enclose your mattress and pillow in hypo-allergenic zipper bags to reduce your exposure to potential allergens.
- Drink plenty of fluids, which may loosen mucus in your lungs and make breathing easier.
- Keep a record of daily treatment, acute-care regimen, and pertinent information about symptoms, treatment and your response to treatment.

What You Can Do

Self-evaluation and self-care are the most important things you can do to control asthma attacks. Discuss a self-care plan with your doctor that includes:

- Daily or routine drug therapy
- A symptom diary
- What medications to take when an attack begins
- When to seek medical or emergency care
- Use of a peak flow meter to help you monitor your asthma status

Final Notes

Often, by eliminating or avoiding triggers in the home, workplace and environment, you can manage your asthma with little or no medication and maintain a normal activity level. The more you know about asthma and the better you become at managing it, the better your quality of life will become.

Asthma

Do these apply:

- You have symptoms of significant respiratory distress, such as a feeling of suffocation, gasping or straining to get a breath
- There is a change in mental status, such as confusion, severe irritability, memory loss, impaired judgement or lack of responsiveness
- Your peak flow is below 50 percent of your personal best, or falling steadily after each treatment
- There is a bluish color to the lips or skin
- You have sharp chest pains
- An asthma attack is out of control

Seek Emergency Care

- You have difficulty breathing, such as shortness of breath or rapid respirations
- Your peak flow is staying between 50 to 80 percent of your personal best despite medication
- Your prescribed regimen for acute attacks provides little relief
- You have chest pain, sputum that is yellow or gray-green, or rust-colored nasal discharge
- You have shaking, chills or high fever, or look very ill

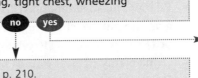

Call Doctor Now

- Peak flow level is below your personal best
- Your use of a rescue inhaler is increasing
- You have asthma and do not have a self-care plan that includes what to do when an attack begins
- You have not been diagnosed with asthma but have developed:
  - A dry cough when you exercise and/or at night
  - Difficulty breathing, tight chest, wheezing

Call Doctor

See **What You Can Do,** p. 210.

Apply Self-Care

Pneumonia

Pneumonia is a general term that refers to inflammation and infection of the lungs. Millions of people in the United States get pneumonia each year. Bacterial pneumonia usually responds well to antibiotic treatment, but virual pneumonia does not (as antibiotics cannot kill viruses). That's just one of the reasons prevention is so important.

Note Your Symptoms

Most forms of pneumonia are characterized by:
- Coughing
- Shortness of breath and labored breathing
- Chest pain associated with coughing or breathing
- Chills and/or fever
- Yellow, gray-green, rust-colored or bloody *sputum* (phlegm)
- Fatigue

Prevention

Pneumococcal vaccine helps protect against the leading cause of bacterial pneumonia and is recommended for all children from 6 months through 2 years of age, people over the age of 65, individuals with chronic illnesses and immune disorders, and people who have no spleen. The influenza vaccine is helpful for preventing viral pneumonia. (See *Influenza*, page 204). Discuss vaccination schedules for yourself and your family members with your healthcare provider or contact your local public health department for more information.

What You Can Do

- Get plenty of rest.
- Take aspirin, acetaminophen (Tylenol) or ibuprofen (Advil, Motrin). **NEVER give aspirin to children/teenagers unless your healthcare provider orders it. It can cause Reye's syndrome, a rare but often fatal condition**.
- Drink plenty of clear liquids unless you're on a fluid-restricted diet.
- Drink chicken soup, bouillon and other salty liquids to restore fluids and minimize dizziness when you stand.

- Ask your doctor about the use of cough suppressants and expectorants.
- Use a cool-mist vaporizer to help loosen secretions.
- Eat according to your appetite.
- Check with your doctor to see if there is a risk of infecting others. Stay home if you are advised to do so.

Pneumonia

Do these apply:

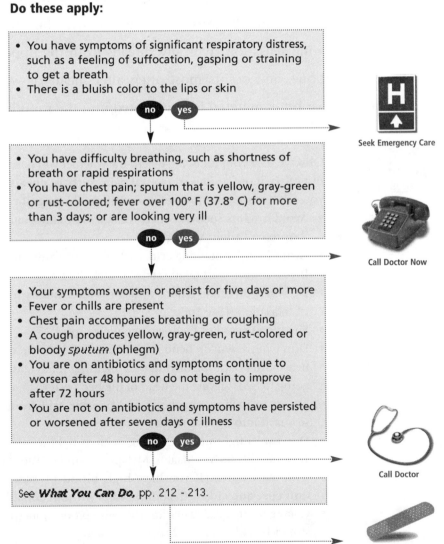

- You have symptoms of significant respiratory distress, such as a feeling of suffocation, gasping or straining to get a breath
- There is a bluish color to the lips or skin

no **yes**

Seek Emergency Care

- You have difficulty breathing, such as shortness of breath or rapid respirations
- You have chest pain; sputum that is yellow, gray-green or rust-colored; fever over 100° F (37.8° C) for more than 3 days; or are looking very ill

no **yes**

Call Doctor Now

- Your symptoms worsen or persist for five days or more
- Fever or chills are present
- Chest pain accompanies breathing or coughing
- A cough produces yellow, gray-green, rust-colored or bloody *sputum* (phlegm)
- You are on antibiotics and symptoms continue to worsen after 48 hours or do not begin to improve after 72 hours
- You are not on antibiotics and symptoms have persisted or worsened after seven days of illness

no **yes**

Call Doctor

See **What You Can Do,** pp. 212 - 213.

Apply Self-Care

Abdominal/Gastrointestinal

Heartburn

Heartburn is caused by the flow of gastric acid from the stomach into the *esophagus*, the food pipe that runs from the throat into the stomach. The pain associated with heartburn (a burning sensation) typically spreads from the upper abdomen into the lower breastbone, and occurs most often after meals or when lying down. Sometimes, sour or bitter material is regurgitated into the mouth.

Observe your symptoms and determine whether you have heartburn by ruling out other, more serious sources of pain, such as a heart attack or angina. If you don't suspect a more serious problem, begin self-care:

- Avoid irritants such as coffee, tea, alcohol, chocolate, mint, aspirin and ibuprofen (Advil, Motrin).
- Avoid foods containing acid, such as citrus fruits and tomatoes.
- If you smoke, start taking steps to kick the habit.
- Do what you can to reduce your stress level and try to make meals a time of relaxation. (See *Stress*, p. 314.)
- Sit—don't stand or lie down—while eating.
- Don't lie down or bend over immediately after eating. If nighttime heartburn is a problem, don't eat anything for at least three hours before going to bed. Elevate the head of the bed with 4- to 6-inch (10 to 15 cm) blocks to incline your body and prevent acid from flowing from the stomach into the esophagus.
- Don't wear tight-fitting clothing, such as tight jeans.
- Take antacids such as Maalox, Mylanta, Gelusil or Tums, which may provide temporary relief. (**If you have high blood pressure or heart disease, don't use antacids with sodium salts without consulting your doctor.**)
- Chew gum after eating to stimulate saliva production, which helps neutralize stomach acid.

- Try acid reducers, medications that decrease the production of stomach acid. These medications include famotidine (Pepcid), ranitidine (Zantac), nizatidine (Axid), cimetidine (Tagamet) and omeprazole (Prilosec). If symptoms persist after two weeks, consult your doctor before continuing use.

People who are prone to heartburn may have gastroesophogeal reflux disease (GERD). Chronic severe symptoms may lead to complications, including a pre-cancerous condition. However, with self-care you can easily treat the symptoms of simple heartburn with no lasting ill effects.

Heartburn
Do these apply:

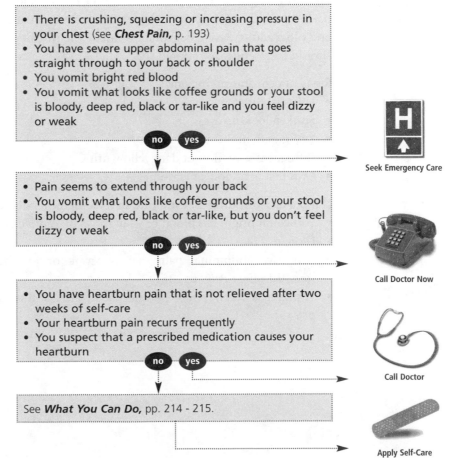

- There is crushing, squeezing or increasing pressure in your chest (see **Chest Pain,** p. 193)
- You have severe upper abdominal pain that goes straight through to your back or shoulder
- You vomit bright red blood
- You vomit what looks like coffee grounds or your stool is bloody, deep red, black or tar-like and you feel dizzy or weak

no   yes

Seek Emergency Care

- Pain seems to extend through your back
- You vomit what looks like coffee grounds or your stool is bloody, deep red, black or tar-like, but you don't feel dizzy or weak

no   yes

Call Doctor Now

- You have heartburn pain that is not relieved after two weeks of self-care
- Your heartburn pain recurs frequently
- You suspect that a prescribed medication causes your heartburn

no   yes

Call Doctor

See **What You Can Do,** pp. 214 - 215.

Apply Self-Care

Nausea and Vomiting

Nausea is most often traced to a viral infection or "stomach flu" that produces a queasy stomach. When nausea intensifies, you may begin to vomit. The condition may also be caused by medications, stress, pregnancy, food poisoning or a head injury. Because nausea and vomiting can be connected with so many medical problems—some of them serious—it's important to watch your symptoms closely.

 The most dangerous threat posed by vomiting is dehydration (see *Dehydration*, p. 236), which can occur quickly, particularly in infants, young children and older adults. Severe dehydration can be life-threatening and symptoms should be carefully monitored.

Signs of dehydration include:
- Unusual thirst
- Sunken-looking eyes
- Dry mouth and cracked lips
- Infrequent urination or dark yellow urine
- Skin that is no longer elastic

Nausea and vomiting may indicate serious medical conditions if:
- You vomit bright red blood or what looks like coffee grounds (see *Peptic Ulcer*, p. 224)
- You have abdominal pain that is severe or localized in one area (see *Abdominal Pain*, p. 238)
- Vomiting is accompanied by a headache and a stiff neck (see *Meningitis*, p. 245)

Some nausea and vomiting can be traced to food poisoning. (See *Stomach Flu and Food Poisoning,* p. 219.) The cause may be a virus, bacteria or toxin that inflames the intestines, found in certain foods that have not been stored or handled properly.

Suspect food poisoning if:
- Your symptoms are shared by others who ate the same food
- Nausea and vomiting begin six to 48 hours after eating food that may not have been stored correctly

Give Your Stomach a Break

- Avoid solid foods.
- For 12 to 24 hours after symptoms begin, slowly sip any of the following:
  - Non-prescription electrolyte supplements such as Pedialyte or Rice-Lyte (found in the infant formula grocery store aisle)
  - Clear liquids such as water and diluted bouillon (unless your doctor has restricted your sodium intake)
- Start drinking a few sips at a time and increase liquids gradually. Do this even if you can't keep anything down for long.
- Suck ice chips if no other liquids stay down.
- As your symptoms improve, try unbuttered rice, potatoes or noodles; crackers or toast; unsweetened hot or cold cereals; soups with rice and meat; and yogurt, bananas and applesauce.
- Do not take aspirin or other pain relievers.

If you are breast feeding, make sure your baby is getting adequate fluids.

While patience and self-care normally do the trick for an upset stomach, it's important to be alert for serious and sudden complications.

See **Decision helper,** p. 218.

Nausea and Vomiting

Do these apply:

- You vomit bright red blood (see ***Peptic Ulcer,*** p. 224)
- You vomit what looks like coffee grounds and you feel dizzy or weak
- You have shortness of breath or a change in mental status
- You have a new headache and a stiff neck (see ***Meningitis,*** p. 245)
- There are signs of dehydration in an infant or a child under age 6 (see ***Dehydration,*** p. 236)
- There is nausea and vomiting with severe abdominal pain or associated with a swollen or tender abdomen
- Vomit contains bile (green-yellow) or fecal-smelling liquid

Seek Emergency Care

no   yes

- Vomiting is severe or occurs in large quantities (see ***Abdominal Pain,*** p. 238)
- Your vomit looks like coffee grounds, but you don't feel dizzy or weak
- There are signs of dehydration in an adult or a child age 6 or older (see ***Dehydration,*** p. 236)

Call Doctor Now

no   yes

- Medication may have caused your symptoms
- You think you're pregnant
- Vomiting is associated with jaundice
- Vomiting lasts more than two days without improvement or becomes recurrent
- You vomit two times or more after a head injury (see ***Head/Spinal Injury,*** p. 56)
- You have abdominal pain concentrated in one area that has lasted longer than a day

Call Doctor

no   yes

See ***What You Can Do,*** p. 217.

Apply Self-Care

Stomach Flu and Food Poisoning

Stomach flu and food poisoning have different causes but many of the same symptoms. However, they both fall under the general category of *gastroenteritis*, which is commonly caused by food-borne bacteria and their toxins, or by viruses spread by improper purification of water or improper handling of food, utensils, etc.

Symptoms—vomiting, diarrhea, abdominal cramping and fever—usually take three to 36 hours to develop, with the resulting illness lasting 12 hours to several days.

For poisoning not related to food, see *Poisoning*, p. 26.

Stomach Flu

- Maximize your resistance to infection with a healthy diet, plenty of rest and regular exercise.
- Wash your hands frequently.
- Keep your hands away from your nose, eyes and mouth.

Food Poisoning

- Wash hands frequently
- Carefully refrigerate (between 34° F [1° C] and 40° F [4° C]) all foods— especially poultry, fish, meats and eggs. Don't eat anything that has been kept between 40° F (4° C) and 140° F (60° C) for more than two hours.
- Defrost foods in the microwave or refrigerator—not on the kitchen counter.
- Avoid foods made with raw eggs, as well as rare or uncooked meats.

- Be especially careful with large, cooked meats like whole turkeys. Refrigerate leftovers as soon as dinner is over. Remove thick bones and cut meat into portions less than three inches (8 cm) thick to speed cooling.
- Thoroughly reheat leftover meats to at least 165° F (74° C) before serving them to destroy any bacteria.
- Wash all utensils, counter tops and cutting boards that have touched raw meat in hot, soapy water before reusing them. Wash your hands frequently.
- Follow home-canning and freezing instructions carefully. Throw out any cans or jars that have leaks or bulging lids. Do not touch the contents and wash your hands after handling the container.

What You Can Do

- Do not eat solid foods while vomiting persists.
- Slowly sip any of the following:
  - Non-prescription electrolyte supplements such as Pedialyte or Rice-Lyte (found in the infant formula grocery store aisle)
  - Clear liquids such as water and diluted bouillon (unless your doctor has restricted your sodium intake)
- As your symptoms improve, try unbuttered rice, potatoes or noodles; crackers or toast; unsweetened hot or cold cereals; soups with rice and meat; and yogurt, bananas and applesauce.
- Do not take aspirin or other pain relievers that may irritate the stomach.
- If you suspect food poisoning, check with anyone else who may have eaten the same food. When possible, save a sample of the suspected food in case analysis becomes necessary.

For additional self-care, see *Nausea And Vomiting* (p. 216); *Diarrhea* (p. 233); *Dehydration* (p. 236).

Many forms of bacteria can cause food poisoning, including *salmonella* (typically found in dairy products, eggs, poultry, red meat and seafood) and *E. coli* (most commonly found in improperly cooked ground meats). A rare but fatal form of food poisoning called *botulism* is usually caused by eating foods with a low-acidity content—such as corn and beans—that have been improperly home-canned.

Decision *helper*

Stomach Flu and Food Poisoning

Do these apply:

- You suspect food poisoning from a canned food (blurred or double vision, difficulty swallowing or breathing)
- There are signs of dehydration in an infant or child under age 6 (see ***Dehydration,*** p. 236)
- There is severe vomiting
- There is bloody diarrhea

no **yes**

H ↑

Seek Emergency Care

- There are signs of dehydration in an adult or child age 6 or older (see ***Dehydration,*** p. 236)

no **yes**

Call Doctor Now

- Vomiting or diarrhea lasts longer than one to two days and is not improving

no **yes**

Call Doctor

See ***What You Can Do,*** p. 220.

Apply Self-Care

Gastritis

Gastritis is a painful inflammation of the lining of the stomach. This may occur more frequently with advancing age.

Causes include bacterial infection (often with H. pylori), acute stress, alcohol abuse, or nonsteroidal anti-inflammatory drugs (NSAIDs), such as aspirin or ibuprofen (Advil, Motrin). Symptoms may include upper abdominal pain or bloating; diarrhea; nausea and vomiting, sometimes with bright red blood or what looks like coffee grounds; or unintentional weight loss.

What You Can Do

- Take over-the-counter (OTC) antacids to provide possible pain relief.
- Moderate your use of tobacco, alcohol and caffeinated drinks. (See *Getting and Staying Healthy,* p. 330.)
- Avoid foods that may trigger gastritis, such as pickles or spices. Food sensitivities vary from person to person.
- Avoid NSAIDs and other drugs that cause or worsen gastritis. (See *Home Pharmacy,* p. 325.)
- Try acid reducers, medications that decrease the production of stomach acid. These medications include famotidine (Pepcid), ranitidine (Zantac), nizatidine (Axid), cimetidine (Tagamet) and omeprazole (Prilosec). If symptoms persist after two weeks, consult your doctor before continuing use.

Final Notes

If over-the-counter (OTC) medications do not relieve the pain, your doctor may recommend a more powerful prescription drug.

Gastritis is generally not serious. In most cases, the pain stops spontaneously or following minor lifestyle changes.

Gastritis

Do these apply:

- There is crushing, squeezing or increasing pressure in your chest (see **Chest Pain,** p. 193)
- You vomit bright red blood
- You vomit what looks like coffee grounds and you feel dizzy or weak

Seek Emergency Care

- You have persistent or moderate to severe symptoms of gastritis, such as upper abdominal pain, diarrhea, nausea and vomiting
- You vomit what looks like coffee grounds, but don't feel dizzy or weak

Call Doctor Now

- Symptoms of gastritis persist or worsen despite the use of over-the-counter (OTC) antacids and other self-care techniques for two weeks or more

Call Doctor

See **What You Can Do,** p. 222.

Apply Self-Care

Peptic Ulcer

Peptic ulcers are craters or eroded areas in the protective lining of the stomach or intestine that are almost always caused by bacterial infection with H. pylori. The most common type of peptic ulcer is called a *duodenal ulcer,* occuring in the upper part of the small intestine. Severe ulcers can lead to pain, bleeding and even perforations—holes—in the wall of the stomach or intestine. **A perforated ulcer is life-threatening and must be surgically treated immediately.**

Most peptic ulcers are caused by infection with the bacteria H. pylori. Other causes include cigarette smoking. The use of certain drugs such as aspirin, ibuprofen (Advil, Motrin) and corticosteroids may also cause them in some people.

Thanks to significant advances in treatment, with antibiotics and acid reducers most people recover from ulcers within four to six weeks.

What You Can Do

To speed the healing process if you have a peptic ulcer:

- Start taking steps to kick the habit if you smoke; also avoid coffee, alcohol, aspirin and ibuprofen (Advil, Motrin).
- Avoid hot or spicy foods if they cause discomfort, but for the most part you can eat a normal diet.
- Try a fast-acting antacid like Bromo Seltzer or Alka Seltzer, unless your doctor has restricted your sodium intake.
- For temporary relief from ulcer pain, try over-the-counter (OTC) antacids such as Maalox, Mylanta, Gelusil or Tums.
- Try acid reducers, medications that decrease the production of stomach acid. These medications include famotidine (Pepcid), ranitidine (Zantac), nizatidine (Axid), cimetidine (Tagamet), and omeprazole (Prilosec). If symptoms persist after two weeks, consult your doctor before continuing to use them.

Tell your doctor if you have a history of ulcers. Common medications taken for other ailments can increase your risk of ulcer recurrences.

Decision *helper*

Peptic Ulcer
Do these apply:

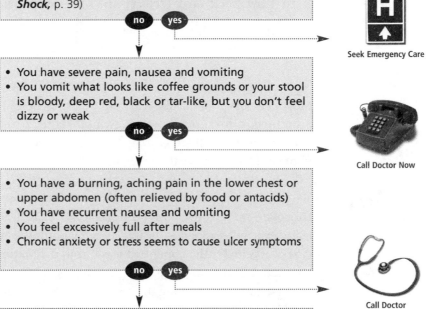

- There is crushing, squeezing or increasing pressure in your chest (see **Chest Pain**, p. 193)
- You vomit bright red blood
- You vomit large amounts of what looks like coffee grounds or your stool is bloody, deep red, black or tar-like, and you feel dizzy or weak
- Your skin is cold and clammy and you faint (see **Shock**, p. 39)

no **yes**

Seek Emergency Care

- You have severe pain, nausea and vomiting
- You vomit what looks like coffee grounds or your stool is bloody, deep red, black or tar-like, but you don't feel dizzy or weak

no **yes**

Call Doctor Now

- You have a burning, aching pain in the lower chest or upper abdomen (often relieved by food or antacids)
- You have recurrent nausea and vomiting
- You feel excessively full after meals
- Chronic anxiety or stress seems to cause ulcer symptoms

no **yes**

Call Doctor

See **What You Can Do**, p. 224.

Apply Self-Care

Hiatal Hernia

Hiatal (or abdominal) hernia occurs when part of the stomach protrudes above an opening in the diaphragm—the muscle wall that separates the chest cavity from the abdominal cavity. The opening is called a *hiatus*. This protrusion allows stomach contents to flow backward (*reflux*) into the *esophagus* (the tube that connects the throat and stomach).

Most people with a hiatal hernia don't have symptoms; others experience a burning pain caused by reflux. Symptoms tend to be more noticeable when a sufferer reclines. Obesity, pregnancy, a low-fiber diet and wearing tight clothes may make the reflux worse.

What You Can Do

To prevent reflux, eat small meals and avoid smoking, acidic foods, chocolate, mint, coffee and alcohol. Elevate your head while sleeping by using extra pillows or a foam wedge, or by putting 4- to 6-inch (10- to 15-cm) blocks under the upper bed legs. Avoid tight-fitting clothing, reclining after eating, and eating or drinking two hours or less before bedtime.

Most cases of abdominal hernia don't require treatment other than antacids or other medications to relieve heartburn. The most common complication of a hiatal hernia is gastroesophageal reflux disease (GERD). **Strangulation of the hernia, in which part of the stomach gets pinched off, is a dangerous situation that needs immediate surgical repair.**

Hiatal Hernia

Do these apply:

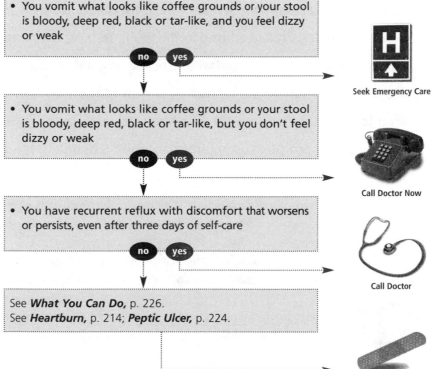

- You vomit bright red blood
- You vomit what looks like coffee grounds or your stool is bloody, deep red, black or tar-like, and you feel dizzy or weak

no / yes

Seek Emergency Care

- You vomit what looks like coffee grounds or your stool is bloody, deep red, black or tar-like, but you don't feel dizzy or weak

no / yes

Call Doctor Now

- You have recurrent reflux with discomfort that worsens or persists, even after three days of self-care

no / yes

Call Doctor

See *What You Can Do,* p. 226.
See *Heartburn,* p. 214; *Peptic Ulcer,* p. 224.

Apply Self-Care

Inguinal Hernia

An *inguinal hernia* occurs when a section of the small intestine protrudes through abdominal muscles, causing a lump in the groin. In men, the hernia often protrudes into the *scrotum*, the sac that holds the testes. An inguinal hernia usually results from weak abdominal muscles and increased pressure in the abdomen. This combination forces a loop of intestine out through the weak area in the muscle wall. Obesity, heavy lifting and prolonged coughing can cause a hernia or make it worse.

Symptoms can include swelling in the groin that goes away when you lie down or when gentle pressure is applied, and groin pain that occurs when you bend or lift.

Strangulation of the hernia, when part of the intestine gets trapped and cannot be reduced, is an emergency and needs immediate surgical repair.

Surgery is the only cure for this type of hernia. Until the hernia is repaired, avoid heavy lifting.

Decision *helper*

Inguinal Hernia
Do these apply:

- You have been diagnosed with a hernia and experience increased or severe groin pain
- A hernia feels very tender, and does not reduce with pressure

no   yes

Seek Emergency Care

- You are unable to push your hernia back into the abdominal wall by applying pressure

no   yes

Call Doctor Now

- You feel increasing pain in the abdomen, scrotum or groin
- Mild groin pain or an unexplained groin bump or swelling continues for more than one week

yes

Call Doctor

Constipation

Constipation is a decreased frequency of bowel movements accompanied by hard, dry stools. However, there is no standard for what constitutes normal bowel movements. Normal for you may be two bowel movements a day or one every three days.

Other symptoms of constipation include difficulty passing stools, abdominal pain and fullness, a feeling of incomplete bowel movements, bloating and gas.

Changes in stools (color, consistency, texture and bulk) generally are not serious. Chronic constipation occurs more frequently in older adults, whose diet and fluid consumption patterns may be inconsistent.

What You Can Do

Constipation often can be successfully treated through self-care:
- If your eating habits have changed (other than for medical reasons), go back to the diet you had before the problems began.
- Improve your diet by adding more high-fiber foods, such as whole grains, bran, beans, leafy and raw vegetables, and fruits—especially dried fruits. A high-fiber diet has the added benefit of reducing your blood-cholesterol level and possibly reducing your risk of colon cancer.
- Drink plenty of fluids, especially water.
- Increase your daily exercise, especially if you sit all day at work.
- Investigate ALL medications you take to see if they cause constipation. (However, DO NOT stop taking a prescribed medication without consulting your doctor).

If these steps don't work, consider over-the-counter (OTC) remedies such as bulk laxatives containing methylcellulose or psyllium, which draw water into the stool; milk of magnesia (**not for individuals with kidney problems**); or stool softeners.

Do not give a laxative to a child without checking with your pediatrician.

A reduction in the frequency of bowel movements with no other symptoms does not necessarily require treatment.

Hemorrhoids

Hemorrhoids are swollen, inflamed veins located around the outside or inside of the anus. They are extremely common and can be caused or aggravated by constipation, straining to move the bowels, obesity, pregnancy or a sedentary lifestyle.

Symptoms may include pain, itching, burning, swelling, bleeding and a sense of incomplete emptying in the rectum. Frequently, hemorrhoidal bleeding is seen as bright red blood on the toilet paper or in the toilet bowl after bowel movements.

Simple self-care is usually the key to initial treatment:

- Keep the anal area clean with pre-moistened towels or "baby wipes."
- Soak in a warm *sitz bath* (hip-high water), which usually proves soothing.
- Avoid sitting for long periods of time, if possible, or sit on a rubber doughnut. Stretch frequently.
- Try over-the-counter (OTC) hydrocortisone cream to reduce swelling and inflammation. Avoid creams with topical anesthetics, since they may slow healing.
- Take steps to avoid constipation and straining to move the bowels. Eat high-fiber foods or take over-the-counter (OTC) fiber supplements. Drink plenty of fluids and exercise regularly. (See *Getting and Staying Healthy*, p. 330.) The occasional use of a mild laxative might be of value, but a better choice is a simple stool softener. Ask your doctor if any medications you take might cause constipation (iron is notorious for this); a stool softener may decrease this side effect.

Decision *helper*

Constipation/Hemorrhoids
Do these apply:

- Your stool is bloody, deep red, black or tar-like and you feel dizzy or weak
- Severe abdominal pain or cramping is accompanied by abdominal swelling, tenderness or rigidity; vomit that is greenish or foul-smelling (bile); and/or fever or chills

Seek Emergency Care

- Your stool is bloody, deep red, black or tar-like, but you don't feel dizzy or weak
- Significant abdominal pain has been present for more than 24 hours

Call Doctor Now

- It has been two or more days since your last bowel movement and you also have abdominal cramping or bloating or leakage of liquid stool
- Constipation is persistent or recurs despite self-care
- A hemorrhoid has become hard and painful
- You have bright red blood mixed with or coating stools
- You think constipation might be a side effect of medication
- There is a persistent change in the frequency, consistency, texture, or color of stools

Call Doctor

See **What You Can Do,** pp. 230, 231.
See **Getting and Staying Healthy,** p. 330.

Apply Self-Care

Diarrhea

Diarrhea (frequent, watery stools) takes place when solid waste is pushed through the intestines before the water in the waste has had time to be reabsorbed by the body. Excessive loss of water, called *dehydration* (see *Dehydration*, p. 236), is the biggest health risk of diarrhea.

Diarrhea is most commonly caused by viral infections. Other causes include bacterial infections and irritation of the digestive tract. It is frequently accompanied by nausea and vomiting. (See *Nausea and Vomiting*, p. 216.)

Many medications cause diarrhea, including antibiotics, blood pressure drugs, digitalis, anti-cancer drugs and nonsteroidal anti-inflammatory drugs (NSAIDs). (See *Home Pharmacy*, p. 325 and *Using Medications*, p. 324.)

Diarrhea in Children

Because of their developing digestive tracts, infants and young children usually experience diarrhea more often than adults. Frequently, runny stools are caused by drinking too much juice or milk or eating too much fruit or too many sweets. If a child seems healthy in every other way, food-intolerance diarrhea is usually not serious and no treatment is required. However, if diarrhea continues, the food or drink that is causing it should be eliminated from the child's diet. Continuing diarrhea may be a sign of some other illness. (See *Stomach Flu and Food Poisoning*, p. 219.)

Because of their small size, children face greater risk of dehydration than adults. Saliva that is dry and sticky may be an early sign. A baby whose diaper has not been wet for several hours also could be suffering from dehydration. (See *Dehydration*, p. 236.)

Infants and Toddlers

- For a child younger than 2 years of age, discuss diarrhea with your doctor.
- To avoid dehydration from persistent diarrhea, see that your infant or child drinks twice as much fluid as usual.

- If your infant is bottle-fed, continue to give the usual mealtime feeding and offer a commercially prepared electrolyte drink or *oral rehydrating solution* (ORS) between feedings. Some popular brands are Pedialyte, Rehydralyte and Infalyte. Check which your pediatrician prefers.
- If your infant is breast-fed, nurse more frequently and give ORS between feedings. Initially offer small amounts (one teaspoon [4.9 mL]) of ORS in a syringe every five minutes. A child with mild vomiting usually can keep down ORS when it is given in this manner.
- Avoid juices or sodas since these can actually worsen diarrhea, cause an imbalance of salt in the blood, and put your child at greater risk of dehydration.
- If toddlers are uninterested in drinking, make it a fun activity by offering small amounts of liquid in special cups, using colorful straws, letting them spoon it for themselves, or using a timer they can set, etc.
- If your toddler eats solid food, the following items are especially good for treating the child's diarrhea: unbuttered rice; potatoes or noodles; crackers or toast (depending on the child's age); unsweetened hot or cold cereals; soups with rice, meat and/or vegetables; bananas and applesauce.
- **Do not give Pepto-Bismol, Kaopectate or other anti-diarrheal medications to infants or young children without consulting your doctor.**

Adults and Older Children

- Slowly sip any of the following:
  - Non-prescription electrolyte supplements such as Pedialyte or Rice-Lyte (found in the infant formula grocery store aisle)
  - Clear liquids such as water and diluted bouillon (unless your doctor has restricted your sodium intake)
- Avoid juices and sodas since these can actually worsen diarrhea, cause an imbalance of salt in the blood, and increase the risk of dehydration.
- As your symptoms improve, try unbuttered rice, potatoes or noodles; crackers or toast; unsweetened hot or cold cereals; soups with rice, meat and/or vegetables; and yogurt, bananas and applesauce.
- Avoid spicy foods, alcohol and foods high in fat for several days.
- Adults: try over-the-counter (OTC) preparations like Pepto-Bismol, Imodium or Kaopectate, which make the stools more solid. However, these medications should be avoided for the first six hours of an illness, since diarrhea sometimes helps speed recovery.

Diarrhea

Do these apply:

- An adult has stool that is bloody, deep red, black or tar-like and feels dizzy or weak
- A child has stool that is bloody, deep red, black or tar-like and appears pale and sweaty or has a belly that is tender when pressed
- Signs of dehydration are present in a child under age 3 (see ***Dehydration,*** p. 236)
- An infant under 3 months of age has had diarrhea and a fever of 100.4° F (38° C) or higher within the past 24 hours, even if it has returned to normal
- Severe abdominal pain occurs (a baby may draw its knees up to its chest and have a rigid, tender, or possibly swollen abdomen; vomiting of greenish or foul-smelling liquid and fever or chills)

Seek Emergency Care

- The stool is bloody, deep red, black or tar-like, but no dizziness or weakness occurs
- Signs of dehydration are present in an adult or child over 3 years of age
- A pregnant woman, diabetic or person with an immune disorder develops diarrhea

Call Doctor Now

- You suspect that a medication might be causing diarrhea
- Diarrhea persists for two days or more
- A child under age 2 has diarrhea
- Diarrhea occurs after travel to a foreign country, eating specific foods or drinking dairy products or specific fruit juices
- Weight loss of 5 pounds or more occurs following the onset of diarrhea

Call Doctor

See ***What You Can Do,*** p. 233.

Apply Self-Care

Dehydration

Dehydration is the excessive loss of water in a body and is a dangerous risk of both vomiting (see *Nausea and Vomiting,* p. 216) and diarrhea (see *Diarrhea,* p. 233). It can occur quickly, particularly in infants, young children and older adults. Dehydration also depletes the body of two essential minerals, sodium and potassium, which are *electrolytes.* Severe dehydration can be life-threatening, and symptoms should be monitored carefully.

Signs of dehydration include:
- Unusual thirst
- Sunken-looking eyes
- Dry mouth and cracked lips
- Infrequent urination or dark yellow urine
- Skin that is no longer elastic
- In young children, early signs of dehydration may include a very dry mouth and lips or diapers that have not been wet for several hours.

What You Can Do

To prevent dehydration or keep it from getting worse:
- Drink clear liquids like water and bouillon after vomiting is under control. (See *Nausea and Vomiting,* p. 216.)
- At the first sign of diarrhea, increase your fluid intake to eight to 10 large glasses of water a day until it stops. Check with your doctor first if you are on a fluid-restricted diet.
- Adults may drink a rehydration fluid like Rehydralyte or any pediatric oral rehydration fluid to replace lost electrolytes. (Because of the sodium content, consult your doctor first if you have high blood pressure, heart disease, diabetes, glaucoma or a history of stroke. Drink plain water if in doubt.)

- To replace electrolytes in children, try Pedialyte or one of the other children's electrolyte fluids. (If a child is vomiting, start with one teaspoon [4.9 mL] of liquid every 10 minutes for one or two hours, then increase the amount.)
- For infants, continue breast- or bottle-feeding (with regular formula) and offer rehydration fluids between feedings.

Dehydration
Do these apply:

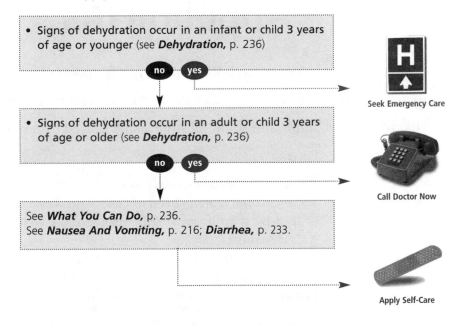

- Signs of dehydration occur in an infant or child 3 years of age or younger (see *Dehydration,* p. 236)

no · · · yes

H ↑

Seek Emergency Care

- Signs of dehydration occur in an adult or child 3 years of age or older (see *Dehydration,* p. 236)

no · · · yes

Call Doctor Now

See *What You Can Do,* p. 236.
See *Nausea And Vomiting,* p. 216; *Diarrhea,* p. 233.

Apply Self-Care

Abdominal Pain

Abdominal pain can be caused by very minor or very serious conditions, and finding out what is causing the pain can be difficult. Locating the pain can help determine the cause:

- Appendix—pain usually occurs in the lower right abdomen
- Gallbladder—pain usually occurs in the upper right abdomen
- Kidney—pain usually occurs in the back

However, it's important to note that abdominal pain can occur for many reasons.

Appendicitis

Appendicitis, the most common abdominal emergency, most frequently strikes people in their teens and 20s. Accurate diagnosis and rapid treatment can greatly reduce the likelihood of complications and death, usually caused by a burst appendix.

Symptoms usually occur in this order:

- Vague discomfort around and just above the navel; later, a sharper pain or tenderness in the lower right quarter of the abdomen that is worse with movement
- Possible nausea, vomiting and loss of appetite
- Fever from 99° F (37.2° C) to 101° F (38.3° C)
- Constipation or, less commonly, diarrhea

Once appendicitis is confirmed, the appendix is usually removed. This surgery, called an *appendectomy*, is relatively low-risk.

If you suspect appendicitis, seek medical attention right away. Do not use laxatives or apply heat to the area. Both can make the appendix rupture more quickly.

See *Decision helper*, p. 241.

Gallbladder Disease

The gallbladder stores bile that is made in the liver, then passes the bile on to the intestines to help digest fats. With a high amount of fat and cholesterol in the system, some of the bile may turn into stones. As the bile flows from the gallbladder to the intestines through the bile ducts, these *gallstones* can block the ducts, causing severe pain, local inflammation or *jaundice* (yellow skin). If the stones stay in the gallbladder, they cause no discomfort.

The pain usually occurs in the pit of the stomach or the upper right side of the abdomen and radiates to the upper right side of the back. It usually begins one to three hours after a large or fatty meal and persists for several hours. It may be accompanied by nausea and vomiting.

The greatest risk factors for gallbladder disease are eating a high-calorie, high-fat diet (which increases bile production), obesity and extreme dieting. Avoid fatty foods and overeating to help prevent a gallbladder attack.

See *Decision helper,* p. 241.

Kidney Stones

Kidney stones are usually chronic, most often affecting adults between the ages of 30 and 40. They vary in size from microscopic to several centimeters in diameter. Most are made primarily of calcium.

- Severe pain in the *flank* (the area between the last rib and the hip), back and/or pubic region
- Nausea, vomiting (usually with severe pain) or abdominal bloating
- Pain traveling along the urinary tract and into the genitals, as the stone passes out of the body
- Chills, fever, and frequent or difficult urination
- Bloody urine

Kidney stones cannot be "cured" by self-care, but increasing fluids to three quarts (about 3 liters) per day and making some dietary modifications (ask your doctor for recommendations) can reduce recurrences in many people. In some cases, prescription medication also helps.

Most kidney stones pass spontaneously, requiring only fluids and a pain reliever, with no further treatment. Medication may be prescribed to help dissolve existing stones and prevent new ones. For a small percentage of kidney stones, additional medical treatment may be required.

See *Decision helper,* p. 241.

Abdominal Pain

Do these apply:

- You have symptoms of shock (see *Shock,* p. 40)
- Sudden, severe abdominal pain goes straight through the body to the back or shoulder
- Severe pain or cramping is accompanied by abdominal swelling, tenderness or rigidity; vomit that is greenish (bile) or foul-smelling; and/or fever or chills
- A blow to the abdomen is followed by severe pain, vomiting of blood, abdominal bruising or blood in the urine
- Lower abdominal pain occurs with pain in one or both testicles

no   yes

Seek Emergency Care

- Abdominal pain persists for more than 24 hours
- You have fever, back or flank pain (the area between the lowest rib and the hip), bloody urine or other symptoms suggestive of kidney stones (see *Kidney Stones,* p. 240)
- You have pain or tenderness in the lower right quarter of the abdomen, or other symptoms suggestive of appendicitis
- There is an inability to urinate or new and significant difficulty urinating

no   yes

Call Doctor Now

- You have abdominal pain and jaundice (yellow skin and/or eyes, dark urine, whitish stools)
- Abdominal pain leads to chronic loss of appetite or weight loss
- You have been diagnosed with gallstones and your symptoms become more frequent or are not improving with self-care

no   yes

Call Doctor

See *What You Can Do, Appendicitis,* p. 238;
    What You Can Do, Gallbladder Disease, p. 239;
    What You Can Do, Kidney Stones, p. 240.

Apply Self-Care

Muscles/Bones/Joints

Arthritis

Arthritis means joint inflammation and refers to several diseases that cause joint pain, swelling and stiffness. There are over 100 different types of arthritis, but most fall within one of the four listed on page 243. Most arthritic conditions cannot be cured, but their harmful effects can be limited with consistent self-care and medical support.

 Prevention

While you can't prevent arthritis, it is possible to delay its onset and slow the process.

- Avoid trauma, overuse and repetitive or jarring activities. Vary your exercise and activity schedule to allow changes in the pressure and stress on joints.
- Exercise regularly. Aerobic exercise increases blood flow to nourish joint tissues. Exercising with weights strengthens muscles that support and protect joints. Stretching and range-of-motion exercise help maintain joint flexibility.
- Control your weight. Excess pounds place stress on weight-bearing joints such as the knees.

What You Can Do

After arthritis has developed in a joint, self-care can help you maintain joint function and decrease pain, swelling and inflammation.

- Take aspirin or ibuprofen (Advil, Motrin) to relieve pain and inflammation. (Follow directions and warnings on package.) **NEVER give aspirin to children/teenagers unless your healthcare provider orders it. It can cause Reye's syndrome, a rare but often fatal condition.**
- Rest sore joints. If you must continue to put weight or stress on the joint, take breaks and rest.
- For inflamed, swollen joints, apply ice for 15 to 20 minutes at a time, more frequently initially, then three to four times a day for up to 48 hours.

ice off for at least 20 minutes between applications. For protection, place a washcloth between bare skin and ice and change the cloth if it becomes wet.

- If the joint is not swollen, apply warm, moist heat for 20 minutes, three or four times a day. Follow heat with gentle full-range-of-motion exercises and gentle massage.
- When joint pain and inflammation subside, continue the prevention measures listed above.
- Become informed about your type of arthritis. Ask your doctor for self-care treatments, and about resources in your community such as support groups, physical therapy, occupational therapy and stores that carry medical supplies.

Major Types of Arthritis

Cause	Symptoms	Commonly Affects
Osteoarthritis		
Cartilage in joints wears out (degenerates)	Pain, stiffness, swelling in joints, especially fingers; may improve with rest; bony growth spurs can occur	Men and women, worsens with age
Rheumatoid Arthritis		
Membrane lining of joint is inflamed; your immune system attacks your own tissues; cause unclear	Pain, stiffness, swelling in joints, with low-grade fever; doesn't subside with rest	Middle-aged women
Gout		
Build-up of uric acid crystals in joint fluid	Pain, stiffness, swelling, especially in big toe, ankle or knee	Men more often, aggravated by foods high in purines (such as organ meats) or alcoholic beverages
Ankylosing Spondylitis		
Inflammation in spine, other joints; thought to be genetically linked	Pain, stiffness in back, neck and other torso joints such as hips	Men and women before age 35

For information about Lyme disease as a cause of arthritis, see *Tick Bites*, p. 143.

Arthritis is a slowly progressive disease that can be managed well with a combination of self-care and medical treatment.

Arthritis

Do these apply:

- You have two or more symptoms that could signify an infection such as unusual or significant redness, red streaks surrounding or radiating from site, pus, increasing warmth, swelling or tenderness, a fever of 101° F (38.3° C) oral or more or swollen or tender lymph nodes

Call Doctor Now

- You experience bothersome side effects from medications
- You have new swelling, tenderness or pain in any of your joints
- You have to use NSAIDs or other pain medications frequently or daily without your doctor's knowledge
- There is an increase in pain lasting longer than 24 hours after exercising or other activities or an inability to resume previous activity level or exercise level after an active arthritis flare-up
- Your arthritis symptoms worsen or are not improved after six weeks of self-care

Call Doctor

See **What You Can Do,** pp. 242 - 243.

Apply Self-Care

Neck Pain

Most neck pain is caused by straining the muscles or tendons in the neck and generally can be treated at home. But there are many reasons for neck pain. Neck pain caused by an accident or injury, such as whiplash from a car accident, can indicate a serious or even life-threatening injury to the spinal cord. (See *Head/Spinal Injury*, p. 56.) Chronic neck pain can be the indirect result of the aging process, resulting in *degenerative* (wear and tear) disk disease.

Other possible causes of neck pain are arthritis (see *Arthritis*, p. 242), meningitis or a pinched nerve.

Meningitis

Meningitis is an infectious disease that can be life-threatening. The classic symptoms are fever, headache and an extremely stiff neck—so stiff that you can't touch your chin to your chest. It can also cause intense muscle spasms in the neck. (See *Decision helper*, p. 247.) **Seek emergency care.**

Pinched Nerve

A pinched nerve can be caused by arthritis or a neck injury. The pain may extend down the arm or cause numbness or tingling in the arm or hand. **If you suspect a pinched nerve, call your doctor.**

Environmental factors—your surroundings—can contribute to or cause neck pain. An uncomfortable mattress, a pillow that's too high, or an ill-fitting desk chair or work area all take their toll on the neck muscles.

If your neck hurts more in the morning:
- Try a firmer mattress on your bed, or use a bed board under your mattress to firm up a softer mattress.
- Use a pillow designed to protect your neck, or no pillow at all.

- Fold a bath towel lengthwise into a four-inch (10 cm) strip and wrap it around your neck; secure it with a safety pin while you sleep.

If your neck hurts more at night:

- Consider whether poor posture may be contributing to your pain. Walk, stand and sit with your ears, shoulders and hips in a straight line.
- Make any necessary adjustments to your office chair or work area.
- Keep your elbows at a 90-degree angle for typing.
- Consider trying some of the following neck exercises every two hours:
  - Sit or stand with an extremely erect posture to stretch the muscles in the back of your neck. Do it gently, repeating six times.
  - Squeeze your shoulder blades together gently six times.
  - Gently roll your head forward and side to side. Repeat six times.

If your neck hurts anytime:

- Aspirin or ibuprofen (Advil, Motrin) can help relieve pain and inflammation. **NEVER give aspirin to children/teenagers unless your healthcare provider orders it. It can cause Reye's syndrome, a rare but often fatal condition.**
- Apply ice for 15 to 20 minutes at a time, more frequently initially, then three to four times a day for up to 48 hours. Leave ice off for at least 20 minutes between applications. For protection, place a washcloth between bare skin and ice and change the cloth if it becomes wet.
- Heat from a heating pad (on the low setting) or shower may be helpful if muscle swelling is not a problem. Limit the use of heat to 20-minute sessions.

See *Headaches,* p. 105;
Temporomandibular Joint Syndrome (TMJ), p. 187.

Decision *helper*

Neck Pain

Do these apply:

- Neck pain is associated with fever, headache and a stiff neck (see **Meningitis,** p. 245)
- Neck pain and/or arm pain occurs with any of the following:
  - Chest pressure
  - Shortness of breath
  - Dizziness
  - Sweating
  - Nausea or vomiting
  - Rapid or irregular pulse
- Any of the following occur after an injury:
  - Weakness or paralysis of the arms or legs
  - Irregular or slowed pulse or respirations
  - Loss of bowel or bladder control
  - Unrelenting neck pain
  - New numbness or tingling
- An accident occurs while under the influence of alcohol or drugs
- Difficulty with jaw movement or swallowing or progressive swelling of the neck occurs

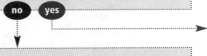

Seek Emergency Care

- Neck pain travels down one arm, or an arm is numb and tingles
- There is no improvement with self-care after 24 hours

Call Doctor

See **What You Can Do,** pp. 245 - 246.

Apply Self-Care

Back Pain

Four out of five adults have back pain severe enough to interrupt their daily routines at least once in their lives. A common and frustrating problem to treat, back pain has no quick, easy cure; recovery is slow, the pain often recurs, and prevention and treatment require life-long commitment.

Self-care is the major factor in preventing and treating back pain. Understanding the anatomy of the back and the most common injuries may help you decrease your risk of back pain. If pain occurs, begin treatment quickly.

Your backbone consists of small, round, donut-shaped bones called *vertebrae*. Stacked in an "S" arrangement, the vertebrae form a protective tunnel for your *spinal cord*. The spaces between vertebrae are filled by *disks*, packets of tough cartilage with a jelly-like filling, that cushion and absorb impact. Your spinal cord, a bundle of major nerves, leaves your brain through the *vertebral tunnel* and sends branches around the disks out to the rest of your body. Large muscles and ligaments support the spine as it twists, bends, stretches, turns and maintains an upright posture.

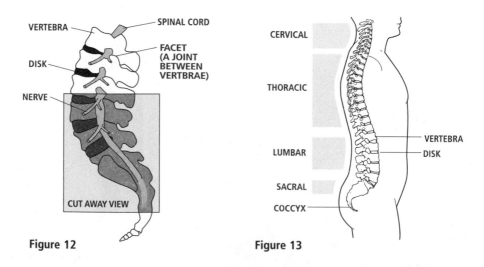

Figure 12

Figure 13

Causes

There are many causes of back pain: muscles can be strained, torn or go into spasm; ligaments and tendons may be overstretched and sprained; disks become worn down, move out of alignment or rupture (*herniated disk*); and bones wear down or change, as in arthritis or a fracture. (See *Osteoporosis*, p. 287.) Occasionally, infection and tumors can be the sources of pain. In addition, back pain may not originate from the back itself but may be *referred pain* from problems in the prostate in men or reproductive organs in women, or from kidney infections or disorders in the stomach and intestines. (See *Kidney Stones*, p. 240.)

Pain from strains, sprains and minor disk damage is usually sudden, sharp and eases over two to three days with self-care. The sharp pain from a herniated disk or fractured vertebra usually lasts several weeks and requires medical care. A steady ache is often a sign of disease, such as arthritis or referred pain.

Any back problem that causes swelling or a shifting in the alignment of the spine can put pressure on a nerve. Numbness, weakness or tingling are signs of nerve irritation. Nerves in the neck produce symptoms in the arms and upper body, while spinal nerves in the middle and lower back affect the back, buttocks, legs and feet. Pressure on the *sciatic nerve* causes sharp, shooting pains down the back of the leg into the foot. Back pain can be constant or come only with movement.

Prevention

- Maintain good posture and keep the right amount of curve in your lower back:
  - Stand tall with your ear, shoulder, hip and ankle in a line. Do not lock your knees. Balance weight evenly on your feet.
  - Avoid wearing high heels.
  - Sit tall with your shoulders back and your lower back supported. Keep knees even with or higher than your hips. Avoid sitting in one position for longer than one hour.
- Use correct posture when lifting:
  - Bend your knees and lift with your leg muscles. Keep your back straight.
  - Never bend forward to lift. Keep the load close to your body.
  - Avoid turning or twisting while holding a heavy object.
  - Avoid lifting heavy loads above your waist.

- Sleep on a medium-to-firm surface. Let comfort be your guide. Provide support for your lower back and beneath your knees if this feels more comfortable.
- Rise up from a prone position correctly. Roll to your side and use your arms and legs to push up.
- Maintain correct body weight. Obesity or a large abdomen can pull your lower back out of alignment.
- Exercise to maintain good muscle tone in your back and abdomen. Walking, swimming and biking are all good activities.
- Learn stress management (see *Stress,* p. 314), muscle-relaxation techniques and strengthening activities such as yoga.

What You Can Do

- Avoid bed rest unless it is ordered by your doctor. Resume normal activity as soon as possible. Immediately stop any activity that causes or increases pain and avoid any activity that puts stress on your back. Complete recovery may take up to six weeks.
- Apply ice for 15 to 20 minutes at a time, more frequently initially, then three to four times a day for up to 48 hours. Leave ice off for at least 20 minutes between applications. For protection, place a washcloth between bare skin and ice and change the cloth if it becomes wet.
- Once the pain has lessened, take warm showers with water directed at the painful area.
- Take aspirin or ibuprofen (Advil, Motrin) to ease pain and inflammation. (Follow directions on the package.) **NEVER give aspirin to children/ teenagers unless your healthcare provider orders it. It can cause Reye's syndrome, a rare but often fatal condition.**
- Sleep on a medium-to-firm surface. Let comfort be your guide.
- Support your back while sleeping. Place a pillow under your knees or lie on your side, knees bent and with a pillow between them. Support the entire length of the leg.
- If back pain starts with no known cause, look for signs of a problem in another area of your body that may be causing referred pain.
- For minor muscle soreness in your back, apply heat for 20 minutes at a time. Place a warm wash cloth, warm water bottle or heating pad directly on the affected area.

Decision *helper*

Back Pain

Do these apply:

- You suddenly lose bladder or bowel control
- Your pulse or respiration is irregular or slow
- There is new weakness or paralysis
- Following an accident, back pain is unrelenting or there is new numbness or tingling
- A back injury occurs while you are under the influence of alcohol or drugs
- You have severe pain in the back and abdomen

Keep still. Avoid movement. Slide firm support under the entire body without moving, if possible.

no   yes

Seek Emergency Care

Apply Emergency First Aid

- You have severe flank (area between the last rib and the hip) pain
- Flank pain is accompanied by chills, fever, nausea or vomiting
- You have had recent abdominal surgery
- Back pain occurs while you are taking medication to slow *coagulation* (blood clotting)

no   yes

Call Doctor Now

- There is numbness or tingling in the leg or foot
- A child has persistent back pain
- Your pain is disabling or you are unable to move your back for more than 24 hours
- Pain worsens or does not improve after 3 days of self-care

no   yes

Call Doctor

See **What You Can Do,** p. 250.

Apply Self-Care

Shoulder/Elbow/ Wrist/Arm Pain

Arm pain usually involves the areas surrounding the joints, such as the shoulders, elbows and wrists. More specifically, the pain usually involves the soft tissues surrounding these joints—the muscles, ligaments, tendons and *bursae* (fluid-filled sacs at the joints that help muscles slide over other muscles or bones).

Bursitis

Through injury or overuse, the bursae can become inflamed and cause considerable pain. This is *bursitis,* which usually develops over several days (sometimes less) from the time of injury or overuse.

Bursitis in the shoulder usually begins with a nagging ache that develops into more severe pain. Sometimes there is swelling at the tip of the shoulder.

Bursitis in the elbow may result in an egg-sized swelling at the end of the elbow. To help relieve the pain and swelling of bursitis, avoid the movements that caused the problem. Rest is the best treatment.

Tendinitis

Tendinitis is a painful inflammation of the tendons and associated muscles of a joint, often occuring at the shoulder or elbow. It is caused by repeated stress and overuse of the tendons and muscles supporting a specific joint.

Rotator Cuff Tendinitis

This irritation of the shoulder often occurs in baseball and softball pitchers and in people who play racquet sports. Pain is often felt sharply when the arm is held in specific positions. Swelling may be difficult to detect.

Tennis Elbow

This form of tendinitis involves the tendons that attach to the bony area on the outside of the elbow. It is caused by repetititve grasping and squeezing activities. Tennis elbow tends to occur in individuals who, through work or recreational activities, use the forearm muscles in a vigorous and repetitive manner. Among the activities that may cause tennis elbow are playing tennis and other racquet sports, hammering, pruning or using a screwdriver.

What You Can Do

If you experience bursitis or tendinitis, you may get relief from:
- Resting the part of the arm that hurts and avoiding the motion or activity that causes the condition
- Putting ice or cold packs on the area. At the first sign of trouble, apply ice for 15 to 20 minutes at a time, more frequently initially, then three to four times a day for up to 48 hours. Leave ice off for at least 20 minutes between applications. For protection, place a washcloth between bare skin and ice and change the cloth if it becomes wet.
- Taking ibuprofen (Advil, Motrin) or aspirin. **NEVER give aspirin to children/teenagers unless your healthcare provider orders it. It can cause Reye's syndrome, a rare but often fatal condition.**
- Maintaining strength and motion by gently moving the affected part through its full range of motion. The goal is to not let your arm get stiff.

Carpal Tunnel Syndrome

Carpal tunnel syndrome results from compression of the *median nerve* (the major nerve) of the wrist. It is usually caused by continuous activities that involve repetitive use of the wrists and hands, such as computer keyboard use or exposure to vibration (using a hand-held sander, for example). The condition also can be the result of a wrist injury.

Hobbies that often cause symptoms include knitting, gardening, weight-lifting, painting and playing certain musical instruments. Medical conditions that result in swelling of the wrist—diabetes, certain thyroid conditions, pregnancy, arthritis and excessive alcohol intake—also may cause carpal tunnel syndrome.

Neglecting this condition can lead to permanent nerve damage and subsequent loss of hand function.

The pain associated with carpal tunnel syndrome is often described as burning and can be accompanied by tingling, numbness or weakness of the hand, as well as shooting pain (particularly in the thumb and first two fingers). The pain is frequently worse at night and in the early morning. Unless an injury has occurred, the pain usually comes on gradually.

If you suspect that you have carpal tunnel syndrome, try to identify the activity causing the symptoms.

If you discover that the cause is job-related:
- Try modifying your work or workspace. Adjust your desk, chair or keyboard height, or use a wrist pad.
- Avoid repetitive hand motions with your wrists bent.
- Take periodic breaks and stretch your hands and fingers.

For relief:
- Apply ice for 15 to 20 minutes at a time, more frequently initially, then three to four times a day for up to 48 hours. Leave ice off for at least 20 minutes between applications. For protection, place a washcloth between bare skin and ice and change the cloth if it becomes wet.
- Rest and elevate the hand and forearm above the level of the heart.
- Splint the wrist in a neutral position to immobilize it. The splint can be worn 24 hours a day if necessary, or in bed.
- Hang your arm over the bed if problems occur while you sleep.
- Limit your salt intake.
- Try using over-the-counter (OTC) anti-inflammatory medication, such as ibuprofen (Advil, Motrin) or aspirin. **NEVER give aspirin to children/ teenagers unless your healthcare provider orders it. It can cause Reye's syndrome, a rare but often fatal condition.**

Shoulder/Elbow/Wrist/Arm Pain

Do these apply:

- Sudden arm pain is accompanied by one or more of the following:
  - Chest pain
  - Confusion
  - Shortness of breath
  - Sweating
  - Dizziness, weakness or faint feeling
  - Nausea or vomiting
  - Rapid or irregular pulse

  See **Chest Pain,** p. 193.
- Sudden arm pain occurs in a person with a history of high blood pressure, coronary artery disease or heart attack

Seek Emergency Care

- You experience signs of infection:
  - Redness around the area or red streaks leading away from it
  - Swelling
  - Warmth or tenderness
  - Pus
  - Fever of 101° F (38.3° C) or higher
  - Tender or swollen lymph nodes

Call Doctor Now

- There is numbness or tingling in the fingers
- You suspect bursitis or a rotator cuff injury and your symptoms fail to improve after three days of self-care
- You suspect carpal tunnel syndrome and your symptoms do not improve after one month of self-care

Call Doctor

See **What You Can Do, Bursitis and Tendinitis,** p. 253; **What You Can Do, Carpal Tunnel Syndrome,** p. 254.

Apply Self-Care

Leg Pain

Most leg pain is caused by injury or straining the muscles and ligaments of the leg. (See *Strains and Sprains*, p. 67.) Other conditions that cause leg pain are thrombophlebitis, intermittent claudication, shin splints and varicose veins.

Thrombophlebitis

Thrombophlebitis is inflammation and blood clots in the veins, which usually make the leg ache. This aching generally occurs after a period of inactivity, such as prolonged bed rest, taking a long plane ride or sitting through a long meeting. Sometimes it makes a vein in the calf feel firm and tender, but not always. Swelling can also be difficult to detect.

The danger is that a blood clot can break off and go to the lungs. This is called a *pulmonary embolism* and is life-threatening.

If thrombophlebitis is suspected, call your doctor as soon as possible.

Intermittent Claudication

When arteries in the legs narrow, the resulting pain is called *intermittent claudication*. The pain is "intermittent" because it's brought on by exercise and stops after a few minutes of rest.

When arteries narrow, blood cannot reach the muscles efficiently. During increased activity, such as vigorous walking, pain occurs. Older adults and heavy smokers are susceptible to this condition and are sometimes bothered even during such mild exercise as walking.

If you suspect intermittent claudication, consult your doctor.

Varicose Veins

Varicose veins are a common condition in which bluish, swollen and twisted veins develop in the legs. They usually begin to appear on the back of the calves or on the insides of the legs when a person is between the ages of 20 and 40. They are almost always more unsightly than they are disabling. While they can't be cured, they can be treated.

Varicose veins are caused by long-term swelling of the leg veins near the skin's surface. This happens when valves in the leg veins fail and the pumping action of the leg isn't sufficient to return all of the blood to the heart. Blood pools and the veins then become distorted and swollen, particularly during prolonged periods of standing. The feet and ankles may swell and the calves and other affected areas may ache or feel heavy. These symptoms may worsen in women before or during menstruation.

In severe cases, the skin around the veins may itch and develop eczema (see *Eczema*, p. 117) or *ulcers* (open sores).

Varicose veins tend to run in families. They can be aggravated by prolonged standing or sitting, by being overweight and by numerous pregnancies.

What You Can Do

Varicose veins are common and usually mild enough for people to treat on their own. To lessen swelling and discomfort and prevent the condition from worsening:

- Walk regularly.
- Wear elastic support panty hose or hose that reach all the way to the knee. Put them on after elevating your legs for 10 to 15 minutes or as soon as you get out of bed in the morning.
- Wear shoes that support your feet well.
- Lose weight if you are overweight.
- Avoid standing or sitting for prolonged periods. If this can't be avoided, develop a habit of contracting and relaxing your calf and leg muscles, knees and ankles several times a day.
- Avoid crossing your legs, wearing tight clothing or doing anything that inhibits the flow of blood from the legs to the heart.
- Never scratch an itchy varicose vein, because an ulcer can develop.
- If symptoms are bothersome, elevate your legs above chest level at least twice a day for 30 minutes each time. Put pillows under your calves (not knees) so your ankles are higher than your heart.

> See your doctor if, despite self-care measures, varicose veins develop ulcers, worsen or interfere with normal activities. Severe pain, tenderness and warmth in the area may indicate a blood clot. Call your doctor **immediately** and elevate the leg until it can be examined. If you suspect a blood clot, DO NOT massage or rub the leg and avoid unnecessary walking.

Shin Splints

Shin splints is a general term used to describe leg pain on the front of the lower leg caused by overuse. It typically develops after a normally sedentary person overexerts (running three miles the first time out, for example).

When the muscles and tendons that originate from the *tibia* (shin bone) become inflamed from repeated stress, pain and tenderness result, normally occuring on the front or the inside of the shin bone about halfway between the knee and ankle.

What You Can Do

- Rest your legs for at least one week after overexertion.
- Apply ice for 15 to 20 minutes at a time, more frequently initially, then three to four times a day for up to 48 hours. Leave ice off for at least 20 minutes between applications. For protection, place a washcloth between bare skin and ice and change the cloth if it becomes wet.
- Take aspirin or ibuprofen (Advil, Motrin). **NEVER give aspirin to children/ teenagers unless your healthcare provider orders it. It can cause Reye's syndrome, a rare but often fatal condition.**
- When the pain is gone, do exercises to gently stretch the calf muscles.
- Wear high-quality athletic shoes, designed specifically for your sport of choice.
- Do not run for two to four weeks, then gradually increase speed and distance.

If symptoms persist, **call your doctor**.

Final Notes

Severe, sharp pain one or two inches (2.54 or 5 cm) below the knee and tenderness in the shin bone are typical symptoms of a *stress fracture*. This tends to occur with an increase in athletic training where the legs are working overtime. Rest is the treatment for a stress fracture. Casts are not used. Complete healing takes four to six weeks. Call your doctor if you have severe leg pain.

Leg Pain
Do these apply:

- There is an area in your leg or calf that is:
  - Distinctly reddened
  - Painful or tender to touch or when walking
  - Hardened like a cord
  - Swollen or warm
- You have a varicose vein with:
  - Bleeding you can't control by applying pressure, or you are on an anticoagulant
  - A rapidly spreading bruise

Call Doctor Now

- You have a new ulcer over a varicose vein or a vein that bled recently
- Your varicose veins are worsening, have failed to improve with medical therapy or are interfering with your daily activities
- Leg pain is brought on by exercise; the pain stops when exercise is completed
- Pain from shin splints continues in spite of self-care

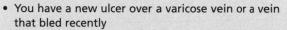

Call Doctor

See **What You Can Do, Varicose Veins,** p. 257;
What You Can Do, Shin Splints, p. 258.

Apply Self-Care

Knee Pain

Knees are very delicate and vulnerable to injury. Ligaments and tendons that attach leg muscles and bones are easily sprained or torn when the knee is overextended, twisted or pushed from the side. (See *Strains and Sprains*, p. 67.) *Meniscus cartilage* (the crescent-shaped cartilage that is the shock absorber of the knee) can wear down, become too soft and tear from overuse or disease. (See *Arthritis*, p. 242.) The kneecap (*patella*) is a thin bone covering the front of the joint that can be broken or displaced.

- Exercises that strengthen and stretch muscles and ligaments around the knee and upper leg are your best prevention. Walking, with warm-up and cool-down exercises, is one of the best choices. (See *Staying Active*, p. 330.)
- Avoid deep knee bends.
- Avoid running downhill.
- Do not wear shoes with cleats when playing contact sports.
- If you have arthritis, take your medicine as directed.
- Wear stabilizing and supportive shoes; avoid or limit wearing high heels.
- Avoid repeated, jarring motions on hard surfaces.
- Control your weight. (See *Eating Right*, p. 331.)

- If knee pain occurs after an injury, rest and immobilize your knee. Start RICE treatment immediately. (See *Strains and Sprains*, p. 67.)
- Pay attention to the pain and avoid any activity that may cause or increase it.
- Use a cane to take weight off the sore knee.
- DO NOT put a pillow under only your knee at night; this may cause the joint to stiffen. Elevate and support the entire leg with pillows.
- If pain is caused by arthritis, see *Arthritis*, p. 242.
- Take aspirin or ibuprofen (Advil, Motrin) to ease pain and inflammation. **NEVER give aspirin to children/teenagers unless your healthcare provider orders it. It can cause Reye's syndrome, a rare but often fatal condition.**

Knee Pain

Do these apply:

- Severe pain follows an injury
- The knee is deformed or bent in an abnormal way
- Bone protrudes or can be seen through the skin

Immobilize the knee. Elevate the leg if possible. Apply a sterile bandage if the wound is open. Apply ice. For protection, place a washcloth between bare skin and ice.

See ***Broken Bones,*** p. 70.

no   **yes**

Seek Emergency Care

Apply Emergency First Aid

- You are unable to bear any weight on the knee
- Your knee is unstable, wobbly or very weak
- A popping sound, snapping or locking sensation occurs during or after a knee injury
- There is knee pain with swelling or pain in the calf
- The knee is red, painful and feels hot when touched
- There is knee pain with fever from no other apparent cause
- Severe knee pain is present even when you're not standing or putting weight on it

no   **yes**

Call Doctor Now

- Moderate knee pain is not improved by 2 or 3 days of self-care
- Knee pain improves but continues after 6 weeks of self-care
- You have been diagnosed with arthritis and new knee pain occurs (see ***Arthritis,*** p. 242)

no   **yes**

Call Doctor

See ***What You Can Do,*** p. 260.

Apply Self-Care

Ankle Pain

Your ankle is a very complex, versatile joint. It is designed to keep your foot aimed in one direction while supporting the total weight of your body when you take a step. When it is not under pressure, the ankle allows the foot to flex and rotate. Problems develop when the ankle rotates under pressure, such as twisting your ankle when you step off a curb. The joint can also be injured by repeated or sustained high pressure, such as running on hard surfaces or supporting excess body weight.

Ankle pain may be due to a sprain in one or more ligaments (see *Strains and Sprains,* p. 67), inflammation in a tendon (see *Achilles Tendinitis,* p. 266), a fracture in the ankle bone (see *Broken Bones,* p. 70), or damage to the sliding surfaces in the joint (see *Arthritis,* p. 242). Whatever the cause of your ankle pain, it is a message to relieve the pressure, rest the joint and provide support. Continuing to walk on a painful ankle without treatment may increase damage and delay recovery.

Ankle Swelling

There is frequently swelling with pain in an ankle injury due to damage to muscles and ligaments. Ankle swelling without pain or injury is often from the accumulation of fluid that has leaked out of the *circulatory* (blood and lymph) *system.* Fluid retention (*edema*) is caused by the build-up of excess pressure in the veins that forces the fluid out into the surrounding tissue.

Anything that interferes with the flow of blood from the legs back to the heart can make the ankle swell. Minimizing certain activities—such as prolonged standing or sitting with pressure on the back of your legs, wearing constrictive clothing such as garters or knee-high stockings—treating varicose veins (see *Varicose Veins,* p. 256), or reducing salt or sodium in the diet may help relieve swelling. When ankle swelling is a sign of a more serious health problem—such as a blood clot (see *Thrombophlebitis,* p. 256), heart failure, liver or kidney disease—treatment requires medical attention with individualized self-care.

Prevention

- Wear shoes, clothing and sporting gear that fit well, have adequate support and are appropriate for each activity.
- Avoid shoes with cleats when you play contact sports.
- Wear stabilizing shoes. Avoid or limit wearing high heels.
- Avoid trauma, overuse or jarring activities such as running on hard surfaces.
- Exercise regularly. Always do warm-up and cool-down exercises.
- Walk or do leg exercises a few minutes every hour when standing or sitting for long periods.
- Avoid wearing clothing that restricts blood flow. Wear support stockings.
- Control your weight and limit sodium in your diet if it seems to be a factor. (See *Eating Right*, p. 331.)
- Take all medications as directed. Check with your doctor before decreasing or stopping any prescription drugs. (See *Using Medications*, p. 324.)

What You Can Do

- If ankle pain follows an injury, start **RICE** immediately. (See *Strains and Sprains*, p. 67.)
- Use a cane or crutches to take pressure off the ankle if necessary.
- Support an unstable ankle with an elastic wrap. Wrap the ankle firmly, not tightly, with an elastic bandage. Start just above the toes, wrapping around the foot and then around the ankle in a figure-eight turn. Repeat figure-eight turns until the foot, ankle and lower leg (not the toes) are bandaged. Do not wrap too tightly or obstruct the blood flow. Loosen and rewrap the ankle periodically if there is any tingling, numbness, a change of color in the toes or increased swelling.
- Do not wrap a child's foot; the risk of cutting off circulation is too high.
- Take aspirin or ibuprofen (Advil, Motrin) to ease pain and inflammation. (Follow instructions on the package.) **NEVER give aspirin to children/ teenagers unless your healthcare provider orders it. It can cause Reye's syndrome, a rare but often fatal condition**.
- Elevate swollen ankles as often as possible with the feet above heart level.
- When pain decreases, exercise the ankle a few times a day:
  - Sit with the leg hanging freely; gently rotate the foot and ankle.
  - As the ankle becomes stronger, support it with elastic wrap and walk on tiptoes, then on your heels, to stretch and strengthen the joint.
  - Gradually increase the duration and frequency of exercise periods.

See **Decision helper,** p. 264.

Ankle Pain

Do these apply:

- Bone protrudes or can be seen through torn skin
- The ankle appears to be twisted, out of joint, or bent in an abnormal position
- Severe pain follows a serious ankle injury

Immobilize the ankle. Elevate the leg if possible. Apply a sterile bandage if the wound is open. Apply ice. For protection, place a washcloth between bare skin and ice.

See ***Broken Bones,*** p. 70.

no   yes

Seek Emergency Care

Apply Emergency First Aid

- You have severe pain or an inability to bear weight for more than two hours
- Immediate pain occurs with a popping, cracking or tearing sound during an injury
- There is a feeling of instability in the ankle
- Swollen ankles occur with chronic kidney, heart or liver disease
- The ankle is painful, red and warm to touch or you have a fever of 101° F (38.3° C) or higher

no   yes

Call Doctor Now

- You have ankle pain and difficulty bearing weight for 72 hours or longer
- Pain and swelling or discomfort occurs in other joints

no   yes

Call Doctor

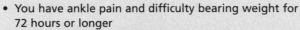

See ***What You Can Do,*** p. 263.

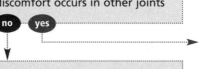

Apply Self-Care

Heel Pain

Most heel pain is due to injury from repeated stress and trauma to the tissues that connect the bones of the feet and lower leg. These tissues bear your total body weight. They get pulled in steps, twists and turns; pounded in activities such as running and jogging; and often are stuffed into poorly fitting shoes with inadequate support. Is it any wonder that they sometimes hurt?

There are three primary causes of heel pain:

Plantar Fasciitis

The *plantar fascia* is a tough band of tissue that stretches from your heel bone to the ball of your foot. It can become inflamed when it is over-stretched or torn by feet that flatten or roll inward with walking; feet with high arches; excessive running or sudden turning.

Shoes that fit improperly, offer inadequate support, or have soles that are too stiff or thin increase your risk of plantar fasciitis. This pain is usually felt in small spots just behind the ball of your foot, right in front of your heel or along either side of the sole. There may be some swelling in the painful areas. Repeated plantar fasciitis or extreme overstretching can lead to the development of calcified fascia splinters or *bone spurs* in the area.

Bursitis

Bursae (*bursa* for one) are little fluid-filled sacs at the joints that help muscles slide over other muscles or bones. The *calcaneal bursae* surround the back and underside of the heel. Inflammation is most often due to pressure from shoes or landing hard on the heel. Pain and swelling are felt directly beneath or on the back of the heel.

Achilles Tendinitis

The Achilles tendon is an elastic, fibrous band that attaches the muscles in the calf of the leg to the heel bone. Inflammation can be caused by shortening and lack of flexibility in the tendon, repeated hard contact or pounding of the foot, or unstable stepping or turning of the foot.

These factors often result from wearing shoes with high heels or inadequate support or shock absorption in the heel; insufficient warm-up and stretching prior to exercising, exercising on hard surfaces, or turning the foot as it strikes the ground. Achilles tendinitis can involve a sharp, burning pain or a dull ache in the lower back of the leg and heel.

Prevention

- Wear shoes that fit properly and have adequate arch support, are flexible and have sufficient padding in the heel cup.
- Wear footwear appropriate to the sport or exercise.
- Ease pressure areas with moleskin patches.
- Remember to stretch and warm up before exercising, including prolonged walking on hard surfaces. (See *Staying Active*, p. 330.)
- Maintain a normal weight. (See *Eating Right*, p. 331.)

What You Can Do

- Rest the area. Stop or decrease any activity that causes heel pain.
- Apply ice for 15 to 20 minutes at a time, more frequently initially, then three to four times a day for up to 48 hours. Leave ice off for at least 20 minutes between applications. For protection, place a washcloth between bare skin and ice and change the cloth if it becomes wet.
- Take aspirin or ibuprofen (Advil, Motrin) to ease pain and inflammation. (Follow directions on the package.) **NEVER give aspirin to children/ teenagers unless your healthcare provider orders it. It can cause Reye's syndrome, a rare but often fatal condition.**
- Wear extra padding in shoes to protect and support the tender area.
- Try slow, gentle stretching of the back of the leg for Achilles tendinitis; stop if the pain starts or increases.

Decision
helper

Heel Pain
Do these apply:

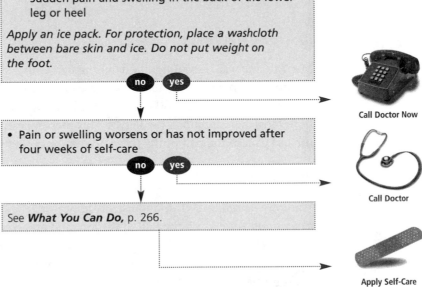

- Heel injury occurs along with any of the following:
  - Severe pain
  - An inability to bear weight after two hours
  - An inability to lift the foot or stand on tiptoe
  - Sudden pain and swelling in the back of the lower leg or heel

Apply an ice pack. For protection, place a washcloth between bare skin and ice. Do not put weight on the foot.

no   yes

Call Doctor Now

- Pain or swelling worsens or has not improved after four weeks of self-care

no   yes

Call Doctor

See **What You Can Do,** p. 266.

Apply Self-Care

Foot Pain

Most foot pain is caused by shoes that do not fit well. Problems can be easily prevented and usually respond well to self-care.

Morton's Neuroma

Morton's neuroma is swelling in one of the nerves that supplies sensation to the front half of your foot and toes. These nerves run parallel along the five long bones in your foot and end in the toes. Tight-fitting shoes squeeze the bones together and pinch the nerves. This pressure can cause swelling with intense pain in the ball of the foot and numbness between the toes.

Plantar Warts

Warts are caused by a virus and usually appear on the surface of the skin. A *plantar wart* appears on the ball of the foot and grows inward so it feels like you are stepping on a pebble. These warts look like an area of thick skin with small black dots scattered throughout and a center core beneath the surface. Unfortunately, they tend to recur. (See *Warts,* p. 136; *Skin Symptoms,* p. 114.)

Calluses

Calluses are hard, thickened layers of dead skin caused by friction. They often follow blisters and are a result of the skin thickening to protect an area against ongoing pressure. The ball of the foot is a very common site for calluses, especially if you wear high heels. Calluses can also occur on the hands, fingers, toes or anywhere friction occurs.

- Wear shoes that fit correctly. Avoid shoes that are too tight or loose, or that rub or slip.
- Wear high heels as little as possible. If unavoidable, alternate with pairs of shoes that have lower heels.
- Ease pressure areas with moleskin patches (available at drugstores).
- Limit your risk of contracting or spreading a foot virus by wearing slippers or bath shoes in public areas and avoiding going barefoot.

What You Can Do

- Take aspirin or ibuprofen (Advil, Motrin) to ease pain and inflammation. (Follow directions on the package.) **NEVER give aspirin to children/ teenagers unless your healthcare provider orders it. It can cause Reye's syndrome, a rare but often fatal condition.**
- For calluses, soak your feet in warm water for 15 minutes, then rub the area with a pumice stone to remove thickened skin. Follow this treatment by applying moisturizing lotion. Repeat the process daily until calluses disappear.
- Warts and calluses can be removed with an adhesive patch containing 40 percent salicylic acid, which is available at most drugstores. Follow package directions.

Decision *helper*

Foot Pain
Do these apply:

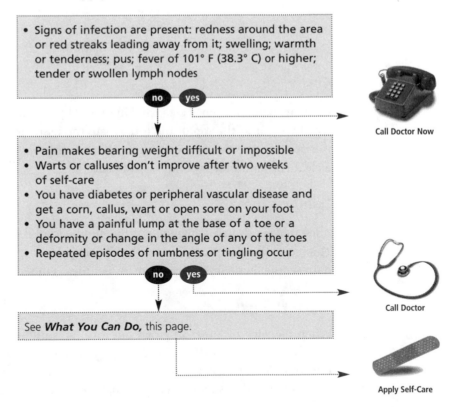

- Signs of infection are present: redness around the area or red streaks leading away from it; swelling; warmth or tenderness; pus; fever of 101° F (38.3° C) or higher; tender or swollen lymph nodes

no   yes

Call Doctor Now

- Pain makes bearing weight difficult or impossible
- Warts or calluses don't improve after two weeks of self-care
- You have diabetes or peripheral vascular disease and get a corn, callus, wart or open sore on your foot
- You have a painful lump at the base of a toe or a deformity or change in the angle of any of the toes
- Repeated episodes of numbness or tingling occur

no   yes

Call Doctor

See *What You Can Do,* this page.

Apply Self-Care

Toe Pain

Although toes are small, they contain many bones, ligaments, tendons and joints. In addition to being susceptible to all the diseases and injuries that occur in larger joints and bones, toes are often pinched, stubbed and jammed, and have things dropped on them. What's more, they usually receive very little attention and care until they hurt.

Bunions

A *bunion* is swelling of the joint at the base of the big toe. The toe turns inward toward the other toes and may even overlap. This forces the joint outward, making it rub against shoes. Thick skin forms in the pressure area and, if the pressure is not relieved, a bony spur develops. The deformed joint often becomes inflamed and very painful.

Corns

Corns are hard, thickened areas of skin caused by pressure or friction. Corns usually occur at the top of the toes where the tissue is squeezed between the bones in the toe and tight-fitting shoes. Corns are usually yellow with a clear core and may become soft, moist or red.

Hammer Toes

A toe that bends up permanently at the middle joint is called a *hammer toe*. This condition is usually caused by wearing shoes that are too tight or narrow. The tendency to develop hammer toes is inherited.

Ingrown Toenails

When the edge of a toenail grows out into the soft flesh surrounding the nail bed, there is usually inflammation, swelling, pain and a high risk of infection. *Ingrown toenails* are caused by trimming the sides of the toenail too short, wearing shoes that are too tight, or injury of the toe or toenail.

Prevention

- Wear shoes that fit properly and have good arch support. Low-heeled shoes with a roomy toe box are best.
- If there is a high risk of trauma or injury to your toes, wear shoes with a reinforced toe box.
- Cut toenails *straight across*. File sides slightly to prevents sharp edges from catching on socks or stockings.

What You Can Do

- Relieve pressure over a painful area by wearing shoes that are roomy or open.
- Cushion the area with moleskin or pads to ease friction.
- Take aspirin or ibuprofen (Advil, Motrin) to relieve pain and inflammation. (Follow directions and warnings on package.) **NEVER give aspirin to children/teenagers unless your healthcare provider orders it. It can cause Reye's syndrome, a rare but often fatal condition.**
- For corns, soak your feet in warm water for 15 minutes, then rub the area with a pumice stone to remove thickened skin. Follow treatment by applying a moisturizing lotion. Repeat this process daily until the corn disappears.
- Corns may be removed with "corn plasters," adhesive patches containing 40 percent salicylic acid, which are available at most drugstores. Put the patch on the area at night after soaking your foot. Remove it in the morning and rub off the whitened skin. Protect with a moleskin patch (available at drugstores).
- For an ingrown toenail:
    - Soak your foot in warm water for 10 to 15 minutes.
    - Wedge a small piece of cotton under the corner of the nail to train it to grow outward.
    - Repeat this process daily until the nail has grown out and can be trimmed straight across.

  NOTE: Do not self-treat corns or ingrown toenails if you are diabetic or have peripheral vascular disease.

See *Decision helper,* p. 272.

272

SECTION 4: HEALTH CONCERNS

Toe Pain
Do these apply:

- Signs of infection are present in an ingrown toenail: redness around the area or red streaks leading away from it; swelling; warmth or tenderness; pus; fever of 101° F (38.3° C) or higher; tender or swollen lymph nodes

Call Doctor Now

- You have a chronic illness such as diabetes or circulatory problems and a corn, wart, callus or open sore appears on your toe
- You have sudden severe pain in the big toe and no previous diagnosis of gout (see **Gout, Major Types Of Arthritis,** p. 243)
- Severe pain interferes with walking or daily activities
- Your big toe begins to overlap the second toe
- Symptoms worsen or do not improve after two weeks of self-care

Call Doctor

See **What You Can Do,** p. 271.

Apply Self-Care

Women's Health

Sound diet, regular exercise and plenty of sleep are key elements of a healthy lifestyle. But even these are no guarantee of lasting health. Every woman needs to make a commitment to herself to screen regularly for potential health problems.

Breast exams, blood pressure screenings and Pap smears are just a few of the preventive tests that could save your life some day. What's more, catching problems early means that treatment is less expensive, least invasive and most successful. See Screening Guidelines, *p. 337.*

Breast Lumps

About half of all women develop a breast lump before they reach menopause. The vast majority of these lumps are harmless. In fact, 80 percent of all lumps that are *biopsied* (tested) are *benign* (not cancerous). But some lumps are *malignant* (cancerous). With early detection, there may be more options for treatment and a better chance to catch any cancer that may spread to other parts of the body.

Although some risk factors for breast cancer have been identified, a large percentage of women who develop the disease have no known risk factors. Having one or more of the following risk factors *does not* mean that breast cancer is inevitable:

- Being over 50 years of age
- Having a mother or sister who has had breast cancer, especially if the cancer was in both breasts or developed at an early age
- Beginning menstruation early and/or going through menopause late
- Having a first child after the age of 30, or having no children
- Having a previous diagnosis of breast cancer

A mass in the breast tissue may be hard or soft and can have a smooth or irregular contour. The size can range from microscopic to quite large. While some lumps are tender or painful, most are painless.

Some women have naturally lumpy breasts (called *benign fibrocystic breasts*). Fibrocystic breasts feel lumpy and tender, and several lumps may be detected. The lumps usually increase in size just before menstruation and then disappear for awhile when your period (*menses*) begins.

Fibroadenomas are also common and are characterized by a rubbery, firm, smooth mass. They are most often found in women under 30 and are almost always benign. Surgical removal of the lump cures the problem.

Screening Program

Monthly breast self-examination

By taking a few minutes to check your own breasts each month, you will become familiar with how they normally feel, enabling you to identify changes. If you still menstruate, the best time to examine yourself is two to three days after your menstrual period has ended. If you no longer menstruate, choose the same day each month to do the exam (the first day of the month, for example). Follow the six steps on page 275. Call your doctor if you discover any lumps or discharge from the nipples or if you have any concerns.

Professional breast examination

Breast exams are recommended for all women during routine checkups every three years beginning at age 20 and annually beginning at age 40 (or age 35 if there is a family history of premenopausal breast cancer in a mother or sister). A discussion of your breast cancer risk factors is advisable at this time.

Regular mammography

A *mammogram*—an x-ray of the breast—is generally recommended for all women beginning at age 40. It is not recommended that women under 40 have routine screening by mammogram unless there is a history of premenopausal breast cancer in one's mother or sister.

Fibrocystic Breast Lumps

Fibrocystic breast lumps do not require treatment. Most associated pain or discomfort can be relieved by:

• Using mild analgesics such as aspirin, ibuprofen (Advil, Motrin) and acetaminophen (Tylenol). **NEVER give aspirin to children/teenagers unless your healthcare provider orders it. It can cause Reye's syndrome, a rare but often fatal condition.**

• Wearing a larger or more supportive bra during the premenstrual phase

Examining your breasts on a monthly basis is very important because the presence of cysts may make it more difficult to find a potentially dangerous lump. However, women who have benign breast lumps or cysts are not at higher risk of breast cancer.

Final Notes

Call your doctor as soon as possible if you think you have a breast lump, or if you have unusual nipple discharge or unusual pain or tenderness in your breast. The call could save your life.

Breast Self-Exam
Make these six steps a monthly habit:

In front of the mirror

1. Stand up straight with your arms at your sides; visually inspect your breasts. Check nipples for discharge or puckering, dimpling or scaling of the skin.

2. Clasp your hands behind your head and press your hands forward. (See Figure 14.) You will feel your chest muscles tighten. Check for any change in the normal shape and contour of your breasts.

3. Press your hands firmly on your hips and lean forward. At the same time, move your shoulders and elbows forward. As in step 2, check for any change in shape or contour that seems different from the way your breasts normally look.

In the shower or bath

4. Raise one arm and with your opposite hand, press your breast firmly with your fingers flat. (See Figure 15.) Make small circles, moving from the outer edge toward the nipple each time until you have worked your way around the entire breast. Check for any unusual lump or mass, especially between the breast and underarm (including the underarm).

5. Gently squeeze the nipple. Check for a discharge. If you have a discharge at any time, call your doctor.

Lying down

6. Repeat steps 4 and 5 lying on your back. Slip a pillow or folded towel under the shoulder of your raised arm. This flattens the breast and makes examination easier.

Repeat steps 4, 5 and 6 for the other breast.

For information from the National Cancer Institute, call 1-800-4-CANCER.
Adapted from the National Institutes of Health

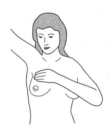

Figure 14

Figure 15

Pap Smear

Examination of the female reproductive organs (a pelvic examination) gives your doctor essential information about your gynecological health. One of the most important elements of this exam is the Pap smear, which tests for the presence of cancer in the cervix.

A *speculum,* a plastic or metal duck-billed instrument, spreads the walls of the vagina so that a scraping of the cervix and a sample of cells from the passage within the cervix can be taken.

These cells are then sent to a laboratory where a trained technician studies them under a microscope and reports the findings to your doctor. Your doctor can help you interpret your results.

Pap smears detect about 90 percent of cervical cancers, making them reliable screening procedures. Since cervical cancers are slow-growing, there is an excellent chance that regular Pap smears will detect cancer before it spreads.

Annual Pap smears are recommended for all women by most national authorities. Women over the age of 65 and women who have had hysterectomies should discuss screening recommendations with their doctors.

A woman should have her first Pap smear three years after the onset of sexual activity, or no later than 21 years of age. (See *Screening Guidelines,* p. 337.)

A woman should not have a Pap smear during her period because menstrual blood obscures the specimen and alters results. For two days before the exam, most doctors advise against douching, sexual intercourse, vaginal lubricants or medication applied within the vagina (unless otherwise directed by your doctor).

Menstrual Cycle

When a woman knows her own body, she knows what is "normal" for her. Women's menstrual cycles can vary from 21 to 40 days from the first day of one period to the first day of the next. Bleeding typically lasts for four to seven days. Changes in bleeding may be normal, as with aging, or abnormal.

Irregular Periods

Bleeding between periods

Most women do not experience bleeding or "spotting" between monthly menstrual periods, but some do. Women who have an *intrauterine birth control device* (IUD) inserted are especially likely to experience occasional spotting.

The key is how heavy the flow of blood is and how often it occurs. If the bleeding is light and occasional, there is probably no cause for alarm. If the bleeding is heavy or occurs for three or more months in a row, a doctor should investigate. Bleeding between periods can be a sign of some serious conditions, such as *fibroids* (benign uterine growths), certain types of cancers or an abnormal pregnancy.

If bleeding is light:
- Use pads or tampons.
- Avoid taking aspirin, which may prolong bleeding.

If bleeding is heavy:
- Contact your healthcare provider.

Missed/irregular periods (*Amenorrhea*)

Pregnancy is, of course, the number one reason for a woman who is not yet menopausal to miss a period. Home-pregnancy kits are fairly accurate as early as six to nine days after a missed period, and a blood test can determine pregnancy nine days after conception.

A positive test response is more likely to be accurate than a negative response. Unless you have another menstrual period, it's best not to believe the results of a negative test until it has been repeated.

Other causes of missed or irregular menstrual periods include:

- Stress: Emotional or physical stress can cause irregular periods.
- Obesity or excessive dieting: Although these may seem like opposites, they have the same result when it comes to missed periods. If either is severe enough, periods may stop altogether.
- Strenuous exercise: Women athletes often have irregular periods caused by hormonal imbalances. This imbalance may contribute to a loss of calcium in the bones. (See *Osteoporosis*, p. 287.)
- Medications: Some medications may cause irregular periods.
- Menopause: If you are in your 40s or older, menopause could be the reason for missed periods. During this time, menstrual periods may be irregular before they stop altogether. Your doctor can determine whether your symptoms are related to menopause. (See *Menopause*, p. 286.)
- Diseases: Some diseases, such as *hyperthyroidism*, can cause missed periods, but these are relatively rare.

What You Can Do

Try to determine why you may be missing periods:

- If your period is more than two weeks late and you've been sexually active (even if you've been using a birth control method), have a pregnancy test to determine whether you are pregnant.
- Lifestyle changes may be in order if you feel the cause is obesity, excessive dieting or exercising. (See *Getting and Staying Healthy*, p. 330.)
- If stress is a factor in your missed periods, focus on the cause of the stress rather than on the symptom. (See *Stress*, p. 314.)
- Keep a good diary with the dates and details of your periods to report to your doctor.

See **Decision helper,** p. 283.

Painful Periods

Menstrual cramps

Menstrual cramps are medically known as *dysmenorrhea*, a Greek term meaning "difficult and painful menstruation." Medicine has finally caught up with what women have known all along—that menstrual cramps are physiological, not psychological.

Some degree of menstrual pain is considered normal, particularly in the first three days of the menstrual cycle.

Primary dysmenorrhea is common and caused by contractions of the uterus. Elevated levels of *prostaglandin,* a chemical produced primarily in the uterus, is thought to be responsible for menstrual cramps and other symptoms. These symptoms may include nausea and vomiting, fatigue, diarrhea, lower back pain, headaches and—in severe cases—fainting.

Secondary dysmenorrhea is the result of an underlying disorder such as endometriosis, pelvic inflammatory disease or fibroid tumors. (See *Endometriosis,* p. 280, *Fibroid Tumors,* p. 280 and *Pelvic Inflammatory Disease,* p. 281.)

More than half of all women have at least mild menstrual cramps and about 10 percent experience severe cramping that interferes with their daily activities.

Symptoms lessen for some women after childbirth or as they get older.

What You Can Do

For relief of menstrual cramps:
- Try over-the-counter (OTC) nonsteroidal anti-inflammatory drugs (NSAIDs), such as ibuprofen (Advil, Motrin) and aspirin, to inhibit the production of prostaglandins and relieve discomfort and cramping. Acetaminophen (Tylenol) may help some women. You may need to try different drugs at different doses to find effective pain relief. NSAIDs and aspirin should not be used by anyone with a history of ulcers, gastrointestinal bleeding or other bleeding disorders without consulting a doctor. (See *Home Pharmacy,* p. 325.) **NEVER give aspirin to children/teenagers unless your healthcare provider orders it. It can cause Reye's syndrome, a rare but often fatal condition.**
- Exercise regularly.
- Eat a healthy diet. Avoid salty foods for a few days before menstruation to help reduce premenstrual bloating.
- Avoid coffee and alcohol, but drink lots of fluids.
- Try applying heat—using a heating pad set to low or hot water bottles; warm baths may also help.
- Try switching to sanitary napkins. Tampons contribute to menstrual cramping in some women.
- If you have an intrauterine device (IUD), consider changing your contraceptive. Some women find that IUDs make menstrual cramping worse. A barrier method or birth control pills may work better for you. Oral contraceptives decrease the production of prostaglandins and may minimize cramps. (See *Birth Control,* p. 303.)

Endometriosis

Endometriosis is a common condition that occurs when *endometrial tissue* (the lining of the uterus) grows outside the uterus, typically in the fallopian tubes, ovaries or pelvic cavity. This tissue responds to monthly hormonal changes just like the normal endometrial tissue inside the uterus, resulting in bleeding and pain. No one knows for sure what causes this condition.

Diagnosis is difficult because the symptoms are not the same in all women. Typical symptoms include pelvic pain, menstrual cramps, irregular bleeding and infertility.

Women whose menstrual cramps become increasingly painful and occur just before and at the beginning of the menstrual flow may have endometriosis. Abnormal uterine bleeding, especially heavy flows, rectal bleeding and pain during sexual intercourse also are common symptoms.

See your doctor if you suspect endometriosis. The objectives of any medical treatment are to control pain and improve or protect fertility. For mild to moderate cases, the common treatment is hormonal therapy. For more severe cases, surgery may be required.

Fibroid tumors

Fibroid tumors—or fibroids—consist of bundles of smooth muscle and connective tissue that develop slowly within the wall of the uterus. These growths are almost always noncancerous and can vary from the size of a pea to that of a grapefruit (the size of the entire uterine cavity).

More than 75 percent of women with fibroids experience no symptoms. When symptoms do occur, they may include:
- Heavy, prolonged or painful menstrual periods
- Frequent urination or incontinence
- Abdominal pain or pressure in the lower back
- Constipation
- Pain during sexual intercourse

Fibroids can remain unchanged for long periods and often stop growing without intervention. On the other hand, they have the potential to develop into multiple, fast-growing tumors, and—in rare cases—can be *malignant* (cancerous).

If you have symptoms of fibroids, call your doctor. Treatment can range from birth control pills (to help control vaginal bleeding) to surgery. Sometimes the tumor itself can be surgically removed (*myomectomy*), but in some cases a *hysterectomy* (surgical removal of the uterus) may be required.

Pelvic inflammatory disease (PID)

Pelvic inflammatory disease is a potentially serious infection of the reproductive organs that should not be ignored.

Pelvic pain with a heavy or foul-smelling vaginal discharge and/or a fever of 101° F (38.3° C) or greater are symptoms of PID. The condition can cause chronic pelvic pain and infertility.

If you have more than one sexual partner you are at greater risk of contracting all sexually transmitted diseases. Some of these can progress to pelvic infection.

Pelvic pain that begins shortly before or during a menstrual period is probably menstrual cramps. If there is any doubt, see your doctor.

See **Decision helper,** p. 283.

PMS and PMDD

Premenstrual syndrome (PMS) is a medical condition involving both emotional and physical symptoms, which generally occurs seven to 10 days prior to menstruation. The precise cause of PMS is unknown, but it is thought to be caused by changes in hormone (*estrogen* and *progesterone*) levels.

An estimated 90 percent of menstruating women experience some form of PMS. About 10 percent of these women have severe problems associated with hormonal monthly changes, called *premenstrual dysphoric disorder* [PMDD]. Most women who suffer from PMS and PMDD are between 30 and 45 years of age.

Note Your Symptoms

Symptoms range from mild to almost disabling, and may vary in severity from month to month. They usually occur a week or so before menstrual bleeding begins and end a few days after the period starts.

Symptoms may include headaches (including migraines), back and muscle pain, swollen or tender breasts, unusual food cravings, bloating, weight gain, diarrhea and/or constipation, extreme moodiness, depression, anger or irritability, anxiety and tension, insomnia and fatigue, reduced concentration or coordination, and a diminished sex drive.

Asking yourself a few questions may help determine whether you are suffering from PMS or PMDD:

- Do you have the same or similar symptoms every month?
- Do symptoms improve or disappear soon after menstrual bleeding begins?
- Do you have at least one symptom-free week each month? Answering "no" may indicate other problems such as endometriosis, vaginal or pelvic infection, or fibroids. (See index, *Women's Health*.)

What You Can Do

- Keep a diary for two or three months, recording the timing and severity of symptoms. This information will help your doctor diagnose your problem and start an effective treatment program.
- Exercise regularly. Aerobic exercise—walking, riding a bike, swimming and climbing stairs—seems to work best to relieve symptoms.
- Eat a diet of fresh fruits and vegetables, whole grains and minimal fat.
- Eat smaller meals every three or four hours.
- Limit salt (to reduce water retention) and sugar (to reduce blood sugar fluctuations).
- Avoid caffeine, alcohol and tobacco.
- Reduce stress in your life as much as possible. (See *Stress*, p. 314.)
- Try over-the-counter (OTC) medication (aspirin, acetaminophen or ibuprofen) to relieve discomfort. **NEVER give aspirin to children/ teenagers unless your healthcare provider orders it. It can cause Reye's syndrome, a rare but often fatal condition.**
- Talk about your problem with your family, friends or other PMS sufferers. Consider joining a PMS or PMDD support group.

Treatment options

Some women's symptoms are severe enough to require professional care. While no cure has been found for PMS or PMDD, and doctors differ on treatment, medications that may be prescribed to relieve symptoms include:

- Diuretics (medications known as water pills that increase fluid loss) to reduce water retention and bloating
- Antidepressant or antianxiety drugs to help ease emotional symptoms
- Progesterone (a female hormone), in combination with estrogen, to treat physical symptoms such as breast pain and bloating

The best defense against PMS and PMDD is to learn as much as you can about the conditions and how either might affect you; then begin experimenting with ways to manage and minimize the symptoms. Within a few months, chances are that you'll notice your symptoms have improved.

Decision *helper*

Irregular/Painful Periods
Do these apply:

- You have sudden, sharp, severe or persistent pain in the lower abdomen or pelvis
- Bright red bleeding saturates one pad or tampon hourly or more frequently, accompanied by dizziness or faint feeling when you stand up

no   yes

Seek Emergency Care

- Vaginal bleeding is heavy and requires an hourly change of tampon or pad
- A pregnancy test is positive and you have vaginal bleeding or spotting, abdominal/pelvic pain or cramps, unusual backache or diarrhea
- You have pelvic pain and a fever

no   yes

Call Doctor Now

- You suspect:
  - Endometriosis (see p. 280)
  - Fibroid tumors (see p. 280)
  - Pelvic inflammatory disease (see p. 281)
- There are unexplained changes in your menstrual pattern

no   yes

Call Doctor

- You are sexually active and your period is more than two weeks late

See *What You Can Do, Bleeding Between Periods,* p. 277; *What You Can Do, Missed/Irregular Periods,* p. 278; *What You Can Do, Menstrual Cramps,* p. 279.

Apply Self-Care

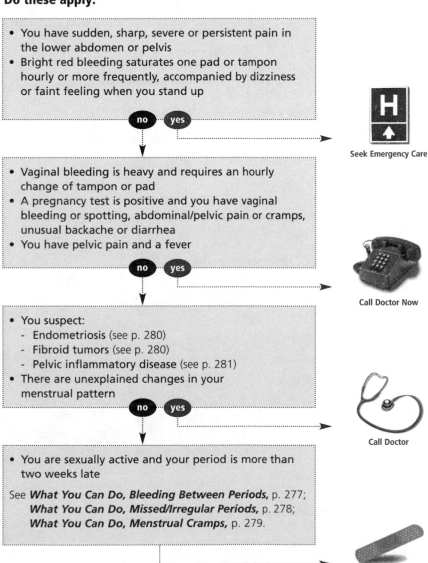

PMS/PMDD
Do these apply:

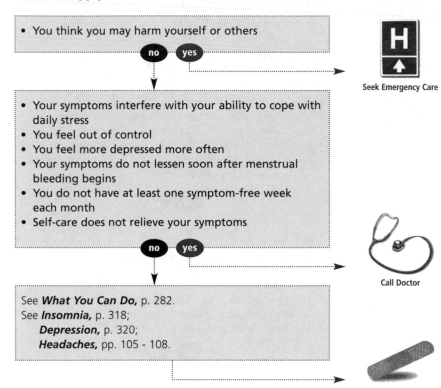

- You think you may harm yourself or others

no · yes

Seek Emergency Care

- Your symptoms interfere with your ability to cope with daily stress
- You feel out of control
- You feel more depressed more often
- Your symptoms do not lessen soon after menstrual bleeding begins
- You do not have at least one symptom-free week each month
- Self-care does not relieve your symptoms

no · yes

Call Doctor

See *What You Can Do,* p. 282.
See *Insomnia,* p. 318;
   Depression, p. 320;
   Headaches, pp. 105 - 108.

Apply Self-Care

Painful Intercourse

Intercourse should be a pleasurable experience, not a painful one. Addressing the condition that causes discomfort may relieve the pain and help you resume an enjoyable sex life.

Painful intercourse, or *dyspareunia*, for women can be caused by:
- Attempting intercourse without sufficient vaginal lubrication
- Vaginal or urinary tract infections
- Vaginal irritation due to an estrogen deficiency related to aging, breast-feeding or birth control pills
- *Endometriosis*, a condition in which uterine tissue grows on other pelvic organs, and which bleed at the same time as the menstrual cycle, causing pain and irritation
- *Vaginismus*, an involuntary contraction of the vaginal muscles with intercourse
- Scarring from surgical procedures, such as *episiotomy* or *vaginal hysterectomy*

Pain in the vaginal canal usually indicates a vaginal problem. Pain that occurs when the penis is already in the vagina suggests a uterine, tubal or other pelvic problem.

What You Can Do

- When the problem is insufficient vaginal lubrication:
  - Try more *foreplay* before intercourse—leisurely, playful massaging and caressing of the entire body (since women tend to become fully aroused more slowly than men).
  - For additional lubrication, try saliva or water-based gels (K-Y Jelly, Replens).
  - Avoid lubricants that are not water-based, especially when you use latex condoms.
- If the cause is recent childbirth or vaginal surgery, nonintercourse lovemaking may be the answer until the vagina has completely healed.

Consult your healthcare provider if you suspect vaginal irritation or infection, urinary tract infection, endometriosis or vaginismus. (See *Pelvic Inflammatory Disease*, p. 281; *Vaginitis*, p. 291; *Urinary Tract Infections*, p. 293; *Endometriosis*, p. 280; and *Menopause*, p. 286.)

Menopause

Menopause, also called the "change of life," is a natural event—not an illness—that marks the end of a woman's menstrual cycles and her ability to bear children. It occurs for most women between the ages of 47 and 55, when production of the female hormone *estrogen* begins to decline.

Menopause can last a few months or several years, and it is considered complete when a woman has not menstruated for a full year. Menopause eliminates the need for any form of contraception, although doctors usually recommend continuing birth control until one year after a woman's last period.

Irregular Periods

Menstrual periods usually become lighter—but can become heavier—and irregular before they stop completely. Keep a written record, including the dates of your periods, in case you need to discuss them with your doctor.

Hot Flashes

Sudden feelings of intense heat, accompanied by sweating and flushing, normally last a few minutes. They are most common at night—although they can occur any time. Hormone imbalance caused by menopause can result in insomnia and subsequent fatigue. (See *Insomnia,* p. 318.) For most women, hot flashes gradually decrease over a period of a few years and eventually disappear.

To manage symptoms of hot flashes:
- Wear loose, lightweight clothing—preferably in layers—that can be easily removed.
- Drink plenty of fluids. Avoid caffeine and alcohol if they seem to bring on hot flashes.
- Exercise regularly to help stabilize your hormones and prevent insomnia.

Vaginal Dryness

Estrogen helps stimulate the production of natural lubricants in the vagina, so the loss of estrogen can result in vaginal dryness—which can make intercourse painful (see *Painful Intercourse*, p. 285) and lead to *vaginitis* (see *Vaginitis*, p. 291) and an increased urge to urinate.

Lubricants that provide relief for many women include water-based gels (K-Y Jelly, Replens). Do not use Vaseline or other petroleum-based products. Many women find that regular sexual activity decreases problems with soreness during intercourse.

Mood Swings

Hormonal and physical changes related to menopause may result in moodiness, depression, lethargy and nervousness. Try to understand that this is a normal part of menopause and to be as accepting of yourself—and your moods—as possible.

Osteoporosis

The thinning of bones (*osteoporosis*) that is caused by reduced estrogen levels results in weakened bones that are easily broken. (This silent disease usually has no symptoms and goes undiagnosed until a bone suddenly breaks.) You are more likely to be a candidate for osteoporosis if you are Asian or white, have a slender body frame, are inactive and have a family history of the disease. Women who smoke or drink are also at greater risk.

To prevent or reduce the effects of osteoporosis*:
- Get plenty of aerobic and weight-bearing exercise—walking, aerobic dance, climbing stairs, weightlifting—to keep your bones strong. (While swimming is an excellent aerobic exercise, it is not particularly helpful in strengthening weight-bearing bones.)
- Make sure your diet includes sufficient calcium (1,200 to 1,500 mg per day) to help reduce bone loss. Low-fat dairy products or calcium supplements are good sources, along with vitamin D, to help your bones absorb calcium.
- Don't smoke cigarettes; keep alcohol consumption to a minimum.

Women at greater risk should begin these measures before menopause.

Treatment Option

Hormone Replacement Therapy (HRT)

The short-term use of HRT (usually a combination of estrogen and progesterone) is the mainstay for treating symptoms of menopause such as hot flashes and night sweats. (These symptoms generally last a few years and then fade away.) HRT can also help prevent vaginal and urethral thinning, and therefore it reduces symptoms such as urinary urgency and incontinence. Other benefits include preventing recurrent urinary tract infections and pain with intercourse.

For some women, HRT also offers protection against *osteoporosis*, a progressive condition that weakens bones, making them fragile and prone to fracture. A class of medications called *bisphosphonates* are also used to prevent and treat osteoporosis in men and women. Medications include alendronate (Fosamax) and risedronate (Actonel).

For many years, HRT was believed to prevent heart disease. Recent studies have cast doubt on its effectiveness for this purpose, however, and it is no longer recommended. Women should consult their doctors about other preventive measures for heart disease, such as lifestyle changes and cholesterol- and blood pressure-lowering drugs.

Deciding whether to use HRT is a very personal matter. It's important to weigh the benefits of HRT against your personal risks for heart attacks, stroke, blood clots, and breast cancer, which may be linked to its long-term use. Discuss the pros and cons thoroughly with your doctor and make the choice that best suits your needs and lifestyle.

Menopause

Do these apply:

- You experience even minor vaginal bleeding and:
  - You haven't menstruated in more than a year and aren't taking hormone replacement therapy
  - You are taking hormone replacement therapy and experience any unexplained vaginal bleeding
- Menopausal symptoms have become intolerable or interfere with your daily life
- You are avoiding social contacts or otherwise are unable to enjoy yourself

Call Doctor

See **What You Can Do,** pp. 286 - 287.
See **Breast Lumps,** p. 273; **Depression,** p. 320.

Apply Self-Care

Vaginal Discharge

Healthy women produce small or moderate amounts of odorless, non-irritating vaginal discharge that may increase at certain times during the menstrual cycle. Abnormal discharge is very common and has many possible causes—some that require a doctor's care.

Symptoms	Possible Cause	Decision helper
White, cheesy discharge; itching; burning with urination	Yeast infection (Candida, monilia) or other forms of nonspecific vaginitis	Apply self-care if you have been diagnosed with a yeast infection before and think you have one now (see *What You Can Do, Vaginitis*, p. 291); if symptoms do not respond to self-care in three or four days, call your doctor
Frothy discharge that is profuse and white, grayish-green or yellowish; vaginal burning and itching; may have urinary-related symptoms (see *Urinary Tract Infections*, p. 293)	Trichomoniasis, a form of vaginitis and urinary tract infection, is most often sexually transmitted; it can also be spread via damp towels, bathing suits and—theoretically—toilet seats	Call your doctor now; if you have trichomoniasis, alert your sex partner(s) and encourage them to see a doctor; abstain from all sexual intercourse until you no longer have symptoms (see *Urinary Tract Infections*, p. 293)
Murky white, gray or yellowish discharge; distinct "fishy" odor; itching	Bacterial vaginosis or nonspecific vaginitis	May go away on its own; apply self-care for vaginitis (see *What You Can Do, Vaginitis*, p. 291); call your doctor if symptoms do not improve in three or four days
Vaginal discharge accompanied by severe lower abdominal pain, fever or recurrent or significant amounts of bloody discharge between periods	May indicate serious conditions ranging from gonorrhea to ectopic pregnancy	Call your doctor now (see *Sexually Transmitted Diseases*, p. 306)
Discharge in a young girl before puberty, or in a postmenopausal woman who is not on hormone replacement therapy	May indicate other problems	Call your doctor

Vaginitis is a Common Cause

Abnormal vaginal discharge is the hallmark symptom of *vaginitis,* which is most often caused by yeast. Vaginitis can be the result of stress, antibiotics (which kill protective bacteria), use of birth control pills, or excessive douching. If you are pregnant or have diabetes you are especially susceptible. Some forms of vaginitis can also be transmitted through sexual intercourse.

In addition to vaginal discharge, symptoms of vaginitis may include burning and itching, general pelvic discomfort, pain during intercourse, and painful or more frequent urination.

Prevention

- Wear cotton underpants that allow for air exchange in the crotch and thighs; avoid tight-fitting pants.
- Avoid douching and the use of feminine deodorant sprays and other perfumed products.
- Wipe from front to back after using the toilet.
- Change tampons at least three times a day during your period. Alternate with pads and be sure to remove the last tampon when your period is over.
- Be sure to remove contraceptive devices after an appropriate length of time.
- If you are prone to vaginitis, consume more acidophilus milk, buttermilk, and yogurt with live cultures to help the vagina maintain its natural chemical balance.

What You Can Do

Some types of vaginitis can be treated with self-care if 1) you have been diagnosed with a yeast infection in the past and you suspect one now; and/or 2) you have minimal symptoms and suspect a non-specific vaginitis.

- For a suspected yeast infection, try over-the-counter (OTC) antifungal creams such as Gyne-Lotrimin or Monistat. (If you have never seen a doctor for a vaginal infection, consult one before using these products.)
- Avoid intercourse—along with douches, spermicides, tampons and contraceptive devices such as the sponge or diaphragm—while you have vaginitis to allow time for vaginal tissue to heal.
- Try not to scratch the area. Apply cold-water compresses or ice packs to reduce inflammation and soothe irritation. For protection, place a washcloth between bare skin and ice. Warm sitz baths (sitting in hip-high water) may also offer you some relief.
- Call your doctor if your symptoms persist or worsen after three or four days of self-care, or if you are unsure what is causing your problem or what you should do.

Final Notes

In most cases, symptoms of vaginitis disappear quickly with treatment. However, vaginitis does tend to recur, and some women simply seem to be more susceptible than others. Complications can be avoided by paying attention to abnormal vaginal discharge and sensations, and getting prompt treatment.

> If you experience burning and pain with urination and feel like you need to urinate more than usual, see *Urinary Tract Infections,* p. 293.

Urinary Problems

Burning or stinging pain with urination, frequent or urgent urination, or blood in the urine may all be signs of an infection in the lower urinary tract or inflammation around the *urethral* opening (the urethra is the tube that carries urine from the bladder and out of the body).

Urinary Tract Infections (UTIs)

Urinary tract infections are also known as *UTIs, cystitis* and *bladder infections.* They are most common among women, but can also affect children, infants and men. (See *UTIs, Men's Health,* p. 298.)

Symptoms may include a frequent and urgent need to urinate, pain or a burning sensation during urination, cloudy, bloody or foul-smelling urine, pain or itching in the urethra, or pressure in the lower abdomen or lower back.

Between 80 and 90 percent of UTIs are caused by *E. coli* bacteria, which are generally found in the digestive system. Because the female anus and urethra are very close together, bacteria can find its way from the anus into the urethra and bladder. Any irritation to the genital area (from sexual intercourse or wearing tight pants) increases the likelihood of developing an infection.

What You Can Do

To prevent UTIs and minimize infection once you begin to feel symptoms:
- Drink plenty of fluids (eight or more glasses of water a day), unless your fluid intake has been limited by your doctor. Cranberry juice and yogurt with live cultures also may be helpful for prevention.
- Avoid alcohol, coffee, tea, carbonated beverages and spicy foods.
- Wear cotton underwear, cotton-lined pantyhose and loose clothing.
- Wipe from front to back after using the toilet (to reduce the spread of bacteria from the anus to the urethra).
- Avoid sexual intercourse when symptoms are present.
- Try to urinate before and after intercourse.
- Empty your bladder frequently.

- Avoid bubble bath or bath oil, especially when symptoms are present.
- Avoid frequent douching and do not use vaginal deodorants or perfumed feminine hygiene products.
- If your doctor prescribes antibiotics, be sure to take the entire prescription as directed to help prevent a relapse or recurrence. (See *Using Medications,* p. 324.)

Urinary Incontinence

Urinary incontinence, or the inability to control bladder function, is two to five times more common in women than in men and is more prevalent with age. The condition affects about 10 to 25 percent of women under the age of 65 and about 15 to 35 percent of women over age 65. The effects of childbirth can make the uterus and pelvic floor sag, putting pressure on the bladder. In women, age-related decreases in hormone levels may also result in a thinning of the tissue lining the urethra, which can make the urethra weaken and leak urine. However, there are many preventive measures and treatments for this condition.

- If you are overweight, losing weight may help reduce pressure on your bladder. (See *Healthy Weight,* p. 331.)
- Check with your doctor to see if your bladder has shifted. A mechanical lift inserted into the vagina may help correct your bladder's position.
- Ask your doctor to check for thinning in the lining of your urethra and vagina. A topical estrogen cream or estrogen supplements in pill form can treat this situation. (See *HRT,* p. 288.)
- *Kegel exercises* strengthen the muscles that surround the openings of the urethra, vagina and anus. Follow these instructions:
  - While urinating, try to stop the flow of urine to identify the correct pelvic muscles.
  - Contract these muscles as if you were stopping your urine stream, but do it when you're not urinating—while sitting, standing, walking or driving.
  - Tighten your rectal muscles as if trying not to pass gas. Contract your anus, but don't move your buttocks.
  - Do these exercises every morning, afternoon and evening. Start with five repetitions and gradually work up to 20 or 30 repetitions each time. Hold each position while slowly counting to five. Try not to move your buttocks, stomach muscles or legs.

- If you take certain medications, such as *diuretics,* or "water pills" (often prescribed for heart failure and high blood pressure to increase fluid loss), ask your doctor about finding an alternative or changing the time of day you take it. They can cause *urge incontinence,* when you feel the need to urinate but can't hold back long enough.
- Check with your doctor if you experience pain, urinary frequency, or blood in the urine; you may have an infection. (See *UTIs, Women's Health,* p. 293.)

See **Vaginal Discharge,** p. 290; **Men's Health,** p. 296.

Decision *helper*

Urinary Problems
Do these apply:

- There is an inability to urinate or you have new significant difficulty urinating
- You have symptoms of a UTI along with: chills, fever, flank pain (the area between the last rib and the hip) or vomiting
- You have a sudden onset of severe flank pain

no · · · yes

Call Doctor Now

- You have symptoms of a UTI or incontinence
- Your symptoms continue to worsen 48 hours after starting antibiotics or fail to improve within 72 hours

no · · · yes

Call Doctor

See **What You Can Do,** pp. 294 - 295.

Apply Self-Care

Men's Health

A lot of men are fond of saying they "hate to go to the doctor." But even those who do should take the time for a few simple preventive exams. Regular physicals, blood pressure tests and cholesterol screenings now could mean fewer, less painful doctor visits in the future. Tests like these could even save your life. See Screening Guidelines, *p. 337.*

Self-examination is equally important. Tracking your genital health takes little time and is well worth the effort.

Genital Health

Three minutes of your time each month can go a long way toward early detection of infections and cancers of the penis or testes. Early detection is the key to successful treatment and cure. (Cancer of the testicle is one of the most easily treated cancers if it is caught right away.)

Washing the penis daily, particularly under the *foreskin* that covers the tip of an uncircumcised penis, can prevent bacterial infection and possibly reduce the already very low risk of developing penile cancer. It's an important routine to teach uncircumsized boys by the time they are 3 or 4 years old.

Once males are in their teens, they should also begin examining their penis and testes each month for any changes that could indicate infection or cancer.

After a warm bath or shower:

- Stand with your right leg on the side of the tub or on the toilet seat.
- Gently roll the right testicle between the thumb and fingers of both hands. Check for:
  - Hard lumps or nodules
  - An enlargement or change in the consistency of the testicle
  - A pain or dull ache in the groin or lower abdomen

- Repeat this procedure on your left side.
- Feel the *epididymis*, the spongy tube on the top and the back side of the testicle. Pain could mean an infection.
- Examine the foreskin and the head of the penis for anything unusual, including sores, warts, redness or discharge.

When to Call Your Doctor

Testicular cancer spreads quickly—within a few months—so it is important to see your doctor to rule it out as soon as possible after you find any testicular lumps or nodules.

Also discuss any enlargement of the testicle, groin pain or penile discharge with your doctor.

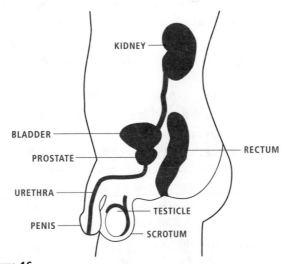

Figure 16

Urinary Problems

Problems with urination—difficulty getting urine started or completely stopped (dribbling), frequent or painful urination, decreased force of the urine stream, incomplete bladder emptying, or blood in the urine—can have a variety of causes, ranging from a urinary tract infection to prostate cancer.

Urinary Tract Infections (UTIs)

Urinary tract infections (also known as *UTIs, cystitis* and *bladder infections*) are most common among women (see *Women's Health, UTIs,* p. 293), but they can also affect men, children and infants. In men, most UTIs are caused by obstructions or structural problems in the urinary tract. In men over 50, the problem is often caused by an enlarged prostate gland, which hinders the flow of urine out of the bladder and becomes the perfect breeding ground for bacteria.

Symptoms may include a frequent and urgent need to urinate, pain or a burning sensation during urination, cloudy or foul-smelling urine, blood in the urine, pain or itching in the *urethra* (the tube that carries urine from the bladder out through the penis), pressure in the lower abdomen, and lower back pain.

- Drink plenty of water to help wash bacteria away, unless your fluid intake has been limited by your doctor. Cranberry juice may be helpful for preventing infection.
- Empty the bladder frequently.
- If your doctor prescribes antibiotics, be sure to take the entire prescription as directed to help prevent a relapse or recurrence. (See *Using Medications,* p. 324.)

Prostate Problems

The *prostate* (see Figure 16, p. 297), which produces some of the fluid in semen, is a donut-shaped gland that sits below the bladder and surrounds the urethra. The three most common prostate problems are prostate infection (*prostatitis*), prostate enlargement (*benign prostatic hyperplasia*) and prostate cancer.

Prostate infection

Prostate infection (*prostatitis*) is an infection of the prostate that may occur with a urinary tract infection as a result of bacteria traveling up the urethra. Prostate infection causes swelling, constriction of the urethra and urinary problems.

Symptoms include difficulty starting or stopping urination, a strong and frequent urge to urinate while passing only small amounts of urine, pain or discomfort in the area behind the *scrotum* (the "sac" of skin that encloses the testes), low-back or abdominal pain, and pain and burning during urination or ejaculation. Fever and chills, a general ill feeling, and blood in the urine or pus-filled discharge are also possible.

The prostate can also become inflamed without bacterial infection, causing chronic pelvic pain syndrome. Symptoms are similar to bacterial prostatitis; the cause is unknown.

What You Can Do

Prostate infection requires a doctor's diagnosis and antibiotics, although self-care may be helpful as well. Chronic pelvic pain syndrome may respond to self-care alone.

- Drink lots of fluids—both water and fruit juices.
- Avoid alcohol, caffeine, carbonated beverages and spicy foods.
- Try warm baths or over-the-counter (OTC) pain relievers: aspirin, acetaminophen (Tylenol) or ibuprofen (Advil, Motrin) to soothe the pain.
- Practice stress-management techniques if you experience anxiety or stress with prostate symptoms. (See *Stress*, p. 314.)

Prostate enlargement

Prostate enlargement (*benign prostatic hyperplasia* or *BPH*) is a noncancerous increase in the size of the prostate gland that appears to be part of the normal aging process; four out of five men between 50 and 60 years of age have this condition. It is not usually a serious problem, but it can become severe enough to compress the urethra and hinder the flow of urine as you urinate.

The hallmark symptom of BPH is *nocturia*, which is the need to get up at night to urinate. Other common symptoms include difficulty starting, stopping or maintaining the flow of urine; a decrease in the force or volume of urine flow; or increased frequency of urination. Symptoms that develop as a result of the condition include increased fatigue, due to difficulty getting back to sleep at night because of nocturia; and mild dehydration (if fluid intake is decreased to avoid having to get up at night).

What You Can Do

- Avoid the use of caffeine, *diuretics* (medications known as water pills that increase fluid loss), alcohol and any over-the-counter (OTC) medications such as decongestants that have warnings related to causing urine retention.
- Take plenty of time to urinate. Sit on the toilet instead of standing.
- Do not limit fluid intake during the day. Try to drink two quarts of water and other fluids throughout the day to help prevent urinary tract infections.
- Don't drink fluids after the evening meal. Empty your bladder before bedtime.
- If you have nocturia, leave a night light on and make sure the path to the bathroom is clear to decrease the risk of falls. You might prefer to keep a urinal at the bedside to avoid getting up at all—especially if you tend to feel dizzy or light-headed when you first get out of bed.

Prostate cancer

Prostate cancer grows slowly in many cases, remaining within the prostate and causing no health problems. In other cases, however, it spreads aggressively and can become life-threatening. (Prostate cancer is the second leading cause of cancer death in men in the United States.)

Symptoms include decreased strength of the urine stream, difficulty getting urine started or completely stopped, frequent and painful urination, hip or lower-back pain, and blood in the urine.

What You Can Do

While prostate surgery is successful in many cases for localized prostate cancer, it can also result in impotence and urinary incontinence. As a result, men who are diagnosed with the disease may face a difficult dilemma: whether to undergo treatment and take the risk of side effects, or opt for "watchful waiting" and risk the possibility that the cancer will spread.

Watching and waiting—a process in which your doctor closely monitors your condition without treating it—may be appropriate in some situations (for example, if your tumor is small and appears to be growing slowly).

If you and your doctor decide to watch and wait, you'll want to discuss how often you need to go in for checkups. Over time, if your doctor notices a steady increase in your prostate-specific antigen (PSA) level (a sign that the cancer could be spreading), it may be time to discuss a different treatment path.

Important questions to ask your doctor:
- What are my treatment options?
- What are the risks, benefits and possible side effects of each option?
- How will treatment affect my sex life?
- Will the treatment be painful, and if so, how will you treat the pain?
- Will I need to change my normal activities? If so, how and for how long?
- How often will I need to have checkups?

> If there is pain associated with urination or ejaculation and an unusual discharge from the penis, see *Sexually Transmitted Diseases,* p. 306. If the question concerns painful or swollen testes or the penis, see p. 302.

Urinary Problems
Do these apply:

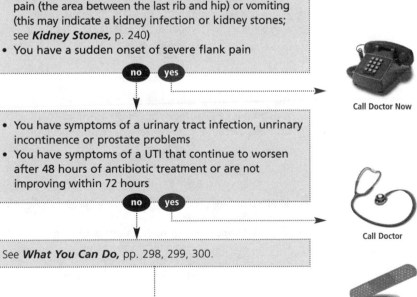

- You are unable to urinate at all or have significant difficulty urinating
- You have symptoms of a UTI along with: chills, fever, flank pain (the area between the last rib and hip) or vomiting (this may indicate a kidney infection or kidney stones; see *Kidney Stones,* p. 240)
- You have a sudden onset of severe flank pain

no   yes

Call Doctor Now

- You have symptoms of a urinary tract infection, unrinary incontinence or prostate problems
- You have symptoms of a UTI that continue to worsen after 48 hours of antibiotic treatment or are not improving within 72 hours

no   yes

Call Doctor

See *What You Can Do,* pp. 298, 299, 300.

Apply Self-Care

Painful or Swollen Testes or Penis

Pain, lumps, swelling or changes of any kind in the testes or penis—even if they do not cause pain—may be signs of a problem that needs prompt attention.

Possible causes include *torsion* (twisting) of the testicle; internal damage to the testicle due to an injury of some kind; infection of the lymph glands; a recent case of mumps; accumulation of fluid; or a cyst or tumor.

Decision *helper*

Painful or Swollen Testes or Penis
Do these apply:

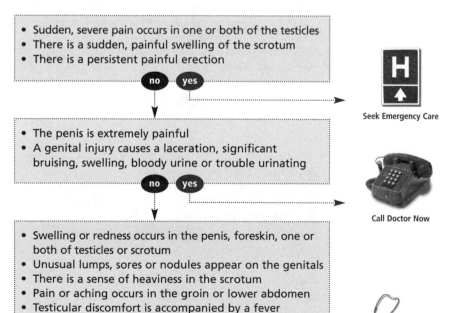

- Sudden, severe pain occurs in one or both of the testicles
- There is a sudden, painful swelling of the scrotum
- There is a persistent painful erection

no   yes

Seek Emergency Care

- The penis is extremely painful
- A genital injury causes a laceration, significant bruising, swelling, bloody urine or trouble urinating

no   yes

Call Doctor Now

- Swelling or redness occurs in the penis, foreskin, one or both of testicles or scrotum
- Unusual lumps, sores or nodules appear on the genitals
- There is a sense of heaviness in the scrotum
- Pain or aching occurs in the groin or lower abdomen
- Testicular discomfort is accompanied by a fever

yes

Call Doctor

Sexual Health

Birth Control

Birth control is a personal decision to be made in the context of your own religious beliefs, health, lifestyle and financial issues. Today's options are varied—from age-old methods to forms that use the latest medical technology. All have benefits and risks that should be considered when making the birth control decision that is right for you.

Birth Control Methods*

Description	Risks	Comments
Birth Control Patch (Ortha-Evra): 99.3 to 99.7% effective		
Skin patch secretes hormones that prevent the release of eggs from the ovaries	Low potential risk for blood clots, high blood pressure, stroke, heart attack	Worn for three weeks each month (replaced weekly); not worn for fourth week to allow menstruation
Birth Control Pills: 99.2 to 99.9% effective		
Pills taken orally by women to prevent the release of eggs from the ovaries; contain hormones such as synthetic estrogen and progesterone	Low potential risk for blood clots, high blood pressure, stroke, heart attack	Must be prescribed by a doctor; used by more than 200 million women worldwide; effectiveness linked to conscientious use
Cervical Cap: 84 to 98% effective		
Similar to a diaphragm; small rubber cup fits over the cervix to block sperm from entering the uterus; must be inserted before intercourse	Prolonged wearing can lead to toxic shock syndrome, a sometimes fatal condition	Prescribed and fitted by a doctor
Condom for Men: 90 to 98% effective (when used with spermicide)		
A thin, glove-like sheath which covers the penis to prevent sperm from entering woman's reproductive system; latex is recommended	No side effects; greatest risk is incorrect usage; may cause irritation	Available without a prescription; low cost; latex condom also reduces spread of HIV and other sexually transmitted diseases

chart continues next page

*Success in preventing pregnancy after one year of correct use.

Birth Control Methods *continued from previous page*

Description	Risks	Comments
Condom for Women: 79 to 96% effective		
Sheath which lines woman's vagina to block sperm from reaching an egg; reduces the spread of sexually transmitted diseases (STDs)	No known health risks; irregular use diminishes effectiveness	Most effective if used with spermicide; insert up to 8 hours before intercourse
Contraceptive Injection (Lunelle, Depo-Provera): 97 to 99.6% effective		
Hormones are injected into a woman's arm or buttocks every one or three months, which prevents release of eggs and causes cervical mucus to thicken and block sperm from reaching an egg	Irregular bleeding, weight gain, cramps; should not be used by women with certain medical conditions	Requires a prescription; usually administered at a doctor's office or clinic
Contraceptive Ring (Nuva Ring): 99.5 to 99.9% effective		
Plastic ring containing hormones inserted into the vagina; suppresses hormones that stimulate ovulation and thicken cervical mucus, blocking sperm before entering uterus; also makes uterine lining less receptive to implantation	Low potential risk for blood clots, high blood pressure, stroke, heart attack	Worn continuously for three weeks; removed at fourth week to allow menstruation; a new ring is required each month; available by prescription
Contraceptive Sponge: 64 to 82% effective		
Donut shaped sponge treated with spermicide; inserted into the vagina before intercourse to destroy sperm	May cause irritation and allergic reaction; sponge can be difficult to remove	Awaiting FDA approval in U.S; available in Canada without a prescription; spermicide may provide some protection against Chlamydia and gonorrhea
Diaphragm: 81 to 94% effective		
Dome-shaped rubber cup that fits over the cervix to block sperm from entering the uterus; must be inserted before intercourse	Usually none; prolonged wearing for more than 6 to 8 hours can lead to infection or possibly toxic shock syndrome, a sometimes fatal condition	Prescribed and fitted by doctor; should remain in place six hours after intercourse; can protect against some sexually transmitted diseases; best if used with spermicide
IUD (Intrauterine Device): 92 to 99% effective		
A copper wire device inserted in uterus; unit may secrete hormones; appears to prevent fertilized egg from implanting in the uterus by causing inflammation of uterine lining	May cause strong cramps, abnormal bleeding; can be linked to PID (pelvic inflammatory disease), which can scar the fallopian tubes and result in infertility	Should be used under doctor's supervision; can pose risk if pregnancy occurs; contraception begins within 24 hours of insertion

Birth Control Methods

Description	Risks	Comments
Periodic Abstinence: 75 to 99% effective		
Abstaining from intercourse during ovulation, a woman's most fertile period; usually 14 days before the onset of menstrual flow	No side effects	Dependent on the user's ability to accurately chart fertile periods; not a fool-proof method
Spermicides: 71 to 95% effective		
Foams, creams or supposi-tories inserted in a woman's vagina to destroy sperm before they can enter the uterus and fertilize an egg	Usually no side effects; can cause skin irritation; irregular use diminishes effectiveness	Available without a prescription; low cost; more effective if used with a diaphragm or condom
Sterilization, Female (Tubal Ligation): 99 to 99.9% effective		
Surgically cutting and block-ing the fallopian tubes so sperm cannot reach egg	Generally not a reversible procedure; causes minor discomfort	Surgical outpatient procedure performed by a surgeon; generally swift recovery
Sterilization, Female (Essure System): 99 to 99.9% effective		
Metal coils implanted into each fallopian tube	Requires special X-ray 3 months afer insertion to be sure the tubes are blocked	Surgical outpatient procedure performed by a surgeon; generally swift recovery
Sterilization, Male (Vasectomy): 99.5 to 99.9% effective		
Surgically cutting the tubes that carry sperm from testicles to penis	Generally not reversible; procedure causes minor discomfort	Outpatient procedure performed by a doctor; generally simpler and safer than tubal ligation
Withdrawal: 73% effective in typical usage		
Withdrawing penis from vagina before ejaculation of sperm	No side effects, but ineffective and not a recommended form of birth control	Reliability is extremely variable; small amounts of sperm-laden semen can leak out before ejaculation

Final Notes

Abstinence from sexual activity is a viable form of birth control for adolescents and young people wishing to abstain from sex prior to marriage. While 100 percent effective, it may be impractical for sexually active individuals.

Sexually Transmitted Diseases (STDs)

Most sexually transmitted diseases (STDs) can be prevented by following basic safe-sex measures. (See *Safe Sex*, p. 312.) AIDS poses special risks, including transmission by needles and from mother to fetus. (See *HIV*, p. 308.) Although genital herpes is an incurable STD, it can be managed with self-care and medical treatment. (See *Genital Herpes*, p. 309.) Always consult your doctor for diagnosis and treatment.

Signs	Diagnosis	Final Notes
Chlamydia: Bacterial		
General pelvic pain; vaginal or penile discharge, discomfort during sexual intercourse; burning urination (which can occur in both men and women)	Pelvic exam and/or test or culture from the cervix or penis	Treated with antibiotics; if untreated, Chlamydia can cause pelvic inflammatory disease (PID), infertility and complications in pregnancy; and prostatitis, epididymitis or urethritis in men
Genital Herpes: Viral		
Clusters of blisters in genital, anal or mouth areas; turn into ulcers or sores and heal in one to three weeks: accompanied by mild flu-like symptoms (see *Genital Herpes*, p. 309)	Physical exam; viral culture	Treated with antiviral medication; self-care includes warm sitz baths, cool compresses soaked in aluminum acetate solution (Domeboro, Bluboro, Burow's), witch hazel compresses, a hair dryer set on low to dry blisters, non-prescription pain relievers
Genital Warts (HPV): Viral		
Small, fleshy growths in genital, anal or mouth areas; singular or in clusters	Physical exam; can be confirmed by biopsy	Cryotherapy, topical medications, surgical removal; genital warts often reappear after treatment
Gonorrhea: Bacterial		
Men: mucous discharge from penis; slow, painful or difficult urination; **Women:** mucous vaginal discharge; vaginal itching; painful or burning urination	Physical exam and culture of discharge	Untreated gonorrhea can lead to pelvic inflammatory disease (PID) or cause arthritis, infertility and other serious problems; treated with antibiotics

Sexually Transmitted Diseases

Signs	Diagnosis	Final Notes
Human Immunodeficiency Virus (HIV): Viral		
See *HIV,* p. 308	Physical exam and lab tests	Multiple drug regimens aimed at prolonging life and preventing replication of the virus
Syphilis: Bacterial		
Painless sore on genitals, anus or in mouth two to four weeks after infection, hardening into a painless ulcer then disappearing; swollen lymph nodes, fever, and/or rashes eight to 10 weeks after infection	Blood test, examination of fluid from sores	Untreated syphilis can lead to blindness, brain damage and heart disease; treated with antibiotics
Trichomoniasis: Protozoan		
Women: may have no symptoms or: painful or more-frequent-than-usual urination; large amount of white, grayish-green or yellowish vaginal discharge that is offensive in odor; possible burning sensation in vagina with spotting of blood; uncomfortable pelvic area; painful sexual intercourse; and itchy vulva **Men:** Generally have no symptoms: possible frothy discharge from the penis and urinary symptoms, scrotal swelling or tenderness	Microscopic examination or culture of discharge	May cause complications such as infections of the urethra or bladder; complications of pregnancy for women; prostate infection for men; treated with a special type of anti-protozoan agent

You can greatly reduce the likelihood of STDs by practicing safe sex:

- Always use a latex condom—if having sex outside of a long-term relationship
- Limit your sex partners
- Ask your partner to be tested for STDs
- Avoid sex with infected individuals

See **Safe Sex,** p. 312.

Human Immunodeficiency Virus (HIV)

The human immunodeficiency virus (HIV) causes acquired immunodeficiency syndrome (AIDS). If you test positive for HIV, you carry the virus and can infect others but may not have symptoms of the illness for some time. For adults, the average period from infection with the virus to development of AIDS is six to 10 years. After AIDS develops, death usually occurs within two or three years.

Millions of people have HIV/AIDS worldwide; the number is growing.

Transmission

HIV is spread by unprotected sexual intercourse; sharing needles or syringes with someone who has HIV; receiving contaminated blood, blood products, organs for transplantation or semen for artificial insemination. It can also spread from mother to fetus during pregnancy or delivery or from mother to infant through breast-feeding.

Note Your Symptoms

Some people experience symptoms of an acute viral infection a month or two after exposure. The symptoms typically last one to two weeks and resemble *infectious mononucleosis*: swollen glands, sore throat, fever, *malaise* (feeling lousy) and skin rash. (See *Mononucleosis*, p. 156 and *Swollen Glands*, p. 161.) Years may pass before illnesses associated with AIDS appear, including:

* Infections of the lungs, brain, intestines, skin, etc.
* Cancers
* Excessive weight loss (wasting)
* Lung diseases such as tuberculosis and recurrent pneumonia
* HIV dementia

Prevention

You can prevent infection with HIV by eliminating risky behaviors:

* Limit your sex partners or abstain from sex completely.
* Avoid unprotected sexual intercourse (oral, vaginal, anal). Always use latex condoms unless you and your partner are intimate only with each other and have both tested negative for HIV for six months or longer.
* Don't use intravenous (IV) drugs, or share needles or syringes.

See *Safe Sex,* p. 312.

NOTE: HIV is not transmitted through saliva, tears, sweat or feces, nor can it be transmitted through mosquito bites, donating blood or contact with inanimate objects such as toilet seats. An infected person who is coughing, talking or eating poses no risk of spreading HIV to others.

Testing for HIV

- Do you suspect you have been exposed to HIV? If so, get tested immediately and repeat the test in six months. Continue testing every three to six months for as long as your high-risk behavior continues.
- Have you had a positive HIV test, but no symptoms of AIDS? Schedule follow-up visits and tests with your doctor.
- Cooperate with your doctor and public health officials in identifying your sex partner(s) so they may be alerted to the possibility of exposure to HIV.

What You Can Do

There is no vaccine for HIV infection and no drug that can cure HIV. Your best strategy for dealing with HIV is to prevent exposure by practicing safe sex or abstaining from sex.

Drug treatments for HIV and AIDS are aimed at prolonging life by preventing replication of the virus. In general, combinations of drugs appear to be most effective. People who test positive for HIV often experience depression and job-security issues, as well as major social and financial challenges. For more information on counseling resources, contact the Centers for Disease Control and Prevention National STD and AIDS hotline, 1-800-342-2437. **Always consult your doctor for diagnosis and treatment.**

Genital Herpes

Herpes viruses can cause conditions such as chickenpox and *mononucleosis*. Herpes simplex virus type 1 typically causes fever blisters/cold sores on the lips and mouth. Herpes simplex virus type 2 causes genital herpes, which infects the genital and *anorectal* (anus and/or rectum) areas.

However, herpes simplex virus type 1 *can* infect the genital area, usually through oral sex, and herpes simplex type 2 can infect the lips or mouth. Once either virus enters the body, you can never be completely free of it. (To avoid genital herpes, always practice safe sex; see *Safe Sex*, p. 312.) You can help limit the spread of infection and reduce the discomfort of an outbreak, however.

During the first outbreak of genital herpes, blisters turn into well-defined ulcers or sores and form crusts that heal within one to three weeks. After the first outbreak, many people experience periodic but milder attacks as smaller clusters of blisters appear and last up to 10 days.

What You Can Do

Although there is no cure for genital herpes, these measures can help relieve your discomfort:

- Take five- to 10-minute sitz baths (soaking in hip-high, warm water), which can soothe and help promote healing.
- Apply cool compresses soaked in aluminum acetate solution (Domeboro, Bluboro, Burow's) or gently dab herpes sores in the genital or rectal area with pads soaked in witch hazel.
- Use a hair dryer set on low to help dry up blisters.
- Take steps to reduce stress and anxiety to help prevent outbreaks. (See *Stress*, p. 314.)
- Try nonprescription pain relievers (aspirin, acetaminophen or ibuprofen). **NEVER give aspirin to children/teenagers unless your healthcare provider orders it. It can cause Reye's syndrome, a rare but often fatal condition.**
- Wash your hands frequently to prevent spreading the disease.

Alerting your sex partner(s)

You will have to tell your sex partner(s) that they have been exposed to the virus so they can be evaluated by a doctor, treated if necessary, and advised to continue checking themselves for herpes outbreaks. If you are hesitant to talk to your sex partner(s), ask your doctor for advice.

Living with herpes

Most people with genital herpes experience itching, tingling or burning in the affected area a day or two before blisters appear. *Acyclovir* (Zovirax) is the drug most often prescribed for outbreaks. Daily treatment does not eliminate the risk of transmitting the virus, however. Until all sores have healed, the herpes virus is highly contagious.

Avoid sex until all the sores have healed. Because the virus can be spread even when there are no apparent sores, always use a latex condom for your partner's safety. Even though infection can still occur if condoms are used, some protection is better than none. Genital sores from any cause increase the risk of HIV or AIDS. Always practice safe sex.

See **Safe Sex,** p. 312.

Final Notes

The Centers for Disease Control and Prevention can provide you with more information about STDs. Call the CDC National STD and AIDS Hotline at 1-800-342-2437.

Decision helper

Sexually Transmitted Diseases (STDs)

Do these apply:

- You have severe lower abdominal or pelvic pain with foul smelling vaginal discharge or a fever of 101° F (38.3° C) or higher

no   yes

Call Doctor Now

- You have general pelvic discomfort, painful intercourse or vaginal discharge
- There is discharge from the penis
- Genital or anal blisters, warts or ulcer(s) occur
- There is urinary burning, stinging or increased frequency; pressure in the lower back or abdomen; or foul smelling, bloody or cloudy urine
- You may have been exposed to an STD or are currently infected

yes

Call Doctor

See *Safe Sex,* p. 312.

Safe Sex

Prevention is the *only* defense against AIDS and the best defense against other sexually transmitted diseases (STDs). Anyone can get AIDS. There is no vaccine to prevent HIV (the virus that causes AIDS) and no cure for AIDS once you have it. It's what you do—not who you are—that puts you at risk.

Prevention

- Eliminate your risk entirely by not having sex with anyone (*abstinence*) or by having sex only with a non-infected partner who has sex only with you (*mutual monogamy*).
- Unless you and your partner are only intimate with each other and have tested negative for HIV for six months or longer (or you and your partner have been intimate with no one else since the late 70s):
  - Use a latex condom each time you have sex.
  - Avoid unprotected vaginal, oral and anal sex.
- Don't use "natural" skin condoms. Only latex condoms protect against HIV/STDs. In addition:
  - Always check the condom for tears.
  - Cover the erect penis with the condom before any sexual contact.
  - Keep the condom snugly in place until sexual contact is over.
- If needed, use a water-based lubricant, such as K-Y Jelly during intercourse. Avoid petroleum-based products, which can weaken the latex barrier.
- Get to know your sexual partner(s) before you have sexual relations, and limit the number of partners you have.

Heterosexual and homosexual behaviors that put you at high risk for contracting HIV and other STDs include having sex with:
  - Intravenous (IV) drug users, or anyone who has had sex with an IV drug user
  - Someone who has or has had numerous sexual partners
  - Someone who has or has had an STD such as genital herpes, syphilis, gonorrhea or any open genital or oral sore

- Someone who has received a blood transfusion or blood products between 1978 and 1985 and has not been tested for HIV
- Male or female prostitutes
- Individuals with questionable HIV status

Although sexual intercourse is the primary means of infection with HIV, it is not the only one. Infants can be born with the virus if their mother is infected, and HIV can be passed to children through breast milk from infected mothers. Always consult your doctor for diagnosis and treatment.

See **Sexually Transmitted Diseases (STDs),** p. 306.

Mental Health

Stress

Anyone who has been late for an important appointment or struggled with family finances knows that stress is a normal and even useful reaction.

In stressful situations or emergencies, our bodies automatically increase the production of certain hormones. This results in a rise in heart rate and blood pressure, a tensing of muscles to prepare the body for action, an increase in perspiration to cool the body, faster respiration to raise the oxygen supply, and a dilation of the pupils to improve vision. These responses, known as "fight or flight," were once vital to the survival of the human race.

Today, we're rarely in life-or-death situations, but our bodies still react to stress in the same old ways. This is particularly clear during times of major life changes such as divorce, death, illness, moving or changing jobs.

Stress in itself is neither good nor bad, but how we react to stress can have a huge impact on our well-being. *Anxiety* is a pronounced reaction to stress. Symptoms of anxiety include insomnia, an inability to concentrate, tension-type headaches and upset stomach. Stress also can cause *depression* that might show itself as avoiding people, irritability or pessimism.

Grief is a response to the loss of a loved one, job or something else dear to us.

In extreme cases of stress, such as war or natural disaster, *post-traumatic stress disorder (PTSD)* can develop. It's characterized by the persistent "re-experiencing" of the stressful event with flashbacks and sometimes hallucinations. Other symptoms include avoiding thoughts and feelings about the event, emotional withdrawal, insomnia, irritability and an exaggerated startle response.

The physical symptoms of stress can be alleviated after you recognize the sources of stress. For example, if job anxiety is continually causing an upset stomach, you won't solve the problem simply by treating the stomach pain. The key is to find ways to minimize or manage reactions to stress.

Look for Creative Solutions

- Would joining a carpool help reduce stress related to commuting?
- Would hiring a babysitter for a few hours a day give you time for yourself?
- Can home chores be rearranged or taken over by others?

Consider These Stress-Management Tools

- Exercise regularly.
- Pursue hobbies.
- Talk things over with a friend.
- Cry if that helps you feel better.
- Try yoga, meditation or muscle-relaxation techniques.

Try to Keep Things in Perspective

- Let go of things that are beyond your control.
- Imagine the worst that could happen in any given situation, the likelihood that it will occur, and how you would handle it if it did.
- Consider whether you will even remember this event in a few years.

During extremely stressful situations, such as the death of a family member, taking time to experience your feelings of sadness and loss is an important step toward emotional healing.

If you feel you can't cope with a problem, talk to a counselor, psychiatrist, clergyperson or healthcare professional. These steps might be particularly helpful if you can't identify the cause of stress but are having troublesome symptoms.

Seek immediate care if you are thinking about suicide or doing physical harm to others. Call your doctor if you are turning to alcohol or drugs to relieve stress.

Other Stress-Related Problems

Hyperventilation Syndrome

Hyperventilation is when you breathe too fast. The result is that too much oxygen is taken into your system and the carbon dioxide level in your blood is lowered. *Hyperventilation syndrome* is when this happens as a result of anxiety.

Hyperventilation makes you feel out of breath and can bring on dizziness or numbness and tingling of the hands, feet and mouth. In severe cases, there can be chest pain, muscle spasms, palpitations or even unconsciousness.

Most common in young adults, hyperventilation syndrome usually is found in anxious or nervous people who develop concerns about their ability to breathe.

Hyperventilation can also be a reaction to severe pain, a reaction to certain drugs, or can be part of a panic attack. The cause needs to be determined in order to eliminate the symptoms.

What You Can Do

If you know someone who has a history of hyperventilating, let him or her know if you notice this tendency. Sometimes people are unaware they are doing it. The goal is to get the person to breathe slower—about one breath every five seconds.

When a person is hyperventilating, he or she should breathe through pursed lips or cover the mouth and one nostril and breathe through the other nostril. Reassure the person that he or she is OK.

Lump in Throat

The feeling of a lump in the throat is a common symptom of anxiety, particularly in young adults. The lump makes it difficult to swallow and usually comes and goes, heightened by anxiety and tension. The symptoms seem worse when the person concentrates on swallowing.

Several serious diseases can cause swallowing difficulties. In these cases, the symptoms usually develop slowly, beginning while eating solid foods, then progressively getting worse. This can result in weight loss and is most commonly seen in those over 40. Call your doctor if you develop these symptoms.

As with any stress-related medical concern, finding the underlying cause of anxiety is important in eliminating the symptom. Relaxation techniques may also be helpful.

Insomnia

Insomnia is the inability to enjoy adequate or restful sleep. It can be defined as difficulty falling asleep, frequent awakenings during the night, or waking too early in the morning.

Acute, *transient* insomnia lasts for less than four weeks and may be due to stress, acute illness or injury, or changes in the sleeping environment.

Chronic insomnia (lasting more than a month) may be caused by depression, anxiety disorders, manic disorders, chronic pain syndromes, heart and circulation disorders, kidney disease, or *sleep apnea*, in which breathing is temporarily interrupted by airway obstruction. More than 300 over-the-counter (OTC) and prescription drugs also can contribute to acute and chronic insomnia, including alcohol, caffeine, cardiac medications, nicotine, amphetamines and decongestants.

Behaviors that can cause or aggravate insomnia include vigorous exercise or mental exertion before bedtime, chronic use of sleeping pills, staying in bed too long in the morning or napping too much during the day.

Practices that promote restful sleep include:
- Exercising on a regular basis (but avoiding exercise within two hours of bedtime)
- Taking a warm bath or drinking warm milk
- A regular bedtime routine that includes relaxing activities such as reading for pleasure
- Reserving the bedroom for sleep and sex
- Avoiding alcohol and smoking before bedtime
- Drinking caffeine in moderation, before noon only
- Not napping

You can gain insights into improving your sleep by keeping a diary of your sleep patterns and behaviors.

Insomnia
Do these apply:

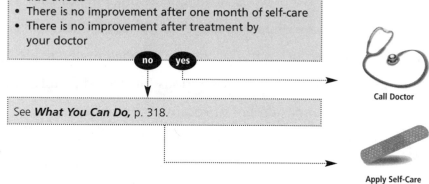

- Medications for sleep are causing bothersome side effects
- There is no improvement after one month of self-care
- There is no improvement after treatment by your doctor

no   yes

Call Doctor

See **What You Can Do,** p. 318.

Apply Self-Care

Depression

Major depression is a potentially life-threatening physical and mental illness. The classic symptoms are a hopeless mood and a loss of pleasure in activities that were once enjoyable. Major depression can be triggered by severe life stresses including the death of a loved one, divorce, serious financial difficulty, chronic illness and chemical dependency (alcohol or cocaine, for example).

Limited periods of sadness and grief are a normal experience for everyone. However, the inability to recover from these episodes signals the likelihood of a potential problem for which professional medical care may help.

While anyone can suffer from depression, individuals at higher risk include women, people under chronic stress, older adults and those who have a relative with depression or another mental illness. Women are at higher risk because hormonal changes involved in pregnancy, menstruation and the postpartum period can affect mood. In the elderly, poor emotional and physical health, social isolation, poverty and grief are factors.

While chronic illness of any sort can cause depression, some illnesses, such as lupus, chronic fatigue syndrome and Parkinson's disease, seem to include depression as one of their symptoms. Depression is also common in people with cancer, heart disease or chronic kidney disease. Certain medications, including some used to treat high blood pressure and Parkinson's disease, also can cause depression.

Unfortunately, despite recent gains, a stigma is still attached to undergoing or seeking treatment for mental illness. Some people may avoid acknowledging their depression to avoid this stigma.

Children sometimes suffer from depression; suicide is the third leading cause of death among American teenagers.

Common signs of depression include:
- Unintentional weight loss or gain
- Abnormal sleeping patterns
- Fatigue

- Feelings of worthlessness or hopelessness
- Excessive or inappropriate feelings of guilt
- Decreased ability to concentrate
- Recurrent thoughts of death or suicide
- A suicide attempt
- Withdrawal from friends and family
- Irritability, anxiety, sadness

People with major mood swings—from depression to elation—may be suffering from a different condition known as *bipolar affective disorder,* previously called manic-depressive illness.

Another form of depression is *seasonal affective disorder,* or SAD. SAD is associated with a lack of exposure to sunlight and often occurs during the winter months in people who live in northern regions.

Symptoms can include lethargy, irritability, chronic headaches, increased appetite, weight gain and the need for more sleep. Episodes may last for several weeks to months.

What You Can Do

Major depression is a chronic, debilitating illness that can last from weeks to years. The majority of people who suffer from depression would benefit from some form of intervention, in the form of medication, psychotherapy (counseling) or both.

Activities that help relieve mild depression include:

- Getting regular exercise
- Joining a support group or getting involved in group activities
- Talking to someone about your problems
- Decreasing or eliminating the use of alcohol or other drugs

Many SAD sufferers benefit from *phototherapy,* a medically supervised treatment program that consists of daily exposure to intense full-spectrum lights (ultraviolet wavelengths are filtered out to protect the skin). Relief usually begins in about a week.

> Seek emergency care if you have serious thoughts of suicide or harming someone else, with or without a specific plan, or if you have made a suicide attempt. If someone you know has threatened suicide, take those threats seriously. Call a crisis hotline or encourage the person to seek help.

Decision *helper*

Depression
Do these apply:

- You have suicidal feelings that are hard to resist, a plan and means to commit suicide now, or a suicide attempt is in progress
- You feel suicidal and are intoxicated or have taken drugs

no   yes

Seek Emergency Care

- You have recurrent thoughts of death and have thought of a method to kill yourself or someone else or have tried to do so in the past

no   yes

Call Doctor Now

- You have recurrent or persistent feelings of depression
- You think about death frequently
- Depression interferes with your ability to enjoy activities, work or school
- You take medication that might be causing depression
- You take antidepressants and are experiencing side effects
- Your symptoms worsen or don't improve
- You and/or your family need emotional support
- Your depression seems seasonal, related to a lack of sunlight
- Episodes of depression alternate with feelings of euphoria

no   yes

Call Doctor

See **What You Can Do,** p. 321.

Apply Self-Care

SECTION 5
Medications

Using Medications

Medications are valuable tools for improving and maintaining health, but they must always be used cautiously and wisely.

Medication Precautions

To get the greatest benefit from your medications, follow these tips:

- Always read the labels of both prescription and over-the-counter (OTC) medications to determine proper dosage and potential side effects.
- Contact your doctor before taking any medication, including OTC herbs, vitamins and supplements (especially if you are pregant or breastfeeding, taking an MAO inhibitor, or being treated for a serious chronic condition such as heart disease, diabetes, asthma or epilepsy).
- Never share or trade prescription drugs with anyone.
- Store all medications out of the reach of children. If you have small children, be sure all medicine bottles have safety caps.
- Take prescription medications as directed by your doctor. This may include instructions on taking the medication with food. (Report any side effects to your doctor.)
- Never abruptly stop taking a medication without first consulting your doctor (even if you begin to feel better). Some medications must be tapered off slowly to be safe. If you take several medications, discontinuing one may require adjusting the others.
- Throw out medications once they reach their expiration date.
- Ask your doctor if an expensive prescription medication can be replaced with a less costly alternative, such as a generic version.
- Refill prescriptions ahead of time so you don't run out on weekends or on holidays, when your doctor may be hard to reach or the pharmacy may be closed.
- When you travel, carry your medications with you; never put them inside the luggage you check. Also, take along enough for an extra day or two, in case your travel plans change.

Home Pharmacy

A properly stocked home medicine cabinet can help you prepare for common complaints and emergencies and help you avoid unnecessary trips to the doctor and pharmacy. The following are some suggested items for your "home pharmacy" and first-aid kit.

Nonprescription Drugs

How it works	Risks	Comments
Acid Reducers		
Decrease gastric acid production	Interact with some medicines and foods and should not be used in the presence of some diseases; read directions carefully	Don't use longer than two weeks without seeing your doctor
Antacids		
Relieve heartburn or stomach upset by neutralizing acid	Some can cause constipation, others loosen stools; some brands are high in sodium and should be avoided by those on low-salt diets	Avoid long-term use
Antidiarrheals		
Relieve diarrhea by thickening stools and/or slowing intestinal spasms	Do not use if you have a fever or blood in the stool; prolonged use can lead to constipation and absorb bacteria that aid digestion. Do not give Pepto-Bismol to children, it increases the risk of Reye's syndrome (due to aspirin-like ingredient). Consult doctor before using attapulgite (Kaopectate) or loperamide (Imodium) for children under 3 years of age	Diarrhea is the body's way of flushing out infection, so use antidiarrheals only when necessary; replace body fluids depleted by diarrhea; drugs with bismuth may darken the tongue or stools
Antifungal Preparations		
Clear up skin fungal infections, such as athlete's foot and jock itch	Few risks; preparations with selenium sulfide can burn skin if used excessively	

chart continues next page

Nonprescription Drugs *continued from previous page*

How it works	Risks	Comments
Antihistamines/Decongestants		
Antihistamines dry mucous membranes to relieve runny nose, watery eyes and itching; decongestants shrink swollen membranes; buy one or the other, rather than a combined medication, to treat specific symptoms	Some antihistamines can cause drowsiness; decongestants can cause agitation, insomnia or high blood pressure; both can cause problems for people with certain medical conditions	Consult doctor before giving either antihistamines or decongestants to children under 12 months of age
Anti-inflammatories [NSAIDs] (aspirin, ibuprofen, naprosyn)		
Help relieve swelling and pain in muscles and joints, as well as fever and headaches	Aspirin and ibuprofen can pose danger to those on blood thinners; do not exceed dosage limits; aspirin can irritate the stomach, cause bleeding or ulcers, and is one of the most common causes of child poisonings. Aspirin and ibuprofen should be taken with food to avoid stomach irritation. **NEVER give aspirin to children/teenagers unless your healthcare provider orders it. It can cause Reye's syndrome, a rare but often fatal condition**	Daily, low doses of aspirin may help prevent heart attack and stroke and may decrease the risk of cancers of the digestive system; ibuprofen is available in liquid for children's use, but can upset the stomach; ibuprofen is the most effective pain reliever for menstrual cramps; naprosyn is similar to ibuprofen in its uses and risks
Antiseptics		
Clean wounds and prevent infection	**Do not use.** Harsh antiseptics like iodine, Mercurochrome, Merthiolate and full-strength hydrogen peroxide can harm delicate tissues and inhibit healing; plain soap and water is all that is needed to cleanse wounds	Wash wounds thoroughly with plenty of soap and running water
Cough Suppressants/Expectorants		
Suppressants may control the cough reflex to reduce dry, hacking coughs; expectorants thin mucus to make it easier to expel phlegm	Some should not be taken by people with certain health conditions; can interact with sedatives and some antidepressants; can contain alcohol; read directions carefully	Coughs help remove phlegm to clear respiratory tract, so suppressing them may be counterproductive; products with guaifenesin are effective expectorants, those with dextromethorphan may suppress coughs; call doctor before giving cough medications to children under 12 months old

Nonprescription Drugs

How it works	Risks	Comments
Laxatives		
Stimulate intestines to prompt bowel movement during constipation; bulking agents soften stool to ease elimination	Few side effects if taken according to directions	Take laxatives with plenty of water; regular use can interfere with the body's absorption of vitamin D and calcium
Nasal Sprays/Nose Drops		
Shrink swollen mucous membranes to encourage free breathing; relieve runny nose and postnasal drip	Should not be used for more than three days in a row; prolonged use can cause more swelling than before spray or drops were used	Less likely than oral decongestants to interact with other drugs; provide temporary relief
Pain/Fever Medication (acetaminophen) — also see *Anti-inflammatories* on previous page (NSAIDs)		
Reduces fever and pain	Excessive use of acetaminophen can contribute to liver damage, especially in heavy drinkers	Acetaminophen is ineffective against inflammation; it is a safe pain and fever medication for children; available in liquid form; milder to stomach than ibuprofen or aspirin; do not exceed dosage limits
Skin Irritation Medication (hydrocortisone)		
Acts as an anti-inflammatory to temporarily relieve itching from rashes, insect bites, hives, poison ivy, etc.	Excessive use can damage the skin; generally safe if used for two weeks or less; should not be used on infected skin or near eyes	Suppresses the itch reflex, but does not cure the rash; use only as much as rubs easily into the skin

If you have any syrup of ipecac in your home, dispose of it by flushing it down the toilet. Syrup of ipecac is no longer recommended for inducing vomiting in someone who has been poisoned. If you suspect a possible poisoning, call the Poison Control Center at 1-800-222-1222. This national toll-free number automatically connects you to your local poison control facility, where trained staff can instruct you on what to do in case of a suspected poisoning. They can also provide information on how to prevent poisoning.

First-Aid Supplies

In addition to over-the-counter (OTC)/nonprescription drugs, a well-stocked home medicine cabinet should include some first-aid supplies and a first-aid manual. You can put together the elements of a first-aid kit by gathering the items listed here, or you can purchase first-aid kits for your home, car, boat or other use at drugstores or through organizations such as the American Red Cross. First-aid manuals are also available at these locations.

First-Aid Items/Uses

Assorted Band-Aids/Butterfly Bandages

Cover and protect small scrapes and cuts from dirt and moisture; butterfly bandages can bring the edges of a cut together

Tweezers

Help remove large dirt particles from wounds and dislodge splinters

Ice Pack

Reduces swelling from injuries; can provide relief from headaches

Cotton/Cotton-tipped Swabs

Useful in cleaning wounds and lifting foreign matter from eyes; do not use inside the ear

Digital Thermometer

Helps detect fever; throw away any mercury thermometers

Gauze Pads/Adhesive Tape

Large bandages for wounds or scrapes that can't be covered with adhesive bandages

Sharp Scissors

For cutting gauze rolls and removing jagged edges from scraped or torn skin

Heating Pad

Speeds the healing process after swelling subsides; may relieve headaches; set to low

Anaphylactic Kit (for people with previous severe allergic reaction)

To treat life-threatening allergic reactions; available by prescription from your doctor

SECTION 6
Prevention

Reader's Note: Prevention is the best medicine, which is why we've included specific preventive information under almost every medical topic in The CareWise Guide. In addition, this section sums up a variety of lifestyle tips for getting and staying healthy.

Getting and Staying Healthy

Health and fitness are big business in America today. But you don't have to spend a lot of money to get healthy and stay that way. Many steps toward wellness don't cost a penny.

Start by using your common sense to prevent health problems and protect yourself. For example, always use your seat belt when you're in a car and make sure you buckle your children into age-appropriate car seats. Always wear a helmet when skateboarding or riding a motorcycle, bicycle or horse.

More tips for healthy living follow. If you'd like more information about any of these topics, ask your healthcare professional for materials that may be available.

Staying Active

Exercise is a crucial element of a healthy lifestyle—no matter what your age. Regular exercise can help lower blood pressure, give you more energy, keep you fit and help you avoid serious illnesses such as diabetes and coronary artery disease (CAD). Numerous studies prove that people who exercise regularly are more likely to cut down or stop smoking cigarettes. Exercise is also a great stress reducer.

The Surgeon General advises adults and children to exercise at least 30 minutes on most, if not all, days of the week. Exercise should be of moderate intensity, and it can be as simple as a brisk walk around the neighborhood. The key to sticking with an exercise program is choosing the type that's right for you—whether it's jogging, swimming, playing tennis, cycling, going to the gym or walking.

Check with your doctor before starting an exercise program if you are not currently exercising or if you have a personal or family history of heart disease or a chronic illness.

Begin exercising gradually. Not only will this help you avoid injury, it will help you stay with your program until it eventually becomes routine.

A well-rounded exercise program should include a warm-up period, stretching, moderate levels of *aerobic* exercise (which raises the heart rate for a sustained period to strengthen the heart and lungs), strengthening exercises such as push-ups or weight training, and a cool-down period. Even during the most strenuous part of your program you should be able to talk or laugh without difficulty.

Don't be discouraged by temporary setbacks—just get back into the routine the next day. If the exercise you've chosen is too strenuous or causes injuries, slow down. Remember that if you can keep up your exercise program for a month, it will most likely become a healthful habit.

Eating Right

For most people, maintaining a healthy weight throughout life lowers the risk of coronary artery disease (CAD) and certain other chronic illnesses.

This means being physically active and following a diet that is low in fat, cholesterol and calories, and high in fiber. Eating right includes an emphasis on fresh fruits, vegetables and whole-grain products and consuming very few processed and "fast" foods, which tend to be high in fat, sugar and sodium.

Evaluating Your Weight

The *body mass index* (BMI), a simple height-to-weight ratio, can help you determine your proper weight range. For most adults, a desirable weight falls within the 19 through 24 "normal" range. People with a BMI of 25 through 29 are considered overweight and a BMI of 30 or more indicates obesity.

To find out your BMI, find the point where your height and weight intersect on the chart on the following page:

BMI	Normal						Overweight					Obese				
	19	20	21	22	23	24	25	26	27	28	29	30	31	32	33	34
Height (inches)	Body weight (pounds)															
60	97	102	107	112	118	123	128	133	138	143	148	153	158	163	168	174
61	100	104	111	116	122	127	132	137	143	148	153	158	164	169	174	180
62	104	109	115	120	126	131	136	142	147	153	158	164	169	175	180	186
63	107	113	118	124	130	135	141	146	152	158	163	169	175	180	186	191
64	110	116	122	128	134	140	145	151	157	163	169	174	180	186	192	197
65	114	120	126	132	138	144	150	156	162	168	174	180	186	192	198	204
66	118	124	130	136	142	148	155	161	167	173	179	186	192	198	24	210
67	121	127	134	140	146	153	159	166	172	178	185	191	198	204	211	217
68	125	131	138	144	151	158	164	171	177	184	190	197	203	210	216	223
69	128	135	142	149	155	162	169	176	182	189	196	203	209	216	223	230
70	132	139	146	153	160	167	174	181	188	195	202	209	216	222	229	236
71	136	143	150	157	165	172	179	186	193	200	208	215	222	229	236	243
72	140	147	154	162	169	177	184	191	199	206	213	221	228	235	242	250
73	144	151	159	166	174	182	189	197	204	212	219	227	235	242	250	257
74	148	155	163	171	179	186	194	202	210	218	225	233	241	249	256	264
75	152	160	168	176	184	192	200	208	216	224	232	240	248	256	264	272
76	156	164	172	180	189	197	205	213	221	230	238	246	254	263	271	279

The BMI does have some flaws. For example, a man with a BMI of 24 is at the upper limit of the normal weight range for a person of his height. However, if he is a muscular athlete, he is well within a healthy weight range, even though his BMI is bordering on high.

For best results, you should discuss your BMI with your healthcare provider, who will take this and any other health factors you may have (such as high blood pressure) into consideration in determining your general health status.

Maintaining a Healthy Weight

If weight loss is a goal for you, avoid the impulse to slim down rapidly. As appealing as this may seem, it frequently leads to a frustrating and unhealthy "yo-yo" cycle of quick weight loss followed soon afterward by weight gain.

By concentrating instead on long-term, sensible dietary changes and regular exercise, your weight should gradually normalize and your health should improve. If you decide to shed a few unwanted pounds, a safe goal is 0.5 to 1 pound (0.25 to 0.5 kg) per week.

Lower Dietary Fat

Reduce the fat in your diet by substituting fresh vegetables and fruits or low-fat yogurt for fat-laden snacks such as potato chips or cookies. Read food packages carefully and try to avoid buying products with more than three grams of fat per 100 calories. Decrease fat when preparing foods by broiling, steaming or poaching instead of frying. Use only small amounts of mono- or polyunsaturated oils when you cook

Good Cholesterol/Bad Cholesterol

Watch your cholesterol. Cholesterol has two major components: low-density lipoprotein (LDL) and high-density lipoprotein (HDL). LDL is called the "bad" cholesterol because it can make cholesterol gather on the walls of your arteries, contributing to coronary artery disease. HDL, the "good" cholesterol, prevents blockage of the arteries by carrying cholesterol away from coronary artery walls. In general, your LDL should be below 130 mg/dL (milligrams per deciliter) and your HDL should be above 40 mg/dL. Your total cholesterol should be below 200 mg/dL. If you have a chronic disease such as diabetes, your doctor will talk to you about what target cholesterol levels are appropriate for you.

To lower your LDL and raise your HDL, exercise regularly and, if you smoke, start taking steps to kick the habit. Also, eat foods with reduced cholesterol or less than one gram of saturated fat per 100 calories. Use fats and oils sparingly and choose those lowest in saturated fat and cholesterol: canola, corn, olive, safflower, sesame, soybean and sunflower. Avoid "trans-fatty acids," which are listed as "hydrogenated" or "partially hydrogenated" fat in the ingredients of many packaged and fast foods and margarines.

Fiber and Salt

Eat more fiber. The fiber in fruits, vegetables, beans and peas helps lower cholesterol and reduce your risk of heart disease. Fiber in whole-grain products provides bulk to give you a "full" feeling, and both types help prevent constipation.

Go easy with the salt shaker. Excess salt can raise your blood pressure and increase your risk of stroke, heart attack or kidney failure. Season foods with spices and herbs instead and watch out for high levels of salt in canned and packaged foods.

Quit Smoking

Snuff out that cigarette. It's hard to quit smoking, but it's worth it. Within 12 hours of your last smoke, your body begins to repair the damage to your heart and lungs. Your risk of lung cancer starts to decline about one year after you quit. In fact, smokers who quit tend to live longer regardless of how old they were when they kicked the habit. Learn about the tools available to help you quit—nicotine gum, patches and other medication products and support groups, for example. Set realistic expectations, and use the support of family, friends and others to help you through the rough spots.

Alcohol and Drugs

Alcohol abuse, abuse of prescription or illegal drugs and chemical dependency not only harm you, they cause family problems, put unborn babies at risk for birth defects and endanger others when you drive under the influence. Many resources are available to help those struggling with alcohol, drug or chemical abuse. Ask your healthcare provider or check your local newspaper or community organizations for the resources available near you.

Identify Risky Behaviors

Does your lifestyle put your health in danger? Certain habits you may take for granted can threaten your health—perhaps even your life—or the life of someone you love. These are a few of the behaviors that can put you at risk:

- Unprotected sex puts you at risk of HIV, the virus that causes AIDS (acquired immunodeficiency syndrome) and a host of other sexually transmitted diseases (STDs). There is no cure for HIV or AIDS and you can have the virus for years without knowing it. Using latex condoms during sex is one way to prevent the spread of HIV. Having only one sex partner or choosing abstinence are also options. (See *HIV,* p. 308; *Safe Sex,* p. 312.)

- Smoking puts you at risk of chronic, often life-threatening illnesses such as coronary artery disease and lung cancer. Smoking also puts those around you at risk of lung disease. (See *Quit Smoking,* previous page.)

- Driving is one of the most dangerous activities we undertake. According to the Centers for Disease Control and Prevention, motor vehicle crashes are the leading cause of injury and death in the United States for people aged 1 to 34. Carelessness, "road rage" and driving under the influence of drugs or alcohol all contribute to accidents. (See *Alcohol and Drugs,* previous page.) ALWAYS fasten your seat belt and make sure that all your passengers do the same. Make sure young children are strapped into child safety seats that meet current federal safety standards and that children up to age 12 ride in the back seat.

- Residential fires claim thousands of lives each year. Check your home regularly for fire safety hazards and make sure every member of your family knows how to evacuate your home quickly and safely, if necessary.

- Basking in the sun or visiting the local tanning booth may give you a deep, dark tan, but these activities also put you at risk for skin cancer—the most common type of cancer in the United States. (See *Skin Cancer,* p. 147.) If you must be exposed, protect your skin by wearing a sunscreen with a sun protection factor (SPF) of at least 15.

Immunizations

Be Smart–Vaccinate

A thorough immunization plan—whether for your child or yourself—is an important lifetime health investment against contracting a number of serious illnesses. To stay current on your immunizations, develop an immunization schedule with your doctor that meets your family's needs and keep a detailed home record of vaccines. Immunization schedules change frequently. Ask your doctor for the most current recommendations.

Most children should get the following immunizations:
- DTaP (diphtheria/tetanus/acellular pertussis)
- Hepatitis A
- Hepatitis B
- Hib (haemophilus influenza type b virus)
- Influenza
- IPV (inactivated poliovirus vaccine)
- MMR (measles/mumps/rubella)
- Pneumococcal vaccine
- Varicella (chickenpox) vaccine

Adults may need the following immunizations:
- Hepatitis A
- Hepatitis B
- Influenza
- MMR (measles/mumps/rubella)
- Meningococcal vaccine
- Pneumococcal vaccine
- Tetanus/diphtheria (booster every 10 years)
- Varicella (chickenpox) vaccine (if not vaccinated as a child)

Screening Guidelines

Catching Problems Early

It's a fact that some medical tests are unnecessary, costly and over-prescribed. Yet others can play an important role in increasing your longevity and quality of life, while saving thousands—or even hundreds of thousands—of dollars in the long run by catching a potentially serious problem early.

Here are a few of the preventive tests that are recommended for healthy adults. If you have a serious medical condition or other high-risk factors, consult your doctor about other necessary tests, or more frequent tests. **Infants, children and pregnant women also need other types of tests.**

Preventive Exams/Tests

Who Needs It	How Often
Complete Physical	
Infants	Birth, 1, 2, 3, 4, 6, 9 and 12 months
Children 15 months to 4 years	15, 18 months; 2, 3 and 4 years
Children 5 to 12 years	5, 6, 8, 10 and 12 years
Adolescents 15 to 20 years	Every two years
All adults	Every one to three years until age 75, then yearly
Sigmoidoscopy, Colonoscopy or Barium Enema (to detect colon/rectal cancer)	
Adults 50 years and over	Every five to 10 years, depending on test
Fecal Occult Blood Testing (stool test for early detection of colon/rectal cancer)	
Adults 50 years and over	Every year
Digital Rectal Exam (to detect prostate cancer)	
Men 40 years and over	Every year
Glaucoma Screen	
Everyone over age 40	Every two years or on your doctor's advice or every year if there is a family history
Pap Smear (to detect cervical cancer)	
All women beginning at age 21 or at onset of sexual activity	Annually. After age 65, or if you've had a hysterectomy, check with your doctor for frequency

chart continues next page

Preventive Exams/Tests *continued from previous page*

Who Needs It	How Often
Professional Breast Exam	
All women during routine checkup; beginning annually at age 40, or at age 35 if a family history of premenopausal breast cancer in mother or sister	Every year (a monthly self-exam is also recommended, see *Breast Self-Exam,* p. 275). Discuss risk factors at professional breast exam appointment
Mammogram	
All women beginning at age 40. It is not recommended that women under age 40 have routine screening by mammogram unless there is a history of premenopausal breast cancer in mother or sister	Every year
Blood Pressure Measurement	
All adults and children	Every two years starting at 2 to 3 years of age
Cholesterol Screening (to detect high blood cholesterol levels, which may lead to atherosclerosis)	
All adults; most important for men over 35 years and women over 45 years. For children and adults over 75, check with your physician	Every five years. More frequently in men 20 to 30 years of age and women ages 20 to 45 if multiple risk factors exist
Glucose	
All adults age 45 or older. Those at high risk, e.g., obesity, family history, members of high-risk ethnic groups, high blood pressure, high cholesterol, women who deliver a baby more than 9 lbs. or are diagnosed with GDM (gestational diabetes mellitus), should be tested at a younger age	If tested normal once, repeated at three-year intervals or on doctor's advice
Electrocardiogram or EKG (to detect coronary artery disease)	
Not recommended for routine screening of people without symptoms	Selectively on your doctor's advice
Exercise Stress Test (to screen for coronary artery disease)	
Not recommended as routine screening of people without symptoms. Men over 40 or women over 50 who have two or more major risk factors for heart disease (high cholesterol, high blood pressure, smoking, diabetes, family history of early-onset heart disease)	Selectively on your doctor's advice
Chest X-ray	
Not recommended as routine screening of people without symptoms	Selectively on your doctor's advice
Common Lab Tests (CBC, urinalysis, thyroid, liver, kidney, syphilis, tuberculin)	
Not recommended as routine screening for people without symptoms or a significant history of exposure	Selectively on your doctor's advice
Osteoporosis Screening	
Baseline test recommended for women at high risk and every two years if no new risk factors exist	Selectively on your doctor's advice

SECTION 7

Working With Your Doctor

Finding the Right Doctor

The first step toward getting the best and most appropriate healthcare is finding a doctor you feel comfortable with and can work with on a long-term basis. Here are a few tips for evaluating and choosing a doctor.

Decide What Type of Doctor You Need

It is usually best to select a primary care doctor who can take care of most of your routine medical concerns and refer you to a specialist, if necessary. Look for someone who is certified in family practice (FP), internal medicine (IM), or *pediatrics* (for children).

Because some family practitioners and internists do not provide routine gynecologic or obstetric care, it may be necessary to select a gynecologist/ obstetrician for women's health concerns.

Find a Few Doctors to Choose From

Ask your friends and family, or other health professionals you may know, for their recommendations. Or call your employer's health plan office for suggestions. Some healthcare plans, such as health maintenance organizations (HMOs), may provide assistance in selecting a doctor. If your insurance plan covers a limited list of doctors, ask them to send you the list to help you make a decision.

Call the Doctor's Office and Ask Questions

After you have identified a few potential doctors, call their offices and ask some questions. Tell the receptionist you want to find a doctor for your ongoing care and are wondering if the doctor is accepting new patients. If the answer is yes, ask if you can get some additional information. Also, if you have children, ask about age limitations (some FPs and internists take only adult patients).

The following are questions you might want to ask:

- Is the doctor board certified in your state? If so, in what specialty?
- Does he or she have practice privileges at accredited hospitals? (If the answer is yes, this indicates that the doctor's credentials have been screened by the hospitals and tells you which facilities would be used if you were hospitalized.)
- If you belong to a managed care organization (MCO), is the doctor a member of that organization? Your insurance may not cover services provided by nonmember doctors.
- Where is the doctor's office located and what are the office hours?
- If you call about an urgent medical problem, will you be seen the same day? What is the average waiting time for a nonurgent appointment?
- What kind of back-up is provided when the doctor is unavailable?
- Is the doctor willing to discuss medical problems over the phone with you? If so, is there a charge?
- Are other medical services (x-rays, laboratory tests, etc.) readily available when needed?
- Is the doctor eligible for maximum payments under your health plan?
- What is the cost of an average office visit?
- Does the doctor's office require payment at each visit?
- What are the terms of payment? Is there a finance charge?

Next, Schedule an Office Visit

Once you find a doctor who seems like a good candidate, schedule an appointment. During the appointment, note whether the doctor:

- Listens to your concerns and obtains a thorough history of your problem
- Answers your questions and explains the treatment plan completely, in terms you can understand
- Discusses treatment alternatives with you and goes over the risks and benefits
- Is willing to make a referral to a specialist if he or she cannot readily diagnose or treat your condition
- Seems aware of cost as well as quality of care
- Is responsive when you express your fears, concerns and preferences
- Is someone you feel you can talk to and work with in the months and years to come

After the Visit, Check Your Bills

- Are the bills or insurance claims processed promptly and accurately?
- Are the charges detailed and readily identifiable? Are there any unexpected or unexplained charges?
- If the doctor's office handles your insurance claims, are they submitted to the insurance company in a timely manner?
- If you must handle the insurance claims yourself, is the doctor's office willing to assist you and provide whatever additional documentation may be required?

Becoming Partners With Your Doctor

Many of us tend to believe that we have little or nothing to contribute to our own treatment program. Think again.

Each of us is the one-and-only possible expert when it comes to:

- Our family history
- Our symptoms and how they developed
- Our opinions about what has and hasn't worked for us in the past
- How we feel about various treatment options
- Our lifestyle and the things that are important to us
- Our preferences, concerns and fears

Doctors report that 70 percent of their correct diagnoses are the result of information provided by the patient. What's more, statistics show that patients who speak up, share information, ask questions and participate in treatment decisions enjoy a noticeable improvement in the quality and appropriateness of their care.

So how do you go about becoming an effective partner with your doctor?

Between Doctor Visits

- Learn to observe your own body and keep a record of your symptoms and concerns so that you're ready to report accurate information to your doctor. For example:
  - **Be able to give your doctor an exact temperature reading**—and ready to report whether it's an oral, *axillary* (taken in the armpit) or rectal temperature. This is much more helpful than saying that you or a member of your family is "burning up." If you don't have a digital thermometer, buy one and learn to use it. Discard mercury thermometers.
  - **Learn to measure pulse rate and its regularity.** Whether you are worried about a feverish child or a spouse who is experiencing heart

palpitations, measuring the person's pulse—which means counting the number of heartbeats occuring in one minute—and noticing whether the rhythm of the beats is regular or irregular, can provide your doctor with useful information. (See *Pulse* in Index.)

- **For women over age 18, make a habit of examining your breasts once a month.** Learn what is normal and customary for you and report any changes—such as unusual lumps or thickening—to your doctor. (See *Breast Lumps*, p. 273.) Once males are in their teens, they should begin examining their penis and testes each month for any changes that could indicate infection or cancer. (See *Genital Health*, p. 296.)
- **Know what your normal weight is.** If it changes, keep track of how much and over what period of time. Knowing about any sudden weight loss or gain can help your doctor diagnose certain illnesses. (Ask your healthcare provider for more information on weight, exercise and healthy diets.)
- **Become familiar with your skin**—moles, warts, bruises, birthmarks, etc., as well as overall tone and color. Learn to notice and track anything unusual—a mole that is growing or a sore that isn't healing—that may need immediate attention.

In short, get to know your whole body—from head to toe—so you will know what is normal for you. Keep a list of any changes, symptoms or areas of concern and bring it with you to your next doctor visit.

- For nonemergencies, check this book before calling your doctor. You may discover some self-care options that can save the time and expense of a doctor visit.
- If you decide to go to the doctor, prepare for the visit. Give some careful thought to your most important health concerns. Get ready to describe them—in order of importance—as completely and concisely as possible. Write down the names of your medications and the questions you want to ask your doctor.

At the Doctor's Office

Begin the conversation with the topics you are *most* worried about—not your minor complaints—and be as honest and direct as possible about your concerns. Keep it short and to the point, but take the time you need to describe your problem.

Taking an Active Role

Whether your doctor suggests putting you on medication, running a few tests, or scheduling a minor procedure or major surgery—it *always* pays off to find out what's going on and participate in the decision-making process.

Yes, your doctor has years of training and offers invaluable medical advice. But only you can really decide if the benefits outweigh the risks— for your particular situation—and if the treatment plan is something you can live with and incorporate into your lifestyle.

Taking an active role in treatment decisions

- Ask your doctor to explain the various treatment options—along with the benefits, risks and costs of each—before going ahead with *anything*: "What is the official name of the test/procedure/medication?" "Why do I need it?" "What will the procedure involve?" "What are the risks and benefits?" "How much will it cost?" "What are the alternatives?" "Would it be possible to just watch and wait for a while?" Take notes if it helps.
- If you don't understand your doctor's explanations, be persistent and ask again: "Could you go over that part again?" "Do you have any material I can read at home?" "Can you show me on paper what will happen?"
- If a prescription drug is suggested, ask about the side effects, and the possibility of using a less expensive but effective generic substitute.
- If a major test or surgery is recommended, ask if there are other treatment options that are equally effective, or if you can watch and wait for a while without putting your health at risk.
- Ask if there will be any restrictions on activity and, if so, how long the restrictions will be necessary. If some treatment is suggested that you know you just can't or won't be able to handle—"I have three kids at home! I can't stay in bed all day!"—speak up. Chances are you and your doctor can work out a suitable alternative.
- Find out if there is anything else—besides or in addition to a prescription or treatment—you can do for *yourself* to help the problem or speed your recovery.

Sorting Through Your Options

- If it's a nonemergency, don't rush into anything! Remember that very few medical procedures are actually emergencies. There is usually time to think about the options and select the one that seems best for you.
- Use this guide to help you understand your medical problem, evaluate your options for care and plan questions for your doctor.
- If you find you have more questions for your doctor, or need additional information, call your doctor's office and ask!

Once Treatment is Determined

- Make sure you understand all the treatment instructions. If not, ask more questions!
- **Carefully follow your treatment program.** For example, write down your medication schedule and each time you take the medicines. Always fully comply with all instructions, and always talk to your doctor before altering your treatment or medication program.
- Keep track of any side effects and call your doctor if you are worried or have any questions, or if something doesn't seem right. (See *Using Medications*, p. 324.)

Index